Irish Boston

IRISH BOSTON

A Lively Look at Boston's Colorful Irish Past

With a Visitor's Guide to Historic Sites, Pubs,
Gift Shops, Museums, Irish Studies Courses,
Genealogy Resources, Irish Music and Dancing,
and More

Michael P. Quinlin

The Globe Pequot Press

GUILFORD, CONNECTICUT

To My Parents
John J. Quinlin and Mary (Campbell) Quinlin

Text design: Tom Goddard
Cover photo credits (left to right): Group of children, South Boston, MA, c. 1919; courtesy of Historic New England/SPNEA. Step dancers take the stage at an Irish festival, 2004; courtesy of Tracy Mallek.

Library of Congress Cataloging-in-Publication Data
Quinlin, Michael P.
    Irish Boston / Michael P. Quinlin.
        p. cm.
    Includes bibliographical references and index.
    ISBN-13: 978-0-7627-2901-2
    ISBN-10: 0-7627-2901-5
    1. Irish Americans—Massachusetts—Boston—History. 2. Boston (Mass.)—Ethnic relations. 3. Boston (Mass.)—History. 4. Boston (Mass.)—Guidebooks. 5. Historic sites—Massachusetts—Boston —Guidebooks. I. Title.
F73.9.I6Q46 2004
974.4'61—dc22

    2004042549

Manufactured in the United States of America
First Edition/Third Printing

Contents

Acknowledgments

IT TURNS OUT you need to befriend numerous strangers and call upon the good graces of friends and colleagues to complete a book like this, and I am very grateful for the assistance I received along the way. I start with thanking Judith Rosen of Cambridge for helping me shape my proposal and for putting me in touch with Laura Strom, my editor at The Globe Pequot Press. Laura found a way to blend two book ideas into one. I thank Mimi Egan, a fellow Pittsburgher, for guiding the book through production with humor and grace, and Doe Boyle for her thoughtful and thorough copyediting.

I am grateful to my sister Margaret M. Quinlin for sharing her publishing expertise at every turn. Experts who commented on individual chapters include Seamus Connolly, Michael Cummings, Kevin Kenny, Henry Lee, L. E. McCullough, and Richard Senier. Professor Thomas O'Connor, who read the entire manuscript, continues to inspire me as a historian and gentleman. David R. Burke, Charles Donovan, Marilyn Halter, Paul Harrington, Patrick Leahy, and Patrick King shared their research with me in a most helpful manner.

I owe an enormous debt of gratitude to the librarians who helped me locate obscure and valuable material for this project. At the Boston Public Library these include Aaron Schmidt in the Print Department; Henry Scannell, Diane Parks, and Nancy Walsh and staff in the Microtext Department; Diane Ota in the Music Department; and Roberta Zonghi and staff in the Rare Books Department. I am grateful to Frances O'Donnell at Harvard University's Divinity School Library; Beth Sweeney at the Irish Music Collection, John J. Burns Library, Boston College; Marie Daly at the New England Historic Genealogical Society; Robert Johnson and Margaret Gonzales at the Boston Archdiocese Archives; Dr. John McColgan at City of Boston Archives; Patricia Burdick at the Miller Library, Colby College; Susan Greendyke at the Massachusetts State House Art Commission; Bridget P. Carr at the Boston Symphony Hall library; Diane Gallagher at Boston University; James B. Hill, Tom McNaught, and Lee Statham at John F. Kennedy Library and Museum; and James Feeney at the Boston Athenaeum.

Finally, my everlasting gratitude goes to my wife, Colette, and son Devin for their love, forbearance, and good humor throughout this project, and to my entire family for their unwavering love and devotion.

Introduction

I MOVED TO BOSTON in 1979 with the common misperception that the city's Irish character was built entirely through politics. Expressions like "the last hurrah" and "all politics is local" were part of the common vernacular. Bostonians referred to long-departed politicians like "Honey Fitz" and James M. Curley as if they had just bumped into them over at Castle Island in South Boston. An Irish ethos dominated the political arena, especially the mayor's office, where Irish Americans held the seat continuously between 1929 and 1993.

I was pleased to gradually discover a rich Irish cultural and social scene set apart from the glare of politics. A non-political tradition, it turns out, dates back to the eighteenth century, when runaway Irish servants and sturdy Ulster Presbyterians were part of the local landscape, introducing their distinct cultural identities into an unwelcoming Puritan milieu. Since then many Irish immigrants to Boston have embraced politics and religion as the touchstones of identity, while others have relied on culture and education. I have tried to include all those elements in this book.

Irish Boston recounts episodes from history that speak to the Boston Irish experience as I have come to appreciate it. Politicians invariably enter the picture, but they usually appear in cameo roles opposite a colorful cast of painters and sculptors, poets and rebels, singers and dancers, and athletes and activists, all of whom captured my imagination.

The cultural experience of the Boston Irish is rooted in individual genius and grassroots expression rather than simply the "militant and triumphant" bastions of powerful institutions. The rigors and revelations wrought by the immigrant experience gave many Irish a creative freedom they may not have had in Ireland, especially those from modest backgrounds. In turn, the artistic expression that came out of that new-found freedom endeared many Bostonians to Irish artists a good two decades before the first Irish mayor, Hugh O'Brien, was elected in 1884.

In selecting who and what to write about, I ultimately relied on my own curiosities and interests. I was guided by the perspective of historian James O'Toole, who wrote in the *Eire Society Bulletin* in 1982 that "the purpose of history is not merely to praise great and famous men; it must also document and reveal the lives of ordinary men, women and children." I have tried to document those lives, with hopes of claiming a value for them in the grand scheme of Boston Irish history.

Included at the end of this book is a guide to Irish Boston that provides dozens of listings for Irish cultural groups, gift shops, pubs and restaurants, and hospitality amenities of interest to visitors and residents alike.

Part One:
A Cultural History of the
IRISH in BOSTON

 CHAPTER ONE

Being Irish in New England
(1700–1770)

E DWARD MURPHY was on the run in Boston. The eighteen-year-old
Irish teenager was last seen wearing a woolen cap and dirty flan-
nel jacket with pewter buttons. He wore light-colored pants, a
checked woolen shirt, brown yarn stockings, and neat leather shoes. He
was described as "blear ey'd" with a "leering look," and his distinguishing feature was "the Irish brogue on his tongue." It was said that he
took along a light-colored wig to avoid detection.

Murphy, an indentured servant, had twice run away from the household of Thomas Craddock of Milton, first in November 1737 and then
again in March 1738. Both times Craddock ran an advertisement in the
New England Weekly Journal, offering a three-pound reward for the Irish
boy's capture and return.

Craddock didn't have much luck with the Irish. In May 1738
another servant escaped: Edmund Ryan, nineteen years old, freckled
face, gray eyes, and sandy hair. "He works well at the nailer's trade,"
Craddock noted, offering a five-pound reward for Ryan, whose unlikely
accomplice in his getaway was fellow servant Edmund Butler, described
as "a good scholar who speaks English, Latin, Greek, and French, a thin
looking fellow of middle stature."

RAN away the 4th Instant from Mr. George Tilley of Boston, a Negro Fellow, named Bristol, aged about 33 Years, he is tall and slim, walks very upright, speaks broken English, he had on when he went away, a Felt Hat, a homespun striped Jacket, and striped Linen Breeches, a Cotton and Linen Shirt, no Stockings, a pair of old Shoes. N B. He has lately been seen with a Frock and Trouzers on. Whoever shall take up the said Runaway, and him safely convey to his abovesaid Master in Boston aforesaid, shall have Forty Shillings Reward, and all necessary Charges And all Masters of Vessels are hereby cautioned against concealing or carrying off said Servant on Penalty of the Law in that Case made and provided.

RAN-away from Mr. Samuel Waldo, of Boston, Merchant, about the 7th Instant, Edward Glasbine, an Irish Man Servant, about 20 Years of Age. He had on when he went away, a black Wig, white Woollen Jacket, an old ragged dark colour'd Coat, Woollen Shirt, dark colour'd Yarn Stockings. Whoever shall take up said Runaway, and him convey to Mr. Samuel Waldo's at Boston aforesaid, shall have Forty Shillings Reward, and all necessary Charges paid. Or any Person inclining to purchase said Glasbine's four Years Service, may have the same on reasonable Terms.

To be Sold by said Waldo, both Flor de Luce Wine in whole, and half Chests, also good Duck.

Ads for runaway slaves and servants frequently appeared together in the 1700s.

Ryan was eventually captured and sent to Boston's Bridewell, a house of correction located at the top of Boston Common where Beacon and Park Streets intersect today. Modeled after England's House of Occupation, Bridewell detained vagrants, juveniles, and runaways and put them to work making products that could be sold on the open market. The jailer on the premises used a whip whenever he deemed it necessary. Ryan escaped from Bridewell in June, forcing Craddock to run the ad again. The five pound reward still stood.

In the eighteenth century no one would have considered Boston the "greatest Irish city in the world," as it came to be called by the turn of the twentieth century. Boston in the early 1700s had a population of 15,000 people, including 1,100 African slaves and about 500 Irish. The Puritan elders still held sway on issues of religion and morality, but sea merchants had taken control of the economy, and many Bostonians were getting wealthy and indulging in surprisingly un-Puritan pursuits, such as fashion and leisure. The coastal city had become Britain's major port for trade in New England and was a key British link to Virginia, Maryland, and the West Indies. Seventy-eight wharves lined the shores around Boston and Charlestown, and shipbuilders were in high demand. Fishermen were reaping record catches, and lobsters were plentiful and cheap. And so too, it turned out, were Irish servants, who could be indentured for four to eight years for an investment of about twelve to fifteen pounds.

Murphy, Ryan, and Butler were just three of the hundreds of Irish who ended up in Boston as indentured servants. In exchange for ship passage, food, shelter, and clothing, they were obliged to work for Boston merchants who owned their contracts. The promise of adventure and prosperity had already become the myth of America and attracted thousands of Irish men and women. Ever since Oliver Cromwell's reign as lord protector of England (1649–1658), during which time the staunch Puritan and ruthless warmonger brutally ravished Ireland, many Irish were propelled to escape their dreary, subjugated existence. Dispossessed of land and even leaseholds, the Irish looked hopefully toward American shores.

Ideally, indentured servants worked out their contracts and then settled in America as free men. Skilled tradesmen were generally well treated and often made a good living after their service was finished. George Washington once hired bricklayer Michael Tracy, shoemaker Thomas Ryan, and tailor Caven Bowe, paying about twelve pounds for each Irishman in exchange for three years of service. The most notable indentured servants in New England were Irish immigrants John Sullivan and his wife Margaret Browne, who settled in Maine in 1740 and raised five sons, all of whom played prominent roles in the Revolutionary War.

Many Irish came to America involuntarily. More than 60,000 adults and children were sent against their will to the American colonies from the British Isles, according to researcher Frances O'Donnell, who notes that while most deportees were felons or vagabonds, political and religious dissenters were also among this group. Cromwell and his troops as well as other British marauding soldiers often sent captured soldiers— Irish and Scots—to New England or the West Indies. This not only eliminated dissenters in the British Isles, it also provided manpower to colonize British holdings abroad. In 1672 Irishman Robert Collins, who had been shipped to America against his will, won a landmark case in Boston's Suffolk County Court and was relieved of having to serve a Bostonian who had purchased his indenture contract. Abbot Emerson Smith, author of *Colonists in Bondage*, describes the practice as "licensed kidnapping on a large scale, with the [English] magistrates and officers of the law conniving at it under some pretense of statutory sanction."

Boston officials kept track of all "foreigners and strangers" coming into town, a difficult task for a capital city and seaport. Newspapers ran regular lists of "Inward Bound" and "Outward Bound" travelers who stayed more than a few days. Those staying too long were ordered to leave, as noted in the selectmen's minutes. In 1719 Mary Newell from Ireland, in Boston for seven weeks, was "warned to depart," and so was John Walker, his wife, and three children, who "came last from Ireland and had then been in this town about one month."

In 1736 the brig *Bootle* was carrying nineteen transports, or prisoners, from Cork to Virginia, when it stopped in Boston to get water and provisions. The Boston selectmen ordered its captain, Robert Boyd, to "keep a strict watch on board his vessel to prevent their escape." Apparently there were already enough runaway Irish roaming the Bay Colony.

Evan Thomas, biographer of naval hero John Paul Jones, notes, "In the [eighteenth] century the world was sharply divided [into] a great chain of being in which you were born to your class." Indeed, most servants had little pleasure in life and were often worked to the bone, not unlike the common man in Britain and Ireland. An Irish person ending up in Boston soon realized that New England was a lot like Olde England. The City on a Hill, as Bostonians proudly called home, was in essence an English town relocated to the edge of the New World. Many English Puritans had a genuine aversion to outsiders, or strangers as they were called in Boston, and treated them poorly. Commenting on this particular trait, Richard Dunn, a historian on the slave trade in the Barbados, suggests that "The English were a narrowly ethnocentric people, exceedingly reluctant to live among foreigners of any sort, even Scots or Irish or Dutchmen."

Perhaps this explains how God-fearing Bostonians could look upon slaves and servants as possessions to be traded with impunity along with other commodities, as demonstrated by an advertisement, placed in 1727 in the *New England Weekly Journal*:

> *To be sold by Augustus Lucus, a Negro man and Negro woman, both young, large and strong, they speak good English. Also, a new copper still, lately arrived from London, containing about 270 gallons, with her cap, worm and worm-tub.*

In 1738 Ephraim Baker was selling cutlery, brushes, men's gloves, saddles, anchovies, books, and other items at a public market, to which he added as a footnote:

> Any person that wants to purchase a fine likely Negro Wench about 22 years old, and a child about four years old, may hear of them by enquiring of the abovesaid Ephraim Baker.

Slaves were permanent property, and owners inherited the children of slaves as property too. Servants, on the other hand, were simply rental property with a restricted time of service. But that didn't prevent Boston merchants from trading them freely. When Samuel Waldo's Irish servant Edward Glasbine ran away in 1738, Waldo offered a 40-shilling reward for his return, then added, "Any person inclining to purchase said Glasbine's four years' service, may have the same on reasonable terms."

Irish servants weren't the only ones absconding. In 1738 Irishmen Michael Dullowin and Patrick Shangasseys ran away from gingerbread baker Thomas Pearson, and Hugh McCan escaped from Bridewell. They were joined on the run by fugitive slave George Tilley, twenty-year-old American Indian Jo Daniels, and twenty-three-year-old Scottish servant William Cobb.

What became of these runaways? Many of them vanished across the Blue Hills into the unwieldy continent, working their way westward along the frontier, avoiding roving bands of Indians or in some cases joining up with them. They might have made their way down the eastern seaboard to warmer climes in Maryland and Virginia. Some of them would have fought in the French and Indian War and in the American Revolution.

Keeping Track of Presbyterians and Papists

Not all Irish came to Boston as indentured servants, of course. Irish who had been small landholders or merchants back in Ireland could afford the passage and the means to live in Boston. The majority of them were Presbyterians from Ulster—the nine northernmost counties in Ireland. As early as 1611 England's King James the First had sent Scottish "planters" to Ulster to subdue the native Irish. Many of the planters' descendants retained their Scottish identity and were commonly known as Ulster Scots.

Along with the German immigrants who had also begun to arrive in Boston, the Ulster Scots altered the singular ethnicity of the English that had predominated in the colonies up to that time. The thirteen colonies were changing—no longer were they a purely English settlement. A diverse community with new customs and religious beliefs was taking shape.

The arrival of the Ulster Presbyterians to Boston in the early eighteenth century altered the Bay Colony, according to historians R. C. Simmons and Henry Jones Ford. Ulster and New England had one aspect in common: each had "served as a refuge for Puritan ministers harassed . . . in Scotland and England," Ford notes. When Ulster Presbyterians began making overtures to bring their congregations to New England in the early eighteenth century, Boston leaders encouraged them, perceiving the newcomers as like-minded religious renegades from Anglicanism. A more practical reason also motivated the Bostonians to welcome the Ulster immigrants: The Bay Colony needed valiant, sturdy colonists willing to settle and protect its frontiers, beyond the Boston pale in New Hampshire and Maine, where Native American Indians and Frenchmen posed a threat. The Scots-Irish, as they came to be known, had experience in settling among indigenous populations that were hostile to them. They had already done so in Ireland.

Some Bostonians, however, had legitimate concerns about the newcomers. Alluding to grain shortages in the city, Thomas Lechmere, an in-law of former Massachusetts Bay colony Governor John Winthrop, complained in 1718, "These confounded Irish will eat us all up, provisions being most extravagantly dear and scarce." Irish passengers often carried contagious disease like smallpox and measles on the ships, putting the entire city at risk.

A large group of Ulster Irish arrived in Boston on August 4, 1718—five boatloads, in fact. These vessels contained about 700 Ulster Irish Presbyterians who appeared in Boston Harbor after having been assured beforehand that they could purchase a parcel of land in the city. To their dismay, they were told by city leaders that they would have to join the Puritans' Congregational Church in order to stay in Boston.

A few of them did, but the rest, at Governor Samuel Shute's suggestion, moved to 12 square miles of land in Casco Bay, Maine, and eventually settled Worcester, Massachusetts, and Londonderry, New Hampshire.

Another decade would pass before Irish Presbyterians managed to gain a foothold in Boston. As the city neared its centenary in 1730, the strenuous tenets of Puritanism had diminished. In 1729 Irishman John Moorhead, formerly of Newtonards, County Down, along with a congregation of thirty believers, established an Irish Meeting House in a converted barn at the corner of Berry Street and Long Lane (now Channing and Federal Street). It was called the Church of the Presbyterian Strangers. As church historian Harriett E. Johnson notes, "Good, quiet, law-abiding citizens . . . they were. [W]ith their sober, steadfast, hard working, moral philosophy of life they constituted an excellent balance to the idealistic, variable [Puritan], who so often preached freedom, but practiced intolerance and bigotry."

The Irish Presbyterians appeared more tolerant than their Puritan neighbors. The congregation's records indicate a number of African-American children being baptized in the church. Between 1737 and 1748 James Mayes baptized "three Negro children, Rosanna, John, and Sarah," all presumably the children of slaves. In 1742 a slave named Jeffrey baptized his son Jeffrey, while church member William Baird had a "Negro boy baptized Thomas." Also in 1742 "Cato and Flora, a Negro man and woman" were married by Reverend Moorhead.

By 1744 the Church of the Presbyterian Strangers had prospered enough to replace the barn with a proper church, and by 1749, twenty years after the church was formed, Reverend Moorhead had baptized more than 1,200 children. The congregation grew prosperous over the years. But in truth most of the Ulster Scots coming to America were now heading to New York and Pennsylvania, where they created towns like Tyrone and Donegal.

Irish Catholics, meanwhile, continued to feel unwelcome in the Bay Colony, even as restrictions against Presbyterians, Quakers, and Baptists eased. In 1700 Cotton Mather, the sour minister associated with the hanging of Irish servant Annie Glover in 1688 for witchcraft, preached against efforts to bring Irish to Boston. He warned that this idea was one of the "formidable attempts of Satan and his sons to unsettle us."

That same year the Massachusetts Legislature voted to eject all Jesuits priests and missionaries from the colony. Any Jesuit caught would be imprisoned for life; if he then tried to escape, he would be executed.

The dispute between English Protestants and Irish Catholics went back to 1560. At that time the British declared spiritual supremacy over Ireland and required all clergy and public officials to take an oath to the Crown. Hatred and fear of Catholics were carried over to the Bay Colony by Puritans who abhorred Catholicism. The ongoing struggle between France and England to claim as much of the New World as possible resulted in the French and Indian War, which lasted from 1756 to 1763. Somehow, the fervor and fear attached to the war increased the paranoia that Catholics were infiltrating Boston.

In 1731 Governor Jonathan Belcher, hearing there were some "papists now residing within the town of Boston," ordered his officers to "break open their dwelling places, shops and so forth and bring them to the court of justice." Rumors flew that local Catholics were planning to hold a secret Mass on St. Patrick's Day, 1732, in the West End, near the present-day Saint Joseph's Church on Cardinal O'Connell Way. Three days later the *Weekly Rehearsal* reported, "We hear that Mass has been performed in town this winter by an Irish priest among some Catholics of his own nation, of whom it is not doubted we have a considerable number of them."

The annual Pope's Day holiday each November 5 was a chilling reminder for any Irish or French Catholic wishing to profess their faith openly. One of those bizarre and archaic pastimes that measure the lack of progress in the human condition, Pope's Day celebrated a failed Catholic plot by Guy Fawkes to blow up the English Parliament in 1605. Groups of men from Boston's South End and North End marched from their respective neighborhoods into the center of Boston, holding effigies they had studiously constructed of the Pope and the Devil. Upon meeting, the two sides, by now fueled by rum and the excitement of old grudges, attempted to destroy the other team's effigies. Often, fights broke out between the two groups of Protestants over who despised the Pope more, and constables had to be called. It wasn't until decades later, during the Revolutionary War, that the brutish pastime died out in Boston, when more immediate enemies were at hand.

Good Deeds: The Charitable Irish Society in Boston

Founded on March 17, 1737, the **Charitable Irish Society** is the oldest Irish organization in North America, created to provide a sense of community for Irish immigrants and to aid the poor within that community. Since 1997, the Society has presented a Silver Key Award to a worthy recipient doing good deeds on behalf of Irish immigrants. It holds its annual banquet on the evening of St. Patrick's Day.

The symbol of the Charitable Irish Society is a silver key bearing the arms of Ireland on one side and those of King George II on the other. The actual key, made of coin silver, about 8 inches long, is engraved with the motto With Good Will Doing Service.

Past presidents of note have included Boston mayors Hugh O'Brien and Patrick Collins, architect Charles D. Maginnis, and historian Henry Lee. Historian Catherine B. Shannon was the first woman elected president in 1990; she broke the Irish glass ceiling for A. Maureen Murphy, who was elected president in 1996, and Paula Carroll, elected in 2002.

The Society's papers, dating from 1737 through 1937, are stored at the Massachusetts Historical Society; more recent papers from the 1930s to the present are kept at the Burns Library at Boston College. For more information, visit www.charitableirishsociety.org.

The Charitable Irish

Hardship and a common need to survive did nothing to soften Puritan hearts toward foreign newcomers. After nearly two decades of Ulster Scots and Irish servants filtering into the town, Boston was in no mood to help foreigners in need. In 1737 the town was suffering a severely harsh winter that temporarily froze the harbor. Food supplies were limited. Ships carrying Irish passengers were quarantined at Spectacle Island whenever measles or smallpox was detected. Boston's poorhouse already held more than one hundred needy people, and about three dozen inmates were imprisoned in Bridewell.

It was during this year that an extraordinary group of Boston Irishmen banded together to help their fellow countrymen and women who were falling upon hard times. On March 17, 1737, twenty-six "Irish gentlemen, merchants and others" came together to form the Irish Society in New England, later to be known simply as the Charitable Irish Society. Their mission was to help their fellow countrymen "reduced by sickness, shipwreck, old age and other infirmities and unforeseen accidents, [and] for the relief of their poor and indigent countrymen." They were mirroring a tradition that had been established eighty years previously, when local Scots formed the Scottish Charitable Society to help their fellow Scotsmen, many of whom had been sent as prisoners to Boston by Cromwell.

Members of the Irish Church formed the nucleus of the Charitable Irish Society, and initially only Protestants could become officers. Dues were ten shillings (or approximately $50) per year and an additional two shillings ($10) each quarter.

In its early years the Society gave out dozens of gifts to people in need. In 1740 Abigail Richardson, an Irishwoman, found herself destitute and resigned to die a lonely death on the streets of Boston. Society member James Downing saw her one night lying in the cold darkness behind his house on Wing's Lane, off Hancock Street in the North End. He picked her up and carried her to his house, then petitioned the Society to help provide relief.

Another recipient was privateer John Ryan, who had been on trial in the 1770s for piracy after sailors from the British frigate *Rose* boarded an American vessel and tried to arrest the crew. Ryan's arm was shattered by a musket in the fracas. His lawyer, the future president John Adams, helped him beat the charge of piracy. The crippled Ryan received a small settlement, but he had to depend upon the Society to survive.

The first Society members came from all walks of life, and many of the early members appear to have been tradesmen. William Hall, the Society's first recorded president, was a leather dresser and town constable; John Little was a groundskeeper, and George Glen was a tailor. Reverend Moorhead remained a member until his death in 1773. Daniel Gibbs was a sea captain, whose ship, *Sagamore*, had brought 408 Irish to Boston Harbor in 1737, where they were quarantined at Spectacle Island for measles. Member Andrew Knox was listed as a mariner.

The Society had an impact in Boston beyond its charitable works:

Many of its members made important, long-lasting contributions. Artist and teacher Peter Pelham, for example, is today regarded as the Father of Fine Art in Boston; Pelham was an early member of the Society. He came to Boston from England in 1726 with the first of his three wives and their three children. Pelham's first work executed in Boston was a copper engraving and oil painting of Reverend Cotton Mather. In 1731 Pelham painted a portrait of Reverend John Moorhead, which he inscribed *Minister of a Church of Presbyterian Strangers at Boston in New-England.* Today the painting hangs at the American Antiquarian Society in Worcester.

In January 1738 Pelham took an advertisement in the *New England Weekly Journal* offering to teach "dancing, writing, reading, painting upon glass and all sorts of needle work." While these were typical cultural pursuits in Europe, they seemed exotic in the New World, even in America's most sophisticated city.

Pelham's time in Boston coincided with the arrival of an Irish woman named Mary Singleton from Quinville Abbey, County Clare, who came from a prosperous family that owned nearly 2,000 acres of Irish land. She arrived in 1735 with her new husband, Richard Copley, "who was probably the son of Alderman Charles Copley, one of the sheriffs of Limerick," writes art historian

---

Tracing Your Irish Roots

Think you could be related to a Murphy, Ryan, Moorhead, Knox, or Copley from the eighteenth century? If you're seeking your local roots, start at the **New England Historic Genealogical Society** (101 Newbury Street, Boston, MA 02111). Founded in 1845, it has a research library of more than 200,000 volumes and was lauded by *Time* magazine as "one of the top three resources in the country" for family research. The Society hosts an Irish Genealogy Conference, organizes tours to Ireland, and schedules genealogy lectures throughout the year. Another organization that can assist researchers is **The Irish Ancestral Research Association** (TIARA) at P. O. Box 619, Sudbury, MA 01776-0619. Established in 1983, the group meets on the second Friday of each month to discuss family and historical research; it also organizes field trips and promotes the exchange of ideas among people interested in Irish genealogy. A booklet entitled *Finding Your Irish Roots in Massachusetts* lists genealogy resources throughout the state. It is published by the **Boston Irish Tourism Association.** To obtain a copy, visit the Web site www.irishmassachusetts.com.

John S. Copley's 1765 portrait of his half brother, entitled Henry Pelham (Boy with a Squirrel), *is displayed at the Museum of Fine Arts, Boston.*

Jules David Prown. Their first and only child, John Singleton Copley, was born on July 3, 1738. According to Prown, the Copley family may have lived for a time on a tract of land owned by Samuel Waldo, a German businessman who regularly transported Irish servants to the Bay Colony.

Richard Copley became ill and died in the early 1840s, leaving his wife and son to fend for themselves in Boston. Mary Copley ran a small shop on Long Wharf, where she sold tobacco and sundries. She met Peter Pelham after his second wife died, and they married in May 1748 at Trinity Church on Summer Street. The following year they had a son, Henry Pelham, who would himself become a gifted artist like his father. Peter Pelham quickly introduced his stepson John Copley to the art and passion of painting, which would one day make John Singleton Copley America's foremost portrait painter.

Rebels and Loyalists Choose Their Sides

As the two boys were coming of age in the 1760s, the town was fast splitting into two camps, those loyal to the Crown and those opposed to Britain's draconian tax acts in the colonies. The Stamp Act, which levied a tax on newspapers and legal documents, and the Townsend Act, which taxed tea and other items, were cutting into the profits that Boston merchants expected to make, and confrontations with customs officials increased. A face off between British officials and Boston merchants was inevitable.

In 1768 British troops occupied Boston to keep order in the town. On May 17 the HMS *Romney* warship, armed with fifty guns, entered Boston Harbor followed by a fleet of warships and two regiments from Halifax, Nova Scotia. The Twenty-ninth Regiment camped on the Boston Common while the Fourteenth Regiment took over Faneuil Hall. A few months later the Sixty-fourth and Sixty-fifth regiments arrived from Ireland.

Like all Bostonians, Charitable Irish Society members had to choose a side: Daniel Malcolm, whom the British described as "a notorious smuggler," Henry Knox, who would become the nation's first secretary of war, and Captain William MacKay, president of the Society from 1784 to 1786, all sided with the colonists. Robert Auchmuty, the Society's president from 1767 to 1769, sided with the British, as did his son of the same name. Reverend Moorhead, though a liberal minister, was a staunch loyalist to the British Crown. Many in his congregation were sea captains and merchants directly affected by the taxes, while others in the church stood to gain from the British presence. When Moorhead died in late 1773, the congregation turned on itself and church services were suspended for several years as the war got under way.

CHAPTER TWO

Tories and Patriots, Pirates and Painters (1770–1800)

APTAIN JAMES FORREST backed the wrong side in the American Revolution. He shared the dilemma of many of his fellow Boston Irish: whether to stay loyal to the British Crown or to join the rebels and try to overthrow British sovereignty. Like many others, Forrest never dreamed that a handful of colonial gentry and a ragged army of indentured servants, felons, immigrants, and other castaways would one day defeat what was then the world's mightiest empire.

In 1761 Forrest had emigrated from Ireland to Boston, where he became a successful merchant and a customs official with strong ties to the British establishment. He joined the Charitable Irish Society in 1772 and was named the Keeper of the Silver Key, a ceremonial position he held from 1772 to 1774.

As relations between Britain and the American colonies continued to worsen, Forrest had to decide whether or not to support the British Crown, which was made manifest at that time by hefty import taxes and the heavy-handed British troops who occupied Boston.

Forrest cast his lot with the British and was quickly branded a Tory. He became ubiquitous in local British circles, tending to socialize with like-minded Irish soldiers in the British Army, such as Captain Brabazon O'Hara of the Fourteenth Regiment and Captain Jeremiah French of the Twenty-ninth. All three men were drinking at the British Coffee House on King Street in September 1769 when patriot James Otis lost a bloody fistfight with loyalist John Robinson, an incident referred to as the Coffee House Brawl by historian Hiller B. Zobel in his masterful book, *The Boston Massacre.*

A few months later Forrest and fellow Irishman Captain Thomas Preston of the Twenty-ninth Regiment attended a party with Major General Thomas Gage, British commander of the occupation of Boston.

Henry Pelham drew the original scene of the Boston Massacre (1770), which Paul Revere then engraved and sold.

According to Zobel, "the average man in the twenty-ninth was over thirty, medium tall, and Irish." It was his friendship with Captain Preston that cast Forrest as a minor player in the infamous Boston Massacre.

The trouble started on Friday, March 2, 1770, when local rope maker Samuel Gray engaged in a scuffle with Private Matthew Kilroy of the Twenty-ninth Regiment. Gray got the better of Kilroy initially, but the two vowed to finish the fight that following Monday, and their respective friends agreed. More scuffles occurred over the weekend, and by Monday the Bostonians and the soldiers were itching for a show-down. Several small confrontations broke out in early evening, and eventually a crowd of 200 to 300 Boston men converged upon the Custom House, which was guarded by a lone sentry, Hugh White of the Twenty-ninth Irish Regiment.

Captain Preston was called in to protect White from the unruly mob, and he arrived along with Corporal William Wemms and six privates—James Hartigan, William McCauley, Matthew Kilroy, William Warren, John Carroll, and Hugh Montgomery. As Preston approached the site, Henry Knox, whose father had been one of the original members of the Irish Presbyterian Church on Long Lane, came out of his bookstore and warned him not to shoot into the crowd, which was throwing snowballs and ice chunks while taunting the soldiers.

Preston ordered his men to present arms to keep the crowd at bay, but the taunting continued. Crispus Attucks, described as a mulatto of African and American-Indian blood, stepped out of the crowd and wrestled Montgomery's rifle away from him. In the confusion that followed, someone yelled, "Damn you, fire!" The troops fired into the crowd. Samuel Gray was the first to go down, shot in the head by a musket ball. Montgomery wrestled his gun back from Attucks and shot him in the chest. Two other Boston men quickly went down: James Caldwell was shot in the back as he turned to run, and seventeen-year-old Sam Maverick was shot on the spot.

Thirty-year-old Patrick Carr, an Irish sailor who had come out of a house on Court Street and was moving toward the ruckus with fellow sailor Charles Connor, was the last man to be shot. (The bullet tore through Carr's hip and backbone, and he suffered for nine days before dying.) The soldiers escaped back to their barracks and the crowd dispersed to a local tavern in absolute shock and anger about the turn of affairs. Captain Preston was arrested and jailed at three o'clock on Tuesday morning, March 6, and the eight soldiers were also rounded up. The town was in an uproar. Distraught at the prospect of his friend Preston getting convicted, Forrest rushed around Boston that Tuesday, begging lawyers to take his friend's case. No one volunteered.

Finally Forrest barged into the law offices of thirty-five-year-old John Adams, the future president of the United States, who would give Forrest his nickname, the Irish Infant. Adams later recalled the encounter in his autobiography:

The next morning, sitting in my office near the steps of the town-house stairs, Mr. Forrest came in . . . . With tears streaming from his eyes, he said, "I am come with a very solemn message from a very unfortunate man, Captain Preston, in prison. He wishes for counsel, and can get none. I have waited on Mr. Quincy, who says he will engage, if you will give him assistance; without it, he positively will not. Even Mr. Auchmuty declines, unless you will engage."

Adams agreed to represent the soldiers, but not without a sense that the decision could harm his career. Even so, he recognized the importance of conveying to the world the capacity of the thirteen colonies to hold a fair trial. He engaged attorneys Josiah Quincy and Robert Auchmuty to assist him. Their opponent in the courtroom was chief prosecutor Robert Treat Paine, who traced his ancestry back to the O'Neill clan of County Tyrone. Assisting Paine was Sam Quincy, the older brother of Josiah Quincy.

As the trial of Preston and his men loomed, an Irish dimension emerged. Local newspapers like the *Boston Gazette* suggested that many of the soldiers the British had sent to Boston were Irish Catholics, feeding into the paranoia about a papist conspiracy extant from the old Puritan days. The *Providence Gazette* even suggested that Pope's Day should take place on the anniversary of the Boston Massacre so as to include Preston and the others in the effigy burnings.

At the same time, defense attorney John Adams described the Bostonians in the melee as "a motley rabble of saucy boys, Negroes, mulattos, Irish teagues and outlandish jack tars . . . shouting and hazing and threatening life . . . whistling, scream[ing] and rending an Indian yell . . . throwing every species of rubbish they could pick up in the street." The term "teague" was and still is a slang and derogatory name for Irish Catholics.

In the end, it was Carr's dying testimony that helped to exonerate Preston and his men. Dr. John Jeffries, who had treated Patrick Carr on his deathbed, became a star witness at the trial. He testified that Carr "was a native of Ireland, and had frequently seen mobs, and soldiers called upon to quell them. . . . He had seen soldiers often fire on the people in Ireland, but had never seen them bear half so much before they fired in his life." As a final gesture of contrition, Carr told Jeffries that "he forgave the man whoever he was that shot him, he was satisfied he had no malice, but fired to defend himself."

On December 5, 1770, nine months to the day after the Boston Massacre, only Kilroy and Montgomery were found guilty of manslaughter for the killing of Crispus Attucks. At their sentencing on December 14, both men invoked a medieval English plea for mercy called "the benefit of clergy," originally offered to clergy and, later, extended to felons facing a first conviction. The plea involved showing their

Remembering the Massacre

The **Boston Massacre Memorial** on Boston Common, along Tremont Street near West Street, was erected in 1888 to honor the five men killed by British soldiers in 1770. The memorial's proponents were surprised to discover opposition to the plan from old-line Bostonians who considered the victims to be nothing more than rabble-rousers.

The memorial proceeded despite the objections. Editor and poet John Boyle O'Reilly, Boston's best-known Irish leader in the late nineteenth century, wrote a poem called "Crispus Attucks," using the occasion to comment on the race relations between blacks and whites. His verses asked "whether we learned what Crispus Attucks knew, when right is stricken, that white and black are one, not two."

The site of the massacre is also marked by a medallion of cobblestones next to the Old State House, at the corner of State and Washington Streets. The Boston massacre victims are buried at the Old Granary Burying Ground on Tremont Street, where their tombstone faces the street.

God-fearing ways by reciting Psalm 51; both Kilroy and Montgomery did so and thus had their execution commuted. Both were branded with an *M* for murder on their thumbs and were released back into their regiment. Years later, when Governor Hutchinson's diaries became public, it turned out that Hugh Montgomery had admitted to his lawyers that it was he who yelled out the fatal call to fire that helped start the American Revolution.

The Fighting Irish

To be sure, evidence is clear that the Irish fought on both sides of the conflict throughout the Revolutionary War. Research confirms, however, that they overwhelmingly sided with the American fight for independence, correctly seeing parallels in the struggles of the Irish and the Americans.

General John Sullivan helped drive the British fleet out of Boston on March 17, 1776.

Patriot Benjamin Franklin recognized this when he journeyed to Europe to establish lasting alliances with France and Ireland during the war. Franklin's sister Mary had married Irishman Robert Holmes, a ship captain from County Fermanagh, who transported many Ulster Scots to New England. In 1778 Ben Franklin wrote a letter from Versailles, France, entitled "To the Good People of Ireland." He noted "the misery and distress which your ill-fated country has been so frequently exposed to," and promised that America would someday find the means to "establish your freedom in the fullest and amplest manner."

The Marquis de Chastellux, who recorded his travels in America between 1780 and 1782, noted the camaraderie between Irish and Americans during this time:

> An Irishman, the instant he sets foot on American ground, becomes, ipso facto, an American. While Englishmen and Scotsmen were regarded with jealousy and distrust, even with the best recommendation of zeal and attachment to their cause, a native of Ireland stood in need of no other certificate than his dialect; his sincerity was never called into question, he was supposed to have a sympathy of suffering.

Thousands of Irish who had settled in the colonies as indentured servants joined the colonial army and navy. English officer Major Joshua Pell wrote in his diary, "The rebels consist chiefly of Irish redemptioners [servants] and convicts, the most audacious rascals existing."

Numerous Irish descendants from the Bay Colony had leadership roles in the colonial army. General John Sullivan of Maine was one of George Washington's most valued officers. So was Henry Knox, the leader at the Battle of Ticonderoga whose family helped form the Irish Presbyterian congregation in 1729. More than 200 Irish-born soldiers fought at the Battle of Bunker Hill on June 17, 1775, alongside Americans of Ulster stock whose families had settled New Hampshire and Maine earlier in the century.

On the naval front, the O'Briens of Maine and the Tracys of Newburyport served as privateers along the New England coast. Hector McNeil of Antrim, an active member of the Irish Presbyterian Church, was a seasoned navy man and close friend of Scottish naval hero John Paul Jones. John Barry of Tacumshane, County Wexford, commander of the ship *Lexington*, captured the first british ship, *Edward*, under the American flag.

It was not uncommon for Irish soldiers to face off against each other in battle during the war. Historians Michael O'Brien and James Cullen each published exhaustive lists of Irish colonists who fought at Concord, Lexington, and Charlestown. The roster at Lexington included three Burkes, five Collinses, eight Kellys, six Kennys, and eight Welshes.

Ironically, these colonial Irish often fought against other Irish soldiers in British uniforms. Colonel Daniel O'Brien's Fifth Regiment of

British Foot Soldiers, composed primarily of Irish soldiers, fought at the Battle of Lexington. After that battle, a cartoon appeared in a local newspaper depicting the retreating British troops as "Irish asses defeated by the brave American militia."

Ever mindful of maintaining the might of the Empire, or the perception of it, the British dutifully planted stories in Boston papers suggesting that all of Ireland was against the American insurrection. In September 1775 *Draper's Gazette* reported, "A brigade of Irish Roman Catholics is forming in Munster and Connaught in order to be sent to Boston to act against the rebels." Indeed, Irish historian Arthur Mitchell notes that seven regiments were sent from Ireland to Boston from 1775 to 1776.

Not all of the soldiers came voluntarily, however. The British employed what they called press gangs to scour the Irish countryside and forcibly conscript young men into military service. A letter printed in a Philadelphia paper during the war and later found by historian Michael O'Brien states, "The recruiting officers were driven out of the towns [in Cork and Kerry] by angry mobs . . . and many of the Irish soldiers in the English regiments destined for America swore they will never draw a trigger against the Americans, amongst whom they all have relations."

In fact, many of the Irishmen pressed into service deserted the British regiments, forcing the British to recruit new soldiers constantly. In New York, British Adjunct General Lord Francis Rawdon, Earl of Moira, led a regiment called the Volunteers of Ireland. On Saint Patrick's Day, His Lordship, hoping to stave off deserters, treated the Irish regiment to a fancy banquet that included "beef and good liquor" in New York City.

A recruiting song, "Patrick's Hearty Invitation to his Countrymen," promised Irish enlistees a life of pleasure in the British army:

> *Our days are contented, our nights pass gaily*
> *For all the girls follow the sound of our drum*
> *Whoever will join us, must sure be the winner*
> *For mirth and good humor is always our plan.*

James Forrest himself remained a steadfast loyalist and seemed to embrace the song's spirit. In June 1772 he was called before Boston's

Selectmen, having been accused of bringing soldiers from the Fourteenth Regiment into Boston from their post at Castle William in South Boston, where they engaged in drunk and disorderly conduct offensive to the townsfolk. The charge was found to be "wholly without foundation" and was dismissed.

In December 1775, Forrest raised a company of ninety-five men and five lieutenants. Called the Loyal Irish Volunteers, they patrolled the streets of Boston with a white cockade, or insignia, on their hats. The duties of this vainglorious group lasted for only about three months, for in March 1776 the British were forced to evacuate Boston when General Sullivan, Colonel Knox, and hundreds of rebels aimed cannons at the British fleet from atop Dorchester Heights in South Boston. The eight-year siege of Boston had come to an end.

Forrest and his fellow Tories fled to Halifax, Nova Scotia, where many of them remained in exile for the duration of the war. In fact, Charitable Irish Society loyalists were so well represented in Nova Scotia that they formed a Halifax chapter; that chapter still flourishes today. Forrest remained active in the war and was captured by American troops while carrying supplies from the West Indies to the British army. He was jailed in Philadelphia for a time. His sons Charles and James fought on the British side, with Charles losing an eye at the Battle of Germantown in 1777. That same year Forrest sunk his life savings into a cargo of tea, which was captured by the Americans on the Delaware River. He later applied for a Tory pension from the British government and was awarded recompense.

The Artists Take on the Revolution

Eventually joining Forrest and the other Tories in exile in and around Halifax was artist Henry Pelham, the talented half brother of painter John Singleton Copley.

A few years earlier, Pelham had gained notoriety as the artist who captured for posterity the Boston Massacre in March 1770, a drawing wrongly attributed to engraver Paul Revere. Revere had stolen the illustration from the twenty-one-year-old artist, engraving, printing, and selling it without any credit to Pelham whatsoever. Pelham wrote Revere a

The Tracys and O'Briens: Irish Privateers

When British ships began to stop American ships along the New England coast in 1775, two Irish families in particular engaged in a daring cat and mouse game with the British fleet. The O'Brien brothers of Maine and the Tracy brothers of Massachusetts were considered pirates by the British, but grateful colonial leaders like George Washington preferred the name privateers for the captains and sailors who joined the struggle for American liberty.

Jeremiah O'Brien and his four brothers—Gideon, William, John and Joseph—started the first naval battle of the Revolutionary War. The sons of Cork immigrant Maurice O'Brien, they captured the British warship *Margaretta* on May 11, 1775, in the waters next to Machias, Maine. The British called it "the first act of Colonial piracy," but the Massachusetts Provincial Congress commissioned the brothers to serve as privateers. During the war they captured numerous British vessels, including the prized schooner *Hibernia.* On September 24, 1900, the United States Navy christened a torpedo boat the S.S. *Jeremiah O'Brien.* A plaque honoring Jeremiah O'Brien was placed at the Massachusetts State House in 1936.

Patrick Tracy of Wexford, Ireland, settled in Newburyport, Massachusetts, in the 1740s and had three sons, Nathaniel, James, and John. Together the father and sons were successful sea merchants who traveled to Europe and the West Indies. When the war began, the Tracy fleet was commissioned for privateering. The Tracy brothers along with their brothers-in-law Jonathan Jackson and Joseph Lee refitted twenty-three of their merchant boats, including their prized vessels *Game Cock* and *Yankee Hero,* with mounted guns. The Tracy vessels captured 120 British vessels and 2,200 prisoners of war. Patrick Tracy's home is today the Newburyport Public Library, located at 94 State Street.

furious letter on March 29, 1770:

> *When I heard that you was cutting a plate of the late Murder, I thought it was impossible, as I knew you was not capable of doing it unless you copied it from mine and as I thought I had entrusted it in the hands of a person who had more regard to the dictates of Honour and Justice than to take the undue advantage you have done of the confidence and Trust I reposed in you. But I find I was mistaken. . . . If you are insensible of the Dishonour you have brought on yourself by this Act, the World will not be so. However, I leave you to reflect upon and consider of one of the most dishonorable Actions you could well be guilty of.*

During this the pre-Revolutionary period and during the war itself, John Singleton Copley had already established himself as a proficient painter and was highly sought after by the Bay Colony's leading citizens. Copley painted portraits of Paul Revere, Samuel Adams, George Washington, and John Hancock, from whom he lived a few doors down on Beacon Street overlooking Boston Common.

But Copley was regarded suspiciously by some radical activists because he had also painted the British elite occupying Boston. Among his subjects was General Thomas Gage, the colonial governor of the Bay State from 1774 to 1775. Copley's reputation was further suspect because in 1769 he had married Susannah Clarke, the daughter of a leading Tory merchant who was the Boston agent for the East India Company. It was Mr. Clarke's shipment of tea that American colonists, disguised as Mohawk Indians, dumped in Boston Harbor on December 16, 1773, in the infamous episode known as the Boston Tea Party.

Distracted by the impending outbreak of war and driven by his desire to study the European painting masters, Copley sailed for Europe in June 1774. A year later, his pregnant wife left Boston on the *Minerva*, the last vessel to leave before the British blockaded the port.

Half brother Henry Pelham stayed behind with their mother, Mary Copley Pelham, but he suffered from poverty and anguished over Boston's state of affairs. In May 1775 Pelham wrote to Copley in London, complaining of the growing rift between colonists and loyalists:

> *Dear Brother, People in [this] country brand every one with the Name of Tory who are not willing to go every length with them in their schemes, however mad, or who show the least doubt of the justice and humanity of all their measures.*

Copley's reply to Pelham on August 6, 1775, laid out his view on the impending crisis:

> *Dear Harry, You must know that I think the people have gone too far to retract and that they will adopt the proverb, when the sword of rebellion is drawn the sheath should be thrown away . . . after they have deluged the country in blood Americans will be a free independent people.*

Pelham worriedly replied to Copley:

> *I am considered a faithful and loyal subject to the most amiable and*
> *injured of sovereigns. I may now have enemies who would [use your]*
> *innocent piece of prudential advice to my disadvantage. I therefore*
> *wish you to exclude all political observations from your letters. . . .*
> *For your observations though intended for my benefit may eventually*
> *prove detrimental, the events of war being precarious and it being*
> *entirely uncertain into whose hands your letters may fall.*

In fact, Pelham was sealing his own fate. After the Battle of Bunker Hill in June 1775, which he apparently witnessed, Pelham was commissioned by General Gage to draw a map he titled *A Plan of Boston in New England and Its Environs,* which put him squarely on the British side of the war.

Henry Pelham's map of Boston was commissioned by the British in 1775.

Like many loyalist Bostonians who felt "a duty to his most gracious Sovereign and Veneration for the British Government," Pelham was in a bind once the British left Boston in 1776. He fled to Halifax and never returned. "All his books, furniture, and personal property was left behind in Boston," according to historian Alfred Jones. His beloved mother, Mary Copley, refused to leave during the exodus and remained in Boston until her death in 1789.

Henry Pelham eventually moved to Ireland, settling in County Clare, where his mother had been born. He married Catherine Butler and worked as a surveyor, completing an intricate map of County Clare for the British Government in 1787. He worked for a time as a land agent for the Marquis of Lansdowne, who owned considerable property in County Kerry. In 1806 Pelham accidentally drowned in the Kenmare River when his boat overturned.

Even though the Boston Massacre illustration remains one of the most popular icons in early American history, Henry Pelham's name has all but vanished from the collective memory of the event and is known to only a few art historians.

His half brother, John Singleton Copley, who died in London in 1815, was treated better by history. Copley Square in Back Bay was named in his honor in 1883, and a plaque at 34 Beacon Street across from Boston Common marks the site of Copley's home. In 1902 the Boston School of Art was renamed the Copley Society to honor the city's most famous painter, and his portraits are cherished by the Museum of Fine Arts, the Boston Public Library, and the Massachusetts Historical Society. In 2002 the Boston Parks Department unveiled a statue of the artist at Copley Square, a testament to the artist's continuing influence on the Boston imagination.

CHAPTER THREE

Claiming South Boston and Charlestown (1800–1840)

EORGE WASHINGTON helped set the stage for the acceptance of Irish Catholics in America. It was Washington, after all, who had stopped the churlish celebration of Pope's Day among his troops at Valley Forge. Colonial soldiers kicking around an effigy of the Pope caused "great indignation among the Irish in the camp," writes historian John Crimmins. Washington himself appeared on the scene and put an end to the pastime, commenting in the process, "I, too, am a lover of St. Patrick's Day."

After the war Washington found support from America's leading Catholic, Bishop John Carroll of Maryland. In a 1790 letter Carroll stated his hopes that "Whilst our country preserves her freedom and independence, [Catholics] shall have a well-founded title to claim from her justice equal rights of citizenship, as the price of our blood spilt under your eyes."

Washington replied, "I hope to see America as the foremost nation in examples of justice and liberality. I hope [Americans] will not forget the patriotic part which [Catholics] took in the accomplishment of their revolution, and the establishment of their government."

Thomas Jefferson also pushed for the separation of church and state and the liberty to worship freely. It was in this post-war environment that Boston Catholics held their first public Mass in 1788.

A Catholic who attended the first Mass later gave this first-hand account:

> We fitted up a dilapidated and deserted meeting house in School Street that was built in 1716 by some French Huguenots . . . and now converted by us into a popish chapel, principally for the use of French Catholics. Money was raised by subscription, with which the sacristy or vestry room was put in order; a pulpit was erected; the

29

Altar furnished; a few benches were purchased for seats and the little temple, which had served as a stable to the British in 1775, was once more consecrated to the uses of religion.

About one hundred people, mostly French and Irish immigrants, attended that first Mass at 26 School Street, where a plaque commemorates the event today, a few feet from the Boston Irish Famine Memorial at the corner of School and Washington Streets.

The support of France during the Revolutionary War had certainly eased some of the animosity toward Catholics, enabling two French priests—Francis Anthony Matignon and Jean DeCheverus—and two English-American priests—John Thayer and Benedict Fenwick—to establish the Catholic Church in Boston.

These clergymen demonstrated their value to the city by their unabashed dedication and loyalty to the citizenry. In 1798, when a yellow fever epidemic hit Boston, DeCheverus "devoted himself day and night to nursing the sufferers," according to Church accounts. "A general panic prevailed, and as soon as the fever appeared in any place, everyone abandoned the house, and the sick person was left with no one to assist or console him. The ministers of other churches in the city fled, or stayed with their families in seclusion, but the despised Catholic priest alone was at the post of danger, braving death with calmness and equanimity."

That bravery paid off, for the following year Bostonians responded generously when DeCheverus started a subscription drive to raise $20,000 for a church. President John Adams kicked off the fund-raising with a generous contribution of $100, and Protestants donated one fifth of the money raised. James Bulfinch, the famous architect who also designed the Massachusetts State House and the new Irish Protestant Church on Federal Street, drew the architectural plans for the church at no charge; he was later awarded a solid silver urn by the congregation.

On St. Patrick's Day, March 17, 1800, church leaders broke ground at a site on Franklin Street for the new church, and the Church of the Holy Cross was completed by 1803, serving as the centerpiece for the Catholic Church in New England. In the 1860s it would be moved to its present site on Harrison Avenue in the South End.

Like DeCheverus, the first Irish priests serving in the Boston area were characterized by their tireless commitment to the poor. In 1817 Bishop DeCheverus ordained Dennis Ryan of Kilkenny who was posted to Newcastle, Maine, to tend to a growing congregation there, and in 1820 DeCheverus ordained another Kilkenny man, Patrick Byrne, who became the bishop's assistant. Thomas Lynch of Virginia, County Cavan, pastor of St. Patrick's Church on Northampton Street in the 1830s, was "probably the best classical scholar at that time in New England," according to the *Boston Pilot*. "But the grand passion of his life was charity to the poor. He fed them, clothed them, and counseled them. They slept in the basement of the church till other shelter could be procured. He always had a store of boots and shoes in his house, and kept many hands busy making up clothes for the immigrant women and children. He cared little for splendid buildings."

Getting to Southie

Just as Presbyterians flourished in Boston after establishing the Church of Irish Strangers on Long Lane more than seventy years earlier, so too did the Irish Catholic community begin to blossom with the completion of the Cathedral of the Holy Cross in 1803. The following year a new neighborhood was established when the state legislature annexed a peninsula that was part of Dorchester and renamed it South Boston. It would soon become synonymous with the Irish.

Drawn by the cheap accommodations and the prospect of working in the neighborhood's burgeoning ship industry, South Boston—called Southie by its residents—turned out to be a perfect place for the Irish. The peninsula's rugged coastline and isolated geography permitted the development of a community akin to an Irish village, and it allowed its citizens to create a distinct, separate culture that remains the hallmark of South Boston today.

In 1810 Thomas Murray, a thirty-six-year-old Dubliner, set up shop in South Boston as an undertaker, and five years later Boston's Board of Health granted Catholics permission to build a cemetery in South Boston. Philip Lariscy, an Augustinian priest, organized a fund-raising campaign and collected more than $600 to purchase the parcel of land

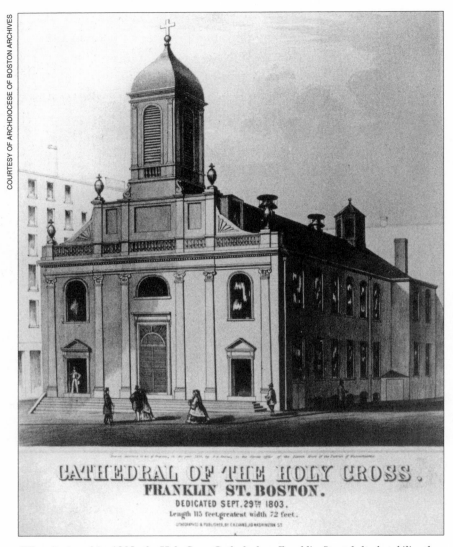

CATHEDRAL OF THE HOLY CROSS.
FRANKLIN ST. BOSTON.
DEDICATED SEPT.29TH 1803.
Length 115 feet.greatest width 72 feet.

When it opened in 1803, the Holy Cross Cathedral on Franklin Street helped stabilize the Catholic community in Boston.

at the corner of Dorchester and Sixth Streets. The cemetery and its small chapel, which opened in 1819, were named for Saint Augustine in honor of Father Lariscy's order.

Up to this time Catholics were buried in one of the city's public cemeteries, like the Old Granary Burying Grounds on Tremont, the

Central Burying Ground on the Boston Common, or Copp's Hill Cemetery in the North End. This was a suitable arrangement, since only 120 Catholics were living in Boston in 1790. By 1820 that population had jumped to about 2,000.

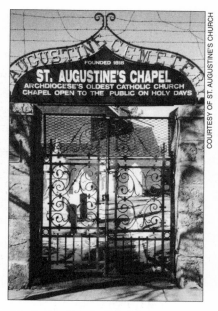

The opening of Saint Augustine's Cemetery caused "over 200 parishioners of Boston's Cathedral of the Holy Cross . . . to transfer the bodies . . . of relatives and friends from local cemeteries to the new Catholic burial ground," writes historian Thomas O'Connor.

Over time, the small mortuary chapel at the cemetery was used to celebrate Mass for the growing population of Irish immigrants. Many Irish Catholics outside of Boston took their loved ones

The Boston Board of Health gave Catholics permission to erect a cemetery in November 1818.

from Irish settlements in Lowell and Chelmsford to be buried at Saint Augustine's, and by the end of the decade, the cemetery was filled.

A survey of the early tombstones by George F. Dwyer indicates that many of the Irish buried there were children who didn't survive past their first year on earth. THIS STONE ERECTED BY CHRISTOPHER CONNOLLY IN MEMORY OF HIS SON, JOHN, WHO DIED APRIL 14, 1825, AGE 16 MONTHS, reads one tombstone. A majority of Irish buried in the cemetery came from Cork, Tipperary, and Kilkenny, followed by Donegal, Longford, Waterford, and Wexford. All thirty-two counties are represented in the cemetery, underscoring the pervasiveness of Irish immigration to Boston in the nineteenth century.

Not only were Irish citizens moving into South Boston, so too were numerous institutions Boston officials didn't want downtown. These included the Massachusetts School for Idiots, the House of Industry, the Almshouse, and detention centers for adults and juveniles. Ironically, the Irish migration to South Boston increased by mid-century, when many of the impoverished immigrants fleeing the Irish Famine ended up in these institutions. In the 1840s neighborhood leaders, mostly Yankees, accused the city of turning South Boston into another Botany Bay, home of the world's most famous penal colony in Australia, and they threatened to secede from Boston. The city eventually transferred several of these facilities to Deer Island in the 1850s, but by then the Irish were well established in South Boston.

Let's Bury Them in Charlestown

In 1832 two Irish children, Florence Driscoll and James Kinsley, paved the way for the establishment of a permanent Irish presence in Charlestown. The 1-square-mile town, which would not be incorporated into Boston until 1874, was separated from downtown Boston by the Charles River and Boston Harbor. Throughout the 1820s Irish immigrants were steadily moving into Charlestown, hoping to settle there permanently.

The people of Charlestown were not in favor of the idea. They watched suspiciously as Father Benedict Fenwick, who had succeeded DeCheverus as bishop, purchased a beautiful plot of Charlestown land in 1825 for the Ursuline nuns, who had been living on Franklin Street across from the Cathedral since 1820. Around 1826 the nuns moved to Charlestown, where they lived in a modest house until their four-story Ursuline Academy was completed in one of Charlestown's loveliest sections. The convent school for the education of young girls became known as Mount Benedict in honor of the bishop.

In 1829 Bishop Fenwick opened Saint Mary's Church on Richmond Street, and in January 1830 he purchased a plot of land behind Bunker Hill for a Catholic cemetery. He must have had an inkling of the trouble ahead when the stable on the cemetery grounds was deliberately burned to the ground. The people of Charlestown were sending a message: they didn't want Irish Catholics buried in their town. In addition to their narrow-minded parochialism, the Charlestown people suffered from actual fear of the Irish. They believed the Irish would bring religious superstitions and disease to their town.

In the nineteenth century the entire world was paranoid about the spread of diseases. Boston had long taken pains to quarantine ailing passengers arriving by ship. Passengers were checked for measles, smallpox, and cholera, and Spectacle and Rainford Islands were used to quarantine ships coming in from Europe. Charlestown had its first smallpox epidemic in 1752 and was always thereafter vigilant against scourges. When faced with cholera epidemics in 1829 and again in 1832, local health officials were successful in preventing the spread of the disease by literally scrubbing down streets, water pumps, and latrines.

Marie Daly of the New England Historic Genealogical Society believes that Charlestown residents developed a paranoia about getting sick through contact with the Irish. Daly, an expert on early Catholic cemeteries around Massachusetts, notes, "In those days, before the development of germ theory, people believed that disease was spread by people emitting fumes that passed from one person to the other. Bostonians considered the Irish to be a very dirty, immoral people who were bringing epidemics to their town. Disease was seen not as a health issue but a moral issue."

The conditions of poverty—poor sanitation, lack of pure drinking water, overcrowded living quarters, and poor nutrition—were characteristic of Irish immigrant life during this time. The mortality rate of the Boston Irish was disproportionately high. In the 1830s the majority of Irish Catholic children died before the age of five. The infant mortality rate was high, averaging 20 percent of Irish babies under age one as late as 1850. A high rate of birth defects also occurred as a result of malnutrition. Those factors may have accounted for the tendency of Irish Catholic couples to have large families, Daly says.

The frequent and early death of Irish children created an urgent need for burial space. When Saint Augustine's Cemetery filled to capacity around 1829, Bishop Fenwick began to bury the Boston Irish in Charlestown. In November 1831 the town selectmen voted to prohibit "the dead bodies of a particular class of people, brought from the city of Boston." The decision expressed concern for the "proper regard for the future health, security and improvement of the town." But it also appeared that Charlestown residents were annoyed "by the frequency and offensive peculiarities of these internments" as a justification for turning the dead away.

What could that mean? Daly believes Charlestown folks were objecting to "the funerals themselves, which were much more demonstrative

This stained-glass window of St. Patrick is at Boston College's Gasson Hall.

than the Yankee funerals and often had a musical band and keeners."
Protestant funerals in Boston, while sometimes filled with pageantry,
were more often somber and restrained occasions.

Keening, of course, was an ancient Irish funeral dirge, said to be
the oldest surviving form of Irish music. The lament, in Gaelic, was typically sung by a woman who was a specialist in mourning, and it consisted of chanting the deceased person's name over and over, praising
the qualities of that person, and finally leading a collective wail or moan
with family and friends.

In his book *How Shall We Sing in a New Land?*, Reverend Thomas
Grimes notes that keening and other Irish funeral traditions were actually bothersome to Catholic priests in America. These rituals usually
occurred outside of Church grounds and often featured an elaborate
wake in which drinking, music making, dancing, and storytelling lasted
for several days. Grimes points out that keening was also fashionable
back in Ireland when going-away parties were held for families immi-
grating to America. Not coincidentally, these parties were known as
American wakes.

Bishop Fenwick immediately contested the selectmen's ruling,
appealing to the Massachusetts General Court in March 1832. His
appeal stated:

More than 100 interments have already taken place . . . tombs have
likewise been marked for the accommodation of families, which have
been purchased. . . . Surely the legislature will not pass a law [to]
forever . . . prevent the ashes of a husband [or] parent from mingling
with those of his once beloved and cherished spouse or of his dear
children.

The state ruled that Charlestown officials had the right to demand that Bishop Fenwick seek permission in writing from the selectmen every time he wanted to bury someone from outside of Charlestown in his new Bunker Hill Cemetery. This was an outrageous notion, and everyone knew that it was intended to prevent burials from ever taking place.

On May 19, 1832, Fenwick attempted to comply with the ruling when three-year-old Florence Driscoll died from teething and three-month-old James Kinsley died from infantile disease. Fenwick requested permission to bury the children and received a reply the same day from Selectman Nathan Austin, who stated, "The object of the town in adopting the rule was to prevent the bringing of the dead from the surrounding towns and country. . . . We feel constrained from a sense of duty to decline giving the permission you request."

Fenwick decided he would test the validity of the state ruling and went ahead and buried the children without permission. The matter went to a higher court, and ultimately the Church was recognized as having the right to bury its dead on its own property. But the victory did not soften the harsh mood that many folks had toward the Irish, and the disdain for Irish-Catholic funerals continued for decades to come.

On June 11, 1837, for example, a brawl ensued in Boston when an Irish funeral procession and a volunteer fire brigade returning to the station reached an intersection at the same time. In what became known as the Broad Street Riot, the volunteer firemen and their supporters chased the Irish along Purchase and Broad Streets into their houses, which were then attacked by the enraged mob. "The air was full of flying feathers and straw from the beds which had been ripped up and emptied into the streets," according to contemporary historian J. B. Cullen. Mayor Samuel A. Eliot ordered 800 National Lancers, a military group, to quell the riot and maintain peace.

Burial Places of Famous Irish Americans

Boston is the final resting place of many famous Irish Americans. The graves of notable politicians, public servants, artists, and athletes can be found in the cemeteries listed here.

Old Granary Burying Ground, Boston
James Sullivan, governor of Massachusetts
John Hancock, governor of Massachusetts
William Hall, Charitable Irish Society founder
Patrick Carr, Boston Massacre victim

Mount Auburn Cemetery, Cambridge
Colonel Thomas Cass, Civil War hero
Fanny Parnell, poet

Forest Hills Cemetery, Jamaica Plain
Martin Milmore, sculptor
Eugene O'Neill, Nobel Prize–winning playwright

Holyhood Cemetery, Brookline
John Boyle O'Reilly, poet
Hugh O'Brien, first Irish-born mayor of Boston
Patrick Collins, second Irish-born mayor of Boston
Rose Fitzgerald Kennedy and *Joseph Kennedy,* parents of President John F. Kennedy

Mt. Calvary Cemetery, Roslindale
John L. Sullivan, boxer
James Michael Curley, mayor of Boston

Saint Joseph's Cemetery, West Roxbury
John F. Fitzgerald, first Irish-American mayor of Boston
John W. McCormack, speaker of the United States House of Representatives
Mary Kenny O'Sullivan, labor leader

During the Famine years, Marie Daly notes, officials in other towns such as Roxbury and Cambridge tried to revive the Charlestown model of obstructing Catholic funerals by transferring authority to local selectmen. In 1849 Boston's Board of Health tried to shut down Saint Augustine's Cemetery, claiming that the graves were too shallow, and the following year the city passed an ordinance to this effect. Once again the ordinance was struck down by the lower courts, and the city appealed to the state legislature to pass what became known as the Paddy Funeral Acts, ceding to town authorities the power to influence who could be buried and who could not. Bishop John Fitzpatrick, who succeeded Bishop Fenwick in 1846, was able to convince the moderate members of the state legislature to let the appeal languish in committee, and burials continued. The Yankees, it seemed, were not just unhappy about the Irish living in Boston and Charlestown. They were also displeased about them dying there.

Chapter Four

Fighting Over the Irish (The 1830s)

T HE DAY AFTER Thanksgiving in 1833, when a mob came to Rodger McGowan's house in Charlestown and tore it to the ground piece by piece, the several thousand Irish Catholics living around Boston had to ask themselves, could it get any worse? The answer was yes, it could get a lot worse, for what happened at McGowan's was just part of an escalating chain of violent episodes directed at the Irish through much of the 1830s.

The troubles began on Thanksgiving, one of the holidays most revered in Massachusetts. Governor Joseph Dudley, after all, had proclaimed Thanksgiving a holiday back in 1713, ordering Bostonians to "attend and perform the duties of the day with a religious and becoming devotion." The Puritans had banned Christmas in Boston, considering it a Catholic holiday with pagan roots, so Thanksgiving had emerged as the city's biggest winter celebration, commemorating the harvest feast shared nearly one hundred years earlier when American Indians had helped struggling Pilgrims survive a harsh winter. In later years Irish humorist Peter Dunne Finley would quip that Thanksgiving "Twas founded by the Puritans to give thanks for being preserved from the Indians, and we keep it to give thanks we are preserved from the Puritans."

As the people of Charlestown sat down to their Thanksgiving feast in 1833, an Irish immigrant named Rodger McGowan and his wife were hosting an Irish ball at their home, which doubled as an unlicensed speakeasy, or *shabeen* as the Irish called it, at the corner of Main and Water Streets. On this night they were charging $1.00 per person, offering dancing and fiddling in two rooms below and refreshments in the bar upstairs. About fifty people attended the affair, mostly immigrants who had walked over from Boston and crossed the Charles River Bridge to enjoy the Irish soiree.

After partaking in a Thanksgiving meal, some of the local Charlestown boys went into town for a few beers in Langley's barroom. Before too long a gang of them, including Ira Greene, Caleb Carter, William Bullard, Benjamin Daniells, and Cornelius Harding, were getting drunk. Around ten o'clock they headed over to the Irish party, looking to cause some mischief. They began to throw rocks, chunks of ice, and snowballs against the house. As the men passed by McGowan's at one point, an Irishman from inside the fence hit Ira Greene on the head with a stick. Then some Irish came around the fence and confronted the Yankees, and threats were exchanged.

Ben Daniells bent down to pick up a club and said sarcastically, "I'll have a shillelagh too." The two groups circled each other tensely. One of the Irishmen, later described as a tall man in a light frock coat and with a cap on his head, pointed at Greene and Daniells and said, "I mark you and shall know you again." The two groups circled each other and then went their separate ways, with the Yankees going back to the hotel for a few more drinks and the Irish going into McGowan's.

Around midnight a few dozen Irish men and women were heading back to Boston, with the men still roiling about the ice-throwing incident earlier that evening. Suddenly the Yankees appeared out of the darkness. As town watchman Cyrus Blanchard later testified, he walked with the Irish back toward the bridge "so that they should not be insulted. . . . The young men followed us down and two or three times sung out, I should think insultingly, to the party. I told the young men to go back and let the Irish people alone."

The Irish men walked the women to the bridge, then suddenly turned and chased down the Yankees. On the wharf next to Davidson's Granary, the two sides caught up with each other a final time. Daniells and Bullard picked up clubs from a nearby woodpile and began swinging them, witnesses recalled.

"They had clubs in their hands about four feet long and as thick round as my arm," one testified in court.

"I came from the woodpile, struck an Irishman with a club, kicked an Irishman and knocked him down," Bullard admitted.

Witness Jacob L. Kean picked up the story from that point: "Two [Yankees] getting clubs from the wood pile . . . came round and went upon the side walk. The Irishmen attacked one of these men and knocked him down; he was dressed in a light dress coat and light pantaloons. I saw one man strike another, afterwards, a second strike him, and after he had fallen, then a third and a fourth." The brawl ended quickly, with the Yankees retreating back to the town and the Irish racing back across the bridge to Broad Street, a notorious Irish enclave in Boston where the poorest immigrants lived and where trouble was routine.

Hearing the noise, the Dailey sisters, who ran a shop right next to the bridge, looked out their window and saw a man lying in the gutter. Ellen Dailey went over to the man, clapped her hands, and began screaming, "It's Ben Daniells," then lifted his head up to help him breathe. "I see no one coming [so] I screeched and I screeched" until others came along.

Dr. Walker, the town physician, arrived upon the scene, where he pronounced Daniells, a thirty-six-year-old married blacksmith, dead from injuries around his head. On the way back home Walker passed McGowan's and was surprised to hear Irish dancing and fiddling still going on. He stopped a watchman and asked him to stop the party, but the watchman said he was too scared to go in. Walker called the police captain, who went into the house and found about twenty-five people there. They told the Irish what had happened, and the party broke up at once.

The next day, rumors of the "cold-blooded murder of an American citizen" spread through the town, and a "just indignation" took hold of the townspeople, the *Bunker Hill Aurora* weekly newspaper later reported. Daniells, people said, was an innocent passerby who met up with a group of Irish who were "undoubtedly intoxicated and armed with billets of wood." There was talk of tearing down McGowan's, where all the trouble had started.

McGowan had heard the rumors and immediately armed himself with "muskets, powder and balls." But the town's selectmen confiscated McGowan's weapons, leaving him defenseless. At about six o'clock in the evening the townies began to assemble outside, whipping up the

Irish Landmarks in Charlestown

❖ The Bunker Hill Monument marks the famous battle of June 17, 1775, in which one hundred Americans died. Historian Michael J. O'Brien, in his book *The Irish at Bunker Hill*, identifies 176 Irish-born colonists and hundreds of Irish-Americans who fought in the battle.

❖ Winthrop Square contains the Bunker Hill Memorial Tablets listing the names of the battle's casualties. It also is the site of the Charlestown Civil War Monument, erected in 1871. The statue of the soldier was created by Irish sculptor Martin Milmore. Across the street from the square, at 34 Winthrop Street, is the home of poet John Boyle O'Reilly.

❖ The Charlestown Historical Society is housed with the National Park Service at 43 Monument Square.

❖ The USS *Constitution* in the Navy Yard became famous during the War of 1812. It was commanded by Charles Stewart, the maternal grandfather of Home Rule leader Charles Stuart Parnell and poet Fanny Parnell.

fury needed to invade the house. Armed with pickaxes, bats, guns, and fire hooks, they threw McGowan and his family out then began to break up the furniture and dump the liquor from the bar onto the street. Several rioters grabbed the fire hook from the local hook and ladder company and pulled down a corner of the house.

Meanwhile, according to newspaper accounts, Judge Soley appeared upon the scene and proceeded to read the Riot Act "amid the uproar and assaults of the rioters." This proved ineffective, so town officials called upon a local battalion of U.S. Marines who marched to the site and were immediately attacked by the rioters. With no direct orders to intervene, the Marines returned to their quarters.

Around eleven o'clock about thirty citizens attempted to quell the riot, coming to the scene with Light Infantry guns, under the command of Captain Pritchard. The mob corralled the citizens with ropes, dragging them away from the scene en masse, where they fled back to Town Hall. Now the rioters had "unlimited sway," according to the *Bunker Hill Aurora*. They found a large cable and attached it to McGowan's roof, and finally managed to demolish the house to the ground. As a final act of defiance, according to the paper, they took two dressed hogs from the kitchen and threw them in the river.

A Decade of Rioting

The McGowan's incident was part of a frenzy building up against the city's growing Irish community. The goodwill that had been established in the early 1800s was quickly fading. As Professor Thomas O'Connor writes, the "veneer of religious and ethnic tolerance was already beginning to wear thin."

What should the Irish do? A few months after the McGowan incident, a letter-writer to the *Catholic Intelligencer* newspaper, who signed his name "A Naturalized Irishman," expressed astonishment at the "apathy with which Irishmen in this city bear the insults that are continually cast upon their religion and their country." Why, he asked, after fighting English tyranny all these centuries, would Irishmen cross the Atlantic and "submit to insult and mockery" in a land where they came to be free?

Why indeed. By 1830, about 11 percent, or 7,000 of the city's 61,000 residents were Catholics, of mostly German, French, and Irish descent, and Boston itself was growing dramatically. The city's second mayor, Josiah Quincy, who served between 1823 and 1828, made great strides in modernizing the city and expanding its infrastructure as the population increased. It wasn't only Irish and German immigrants who pushed the city to its limits; rural workers from New England and the Maritimes were also pouring into Boston looking for work.

Quincy, who had been a close friend of Bishop DeCheverus, seemed sympathetic to the immigrant plight, and he made great strides in improving sanitary conditions in the city by putting restrictions on livestock, collecting garbage regularly, and cleaning the streets. The rapid expansion of the city brought the attendant urban ills. Crime was on the rise, and so were public drunkenness, arson, prostitution, and vagrancy. Rioting seemed to come into fashion as rival volunteer fire companies, neighborhood gangs, and other public audiences engaged in fights as if they were sporting events. Much of the rioting was directed against the newcomers. As Professor Jack Tager writes in his book *Boston Riots,* "hatred against Catholicism by Yankee plebeians was an intrinsic part of their heritage."

The Boston Irish seemed timid, trying not to draw attention to themselves. Perhaps they were falsely optimistic that the situation might improve if they kept their heads down. As the goodwill established after the Revolutionary War continued to deteriorate, Irish Catholics had become the whipping post for the city's collective fears, anxieties, and resentments.

Conservative Protestant preachers kept the emotional flames high. Professor Tager points out that in the 1830s a "nationwide evangelical movement" was targeting Catholicism and liberal Protestantism as "a danger to American democracy." The movement, called the Second Awakening, was a sequel to Reverend Jonathan Edwards' Great Awakening of the 1740s, which sought to restore a pure Puritanism to New Englanders. The stern, rigorous outlook some Bostonians yearned for seemed to personify the quip journalist H. L. Mencken made about Puritanism: the haunting fear that someone, somewhere, may be happy.

The Jesuits Keep Watch

The Catholic community received a shot of self-esteem in 1829 when Bishop Fenwick established the first Catholic newspaper in Massachusetts initially called *The Jesuit or Catholic Sentinel.* The editor was Reverend Doctor Thomas J. O'Flaherty, a scholar and physician from County Kerry who had studied theology and medicine in Dublin and Rome. He had translated a tome on the Spanish Inquisition and was said to be the intellectual equal of any preacher in town. In 1830, when Reverend Henry Ward Beecher began a series of anti-Catholic sermons, O'Flaherty rose to the occasion and challenged every one of the sermons, pointing out the theological flaws and the non-Christian attitude toward Catholics.

Joining O'Flaherty in the fray was Patrick Donahoe, who had arrived in Boston from Munnery, County Cavan, in 1825 at the age of fourteen. A Catholic, Patrick was a novelty at the predominantly protestant Adams School in Boston, and the older boys liked to chalk a cross on his back, according to historian Robert Walsh. He took a job as a typesetter with the local paper, the *Columbian Sentinel,* and by the time he was twenty-four had established the first boat ticketing service between Ireland and America. In 1834 Donahue took over *The Jesuit* newspaper, which had undergone many name changes since 1829, then rechristened it the

Boston Pilot, which became the most influential Catholic newspaper in the United States. Donahoe ran the *Pilot,* serving as both publisher and occasional editor, through the end of the century.

In the 1830s Irish activities in Boston continued to increase. A literary group named the Hibernian Lyceum held weekly meetings at Columbian Hall behind the courthouse. The Boston Roman Catholic Mutual Society brought Irish businessmen together. Thomas Mooney's bookstore, at the corner of Federal and Franklin Streets, opened a Singing School for young Catholics, using the new *Catholic Music Book* that Bishop Fenwick had paid to publish.

LIBRARY OF MICHAEL P. QUINLIN

The Charitable Irish Society was approaching its centennial and had been energized by James Boyd, an Ulster Irish Presbyterian who patented the first fire hose in America. President of the Society from 1836 to 1837, Boyd delivered a rousing oratory on

Patrick Donahoe was publisher of the Pilot.

the Irish at the centennial dinner. The Society, which had started as a Protestant group, began selecting Irish Catholics as its presidents. Among these were businessman Thomas Murphy, Bernard Fitzpatrick (the future bishop of Boston), and Reverend O'Flaherty.

The increasingly visible Catholic activities did not likely comfort the plebeians and preachers who were calling for a return to Puritanism and were often inflamed by the spectacle of Irish worship. On Saint Patrick's Day, 1833, for example, the Cathedral of the Holy Cross overflowed with parishioners, and hundreds more waited outside hoping to get in. Reporting on the occasion, *The Jesuit* noted, incorrectly, that the scene "afforded great edification to the good citizens of Boston, who beheld them, as they passed, at prayer, and all of them kneeling reverently with their faces turned toward the altar, on the hard pavement, and in the open street, in front of their church."

In November 1833, just a few days before the Thanksgiving incident at McGowan's, the first Catholic concert was held at the Masonic Temple. "Never was the Masonic Temple more densely crowded; and great were the numbers who could not gain admittance," *The Jesuit* reported. Organizers vowed to hold another concert on the Sunday before Christmas.

Support for the Irish

While many plebeians and preachers appeared intolerant, the Irish had garnered sympathy from Boston's intelligentsia, at least as far as Ireland's plight was concerned. Nineteen-year-old poet and abolitionist John Greenleaf Whittier wrote a poem in 1826 entitled "The Emerald Isle," in which he mourned Ireland's "stern patriots in vain to the tomb ye descended" while condemning "the hand of the tyrant extended over the land of your fathers."

In 1832, John Quincy Adams, who was then a Massachusetts Congressman after having served as president of the United States (1825–29), published a lengthy poem called "Dermot McMorrogh, or the Conquest of Ireland, an historical tale of Ireland in the Twelfth Century." The poem supported Ireland's quest for independence while criticizing the bloody conquest of Ireland by the British. One stanza in particular captures the public perception of the Irish during that period:

> And then, the people were, as they are now,
> A careless, thoughtless, brave, kind-hearted race:
> With boiling bosom and with dauntless brow
> With shrewdest humor, and with laughing face;
> The women, purer than the virgin's vow,
> Blooming in beauty, and adorned with grace . . .

Writer Francis J. Grund, who published a two-volume book in 1837 called *The Americans, in Their Moral, Social and Political Relations,* complimented the Boston Irish as "a remarkably orderly people . . . not usually given to intemperance but on the contrary willing to aid in its suppression." Grund sympathized with their impoverished plight, but he thought they had made a "noble beginning in Boston." If he had one piece of advice, it was this: "Let the Irish, on their arrival in the United

The Ursuline Convent in Charlestown was burned to the ground in 1834.

States, be, above all things, careful not to disturb the peace of the citizens by revels of any kind." But very often it was Bostonians who disturbed the peace.

In 1834 the Ursuline Convent at Mount Benedict in Charlestown was set afire. The frightened nuns and their young female boarding students (most of them, ironically, Protestants) rushed from the school as it went up in flames, with the bloodthirsty mob intent on burning it to the ground. A newspaper later reported that the "pianos and harps, thrown from the windows when the Convent was set on fire, were subsequently burnt, and nothing but an old chair and one or two worthless articles were saved from destruction."

Many public leaders condemned the mob of Yankee workmen who had burned the school. Lynde Walter, editor of the *Boston Transcript*, wrote an editorial denouncing the episode:

> *We passed the ruins of the Ursuline Convent this morning. [It] was indeed a melancholy and mortifying sight. We hung our heads in shame whilst our spirit was indignant. We felt a great sense of degradation whilst we could have leapt into burning flames to seize upon the atrocious villains who had brought this disgrace.*

Assaults against the Irish continued through the decade. In 1837 the Broad Street riots occurred when a fire brigade and Irish funeral procession clashed at an intersection. Mayor Samuel Eliot stepped in to keep the Yankees from burning down Irish homes. Later that year an Irish voluntary militia group was attacked by other brigades during the annual brigade mustering on Boston Common. The Irish group called themselves the Montgomery Guards after Irish-born Revolutionary War hero General Richard Montgomery. When the Irish regiment arrived on the Common, the other groups walked off the parade ground in protest and then marched through the streets of Boston playing "Yankee Doodle" on their fifes and drums. As the Montgomery Guards returned to their barracks near Faneuil Hall, a mob attacked them, pelting them "with stones, coal, and sticks of wood all along their line of march." The Irish held formation and marched quickly to their armory, which was surrounded briefly by several thousand Bostonians. Mayor Eliot again intervened.

By the end of the decade, many Bostonians wondered whether their City on a Hill would now be destroyed by reckless, desperate Irish Catholics. Could the problem get any worse? The answer was yes. In 1840 the ship company, the Cunard Line, subsidized by the British government, built a pier in East Boston and began direct routes from Britain to Boston, using the port as the best way to distribute mail throughout North America. As historian Oscar Handlin writes, "The line itself did not engage in the immigrant trade until 1863; but by engrossing other passenger business almost at once, it forced the established packet lines to devote themselves to the least desirable customers."

That would be the Irish. Ireland continued to fare poorly under the administration of the British government. In 1836 a British report by George Nicholls suggested that emigration was a possible remedy for Irish destitution. In the 1840s Ireland remained embattled by political unrest and economic instability caused by the policies and practices of the British government and by a series of potato crop failures. Between 1845 and 1849 all of those conditions would work against the Irish, and they would be forced to flee Ireland, hopping aboard rickety ships in hopes of avoiding disease and death. Unfortunately they couldn't escape either. Instead, they brought both with them.

CHAPTER FIVE

Invasion of the Fruitful Barbarians (The 1840s)

TWO IRISH immigrants, each named Patrick Sullivan, left their homes in the year 1847 and took passage to Boston. One of them flourished there; the other perished.

The Sullivan who survived had boarded the good ship *Unicorn* in London on July 22, 1847, and sailed into Boston that August. His only skill was dancing, so he set up a dance academy and taught boys and girls "the fine art of symmetry, of grace, of rhythm," as it was later described. He married Swiss immigrant Andrienne List, a classically trained pianist, and they settled at 22 Bennett Street in the South End, where the New England Medical Center is today.

The other Patrick Sullivan spent his final days on this earth quarantined at Deer Island in Boston Harbor. He died on November 11, 1847, of diabetes at age 33. He was the 260th Irish immigrant to die at the quarantine hospital since its opening on May 29 of that year. He was one of nine Sullivans who died on the island between June and December 1847.

In September 1856 Sullivan the dancer and his Swiss wife had a son whom they named Louis, who became the nation's foremost architect and is regarded as the Father of American Architecture. In his 1924 book *The Autobiography of an Idea,* Louis Sullivan described his father's remarkable odyssey through life. When Patrick was twelve he became separated from his father at an Irish county fair and never saw him again. "Thus he was thrown upon the world to make his way," wrote Louis. "With a curious little fiddle, he wandered barefoot about the countryside, to fiddle here and there for those who wished to dance . . . [eventually] his attention focused on dancing as an art." He moved to London, where he taught dancing "as a social art of grace, of deportment, and of personal

Famine Memorials around Boston

A number of Irish Famine memorials have been built in the Boston area to commemorate the Great Hunger that devastated Ireland from 1845 to 1849.

❖ Boston Irish Famine Memorial, unveiled in 1998, is at the corner of School and Washington Streets.

❖ Cambridge Irish Famine Memorial, unveiled in 1997, is on Cambridge Common near Harvard Square.

❖ Cohasset Celtic Cross, unveiled in 1914 in Central Cemetery, commemorates the Galway passengers aboard the famine ship *St. John,* which perished during a storm in 1849.

❖ Deer Island Irish Famine Memorial honors more than 700 famine refugees who died and were buried on the island at Rest Haven Cemetery.

❖ Providence Irish Famine Memorial honors the Irish famine refugees who settled in Rhode Island.

❖ Lawrence Irish Famine Memorial at St. Mary's Cemetery in Lawrence, Massachusetts, honors the Irish famine refugees who settled in the Merrimack Valley.

For more information, visit the Web site www.irishheritagetrail.com.

carriage . . . [H]e was [considered] no gentleman, as that technical term went, but essentially a lackey, a flunkey or a social parasite."

"It is probable that about this time," Louis continued, "the lure of America, goal of the adventurous spirit, the great hospitable, open-armed land of equality and opportunity, had been acting on his imagination." The rest, as they say, is history.

But the Patrick Sullivan who languished on Deer Island is also part of our history. He was one of several hundred men, women, and children who suffered a sad, painful, lonely death at a quarantine station in a harbor 3,000 miles away from home. Fate has always had a hand in Irish history, and it's worth pondering what this Patrick Sullivan and the other Sullivans might have become had they actually made it to the Promised Land, which shimmered just 5 miles in the distance on the shores of America.

It is impossible to downplay the utter tragedy of the Irish Famine, known as the Great Hunger, which occurred in Ireland between 1845 and 1849. Out of Ireland's population of eight million, nearly one million people died, and another two million fled the island, many of them in abject poverty, selling the clothes on their backs to get ship passage and often arriving at their destination—Quebec, Boston, New York—distraught, diseased, and, in many cases, dying or dead.

Bostonians were entirely unprepared for what happened in 1847, known in Irish history as Black '47. How could they be otherwise? On New Year's Day, when the *Boston Daily Bee* cheerfully wished readers "health and prosperity . . . that they may increase and multiply," who could have imagined that the fallout from an impending calamity—of such scale that it could only be described in the most extreme terms— was about to descend on Boston?

Details of the dying taking place in Ireland were described in con- temporary accounts in language that strikes modern readers as apoca- lyptic. "Children have been found lying dead on their mother's breasts which they had gnawed in twain to procure the nourishment that was not there; and men and women devour the mantling filth of the gutters to alleviate the pangs of the awful hunger which oppresses the whole people," wrote the *Boston Bee* in February 1847. The magnitude of the despair and desperation cannot be overstated.

Over a period of twelve months, more than 100,000 Irish refugees fleeing from famine landed in Boston in the most pitiful condition imaginable. Irish paupers lay on the streets, their tongues swollen from ship fever, signaling for help with their eyes. Irish vagrants broke into people's homes and stole from shops. Irish children whose parents had died on route to Boston were put in orphanages. Fifty refugees camped out on Boston Common, with nowhere else to go. A family of seven who landed in Quebec walked the 400 miles to Boston and, exhausted, ended up at the quarantine station. Some Irish, distraught by the carnage they had witnessed, committed suicide by jumping out of windows or by slitting their throats with a razor. Others, simply unable to cope, broke down and were placed in the lunatic asylum in South Boston.

It was a year of ironies and mysteries of the human condition that neither the poet, the pundit, nor the preacher could fully comprehend, much less articulate. The swollen tongues and shrunken stomachs caused by ship fever rendered the Irish speechless and unable to eat when they arrived. Freedom of speech in the land of plenty was lost on these Irish. In Boston, Protestant ministers like Reverend Kirk charged the English government and the Catholic Church of doing to the Irish what Americans were accused of doing to the slaves.

THE
BOSTON MEDICAL AND SURGICAL JOURNAL.

VOL. XXXVII.   WEDNESDAY, JANUARY 19, 1848.   No. 25.

CLINICAL NOTES AND POST-MORTEM ILLUSTRATIONS OF TYPHUS OR SHIP FEVER, AS IT OCCURRED AT HOUSE OF INDUSTRY AND DEER ISLAND HOSPITALS IN 1847.

By J. B. Upham, M.D., Boston.

[Communicated for the Boston Medical and Surgical Journal.]

THE following illustrations of maculated typhus or ship fever were obtained during a period of four months' observation at the hospitals connected with the House of Industry at South Boston, and subsequently of four weeks in the fever wa... ... ...nd. During this time about 700 cases of that disease w... ...ted are a few from a multitude of records ... ...e or interest of the case dictate... ...ances some will be submitted a... ...others will be made, or the path...

It is presumed no apolo... ...e in a few numbers of this Jou... ...me of them may seem at first ... ...e subject demands the attenti... ...disease among all classes and c... ...particu... larly fatal in this count... ...our pr...

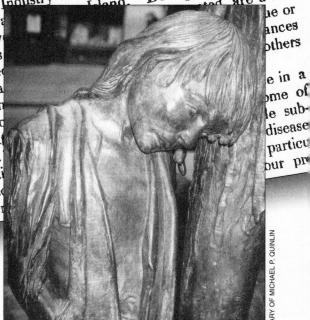

This image of a starving boy is seen at the Boston Irish Famine Memorial.

And yet, in the midst of utter depravity and human suffering were wondrous triumphs of humanity. Even as narrow-minded Bostonians added insults to the injuries of the Irish, big-hearted Bostonians proved to be among the most generous and compassionate citizens in the entire nation. As nativists threatened to burn down the quarantine station where hundreds of immigrants battled death, the city's finest Yankee physicians were at the hospital, tending to their patients at personal risk to their lives.

The USS *Jamestown* Sails to the Rescue

When the full extent of the crisis became known in Boston, both the Irish and the Yankee communities sprang into action. On February 7, 1847, Bishop John Fitzpatrick gave an emotionally charged sermon from the pulpit of the Cathedral of the Holy Cross, and parish priests followed suit. By the end of the month the Boston Archdiocese had raised $20,000 for Ireland. Workmen were sending in $5.00 bills, and schoolchildren were giving over their paltry savings for this urgent, desperate cause.

The city's Yankee leaders, meanwhile, called a meeting at Faneuil Hall on February 17; it was attended by 4,000 people. Harvard President Edward Everett and Boston Mayor Josiah Quincy Jr., along with the city's leading merchants, made a passionate appeal to aid the starving people of Ireland. They formed the New England Relief Committee, which raised more than $150,000 in three weeks to purchase supplies.

Four days later Robert Bennet Forbes, a wealthy China trade merchant from Milton, petitioned Congress for the loan of a naval ship to bring supplies to the people of Ireland. Permission was granted, and the USS *Jamestown*, then anchored at the Charlestown Navy Yard, was designated to Boston, while the USS *Macedonian* was given over to Captain George DeKay for a similar enterprise in New York.

The notion of sending a ship filled with food and provisions to Ireland at once captured the imagination of the entire state, and donations came pouring in. People recalled that in 1676 the Irish ship *Katherine* brought relief supplies to Plymouth, when the colonists were fighting the Indians during King Phillip's War. According to Forbes's memoirs, this recollection was brought to his attention by Reverend R. C. Waterston, who wrote in a letter, "It is an interesting fact that the people of Ireland, nearly 200 years ago, thus sent relief to our Pilgrim fathers in their time of need, and what we have been doing for that famishing country is but a return for what their fathers did for our fathers."

Rev. Waterston went on to write, "I consider the mission of the *Jamestown* as one of the grandest events in the history of our country. A ship-of-war changed into an angel of mercy, departing on no errand of death, but with the bread of life to an unfortunate and perishing people."

The Catholics were equally impressed with the *Jamestown* mission. On April 4 the *Pilot* wrote, "Captain Forbes is one of our most eminent merchants and retired sea captains. He has done himself infinite credit by his untiring exertions throughout, and his name will long be remembered by every friend of Ireland."

Henry Lee's book *Massachusetts Help to Ireland During the Great Famine* gives a masterful account of this extraordinary episode in Boston's history:

> *Contributions of food continued to arrive from all over New England. So great was the feeling of those with relatives in Ireland, that numbers came carrying sacks of flour or potatoes entreating the crew to let them be put on board . . . . [T]he cargo consisted largely of Indian corn and bread but included also hams, pork, oatmeal, potatoes, flour, rye, beans, rice, fish and sixteen barrels of clothing.*

Irish longshoremen helped load the vessel on March 17, and on the morning of March 28 the USS *Jamestown* set sail for Cork carrying 800 tons of supplies, with Captain Forbes at the helm and thirty-eight men who signed on as the crew. Crowds lining the wharf and the shores cheered as the ship headed out to the open seas. The fifteen-day voyage faced foul weather and a blend of rain, sleet, wind, and fog requisite for that time of year, but finally, Forbes later wrote, "we cast anchor in the outer harbor of what had been known as Queenstown."

Back in Boston, the papers enthusiastically reported on the trip, failing to note the cruel irony that became apparent when the provincial rulers greeted the crew with an invitation to a sumptuous arrival dinner. "A deputation of the gentry of Cork visited the ship. After some conversation the deputation withdrew, having previously invited Captain Forbes and officers to a public dinner, which the gallant gentleman kindly accepted. The dinner was a very special affair, and attended by the most influential classes in and around Cove," the papers reported. Forbes and his crew found this banquet most embarrassing, however, as Irish citizens lay dying in the streets nearby.

According to Lee, "Forbes strongly urged that all public demonstrations be dispensed with on account of the prevailing distress, [but] his hosts were not to be denied the satisfaction of showing their gratitude to New England and America . . . . It should be remembered that one of the terrible anomalies of the famine years—and one which greatly surprised the Americans—was the availability of food to those who could afford to buy it."

The *Boston Daily Bee* reported, "The tables were sumptuously spread, the company most honorable, and the sentiments drank were of a high order." But Forbes was more interested in seeing firsthand the suffering everyone had heard so much about. He was escorted around Cork by Father Theobald Mathew, the famous temperance priest. Forbes later wrote,

> *I went with Father Mathew only a few steps out of the principal streets . . . into a lane . . . . [I]t was the valley of death and pestilence itself. I would gladly forget, if I could, the scenes I witnessed . . . [of] more actual distress and apparent poverty than I ever saw in my whole life . . . yet I am told that I saw nothing compared to the indoor suffering and the suffering in the country.*

Forbes was overwhelmed by the gratitude he received from the people of Cork but more so by the plight of the dying, and when he returned home, arriving at the Navy Yard on May 16, he immediately set his sights on the USS *Macedonian,* which sat in New York harbor only partially filled with supplies. According to Lee, Captain Forbes and the Boston Committee took over the task of funding and organizing the ship, which sailed for Cork on June 19, arriving there on July 16, 1847.

More humanitarian aid was sent to Ireland over the next three years, including a donation of $710 by the Choctaw Indians, according to a *Connecticut Courant* article published in 1847. The *Boston Pilot* reported that the Shakers of New Lebanon contributed $700 worth of clothing, while the *Merrimack Courier* bragged that the mill workers of Lawrence, mostly Irish immigrants, gave $2,000 for famine relief.

But the two famine relief ships organized by Forbes and others remained in the collective memory of Bostonians for years to come and became part of Irish lore. Samuel Lover, one of Ireland's leading poets and songwriters, penned a song in 1847 called "War Ship of Peace." It captured the spirit of Irish gratitude toward the United States, which is referred to as Columbia in the lyrics:

> *Sweet Land of Song, thy harp doth hang upon the willows now*
> *While famine's blight and fever's pain stamp misery on thy brow*
> *Yet take thy harp and raise thy voice, Tho faint and low it be*
> *And let thy sinking heart rejoice, in friends still left to thee.*
>
> *Look out! Look out across the sea that guards thy emerald shore*
> *A ship of war is bound for thee, but with no warlike stores*
> *Her leader sleeps tis mercy's breath that wafts her o'er the sea*
> *She goes not forth to deal out death but bears new life to thee.*
>
> *Thy wasted head can scarcely strike the chords of grateful praise*
> *Thy plaintive tear is now unlike thy voice of prouder days*
> *Yet in her sorrow, tearful still, let Erin's voice proclaim*
> *In bardic praise on every hill, Columbia's glorious name.*

The Poor House of the World

During the forty-nine days when Forbes was away, Boston's public opinion of the Irish Famine had undergone a dramatic shift. Historian Cecil Woodham-Smith comments on this changing dynamic in her classic book *The Great Hunger:*

> *By a curious piece of reasoning, the Irish starving in Ireland were regarded as unfortunate victims, to be generously helped, while the same Irish, having crossed the Atlantic to starve in Boston, were described as the scourings of Europe and resented as an intolerable burden to the taxpayer.*

The Forbes House

Robert Bennet Forbes (1804–1889) was a China trade merchant described as having "the most original brain and attractive personality of any merchant of his day." In 1833 he built a Greek Revival mansion in the town of Milton, Massachusetts; it had a full view of Boston Harbor and the cargo ships coming in from the Far East. In 1967 the *Captain Robert Forbes House* at 215 Adams Street was designated a National Historic Landmark and was made into a museum that focuses "on social, cultural and historical context of the 19th century." The museum contains many of the artifacts associated with the voyage of the USS *Jamestown* and with the Forbes family's friendship with the Irish through the end of the century. For more information, call (617) 696–1815 or visit the Web site: www.key-biz.com/ssn/milton/forbes.html.

Even as the *Jamestown* unloaded its provisions, the dying Irish whom Forbes had seen in the back lanes of Cork were now turning up at Boston Harbor. Many of them had sold everything they had to get a one-way ticket, which cost $12. Others had been rounded up by their landlords and sent overseas to become someone else's problem.

The debate went up a notch when a new paper published by Reverend Dennison and named the *American Signal* hit the newsstands on May 20, 1847, keeping up a relentless attack on the immigrants:

> *Is this Boston? Or is it Dublin? Did our Pilgrim Fathers land on Plymouth Rock or was it in the Cove of Cork? Have we a right to the streets of the city where we were born or do they belong to his holiness, the Pope? Must we submit to be overrun by the paupers of English government? Shall our beloved country be forced by despots to become the POOR HOUSE OF THE WORLD?*

It seemed that the indelible fears that Bostonians carried with them since the Puritan days—of economic uncertainty, religious instability, and the spread of disease—had exploded to the surface in a raucous debate that threatened to undermine civility and authority. The spread of disease was the most potent fear because it combined both medical ignorance and religious superstition, as a report of the Boston Society for the Prevention of Pauperism later acknowledged in 1865:

> *Good health and clean living were synonymous in the mid-19th century. . . . [I]t was still acceptable in certain quarters to characterize*

*contagious diseases as God's form of moral cleansing, and there were
many instances where the lack of moral character of the Irish was
blamed for their medical woes.*

Thankfully for the Irish, a group of Yankee doctors stepped forward
to help the dying refugees in the face of a growing nativist revolt. The
names of Dr. Albert G. Upham, Dr. Joseph Moriarty and his brother Dr.
John Moriarty, Dr. Thomas Welsh, Dr. C. A. Walker, Dr. Henry Gratton
Clark, and Dr. Jabez Baxter Upham may have been forgotten in Boston
through the passage of time. But they, along with their dedicated nursing staff, most of whom were Irish immigrants, saved thousands of Irish
lives, provided physical comfort and solace to the dying, and advanced
the medical knowledge of ship fever to benefit future generations. They
became the unsung heroes of the Boston Irish. Several of the doctors,
including Clark and Upham, kept careful notes and later published
their findings in medical journals like the *Boston Medical and Surgical
Journal,* the forerunner to the *New England Journal of Medicine.*

The setting for their brave and risky work was Deer Island, a 200-
acre island about 5 miles from downtown Boston. The island had been
so named by seventeenth-century colonists because of "the deare which
often swimme thither from Maine, when they are chased by the wolves."
In 1717, when the first wave of Ulster Irish began arriving in the
Harbor, the town selectmen had voted to build a hospital on the island
to contain the spread of diseases like measles and smallpox. The crisis
passed, however, and the hospital wasn't built.

More than a century later, in May 1847, city officials designated
Deer Island as the site of the city's quarantine hospital, as the threat of
a typhus fever epidemic loomed. The almshouse in South Boston had
already filled to capacity, and an average of five patients, mostly females,
were dying each day. Irish people were literally huddled on the streets
of Boston, waiting to die. On May 27 the first famine ship, the *John
Clifford,* was sent to quarantine, and by the end of the week more than
100 patients were in the Deer Island Hospital. The first patient to die at
the hospital was six-year-old Mary Nelson, who succumbed to typhus
fever on June 1, followed on June 3 by one-year-old Mary Connolly. The
city created a cemetery on the island and named it Rest Haven. It would
eventually hold several hundred Irish famine fatalities.

The Deer Island Hospital was directed by Dr. Joseph Moriarty, who came from a merchant family in Salem and had married the niece of John Hancock. Moriarty was assisted by Dr. Thomas Welsh, according to Dr. John McGolgan of the City of Boston Archives, along with a "support staff about fifty strong [which] consisted of eighteen nurses, a store keeper, a boatman, a farmer, teamsters, laborers, cooks, kitchen boys, chamber girls, a table girl, ten washerwomen, a baker, a seamstress and a teacher." Quoting from city records, McGolgan notes that the hospital was run with compassion:

> *Health aides . . . were to receive patients when brought to the island, and see that they are properly prepared . . . . [T]hat they are kindly treated, and their food is properly served and distributed, that their apartments are kept clean and in good order and properly warmed and ventilated.*

The disease most fatal to the Irish was typhus fever, also known as ship fever. Typhus, from the Greek word *tuphos,* meaning "mist," was a term coined in the eighteenth century to describe the clouded mental state of the patient. In the first six months at the Deer Island hospital, it killed 188 people. Another seventy died of complications related to the disease: dropsy, diarrhea, and dysentery.

The fever, Dr. Clark reported, attacked its victims suddenly, causing chills followed by "morbid heat of the skin, in many cases very intense and pungent." It caused pains in the head, back, and limbs, dizziness, deafness or ringing in the ears, and put victims in a stupor. It was, Clark explained, "a disease of debility . . . one characteristic is the great indifference the patient manifests."

In his medical notes, Dr. J. B. Upham reports treating a patient named John Salter, age forty-five, on the day after Christmas in 1847: "a strong muscular man, in an advanced stage of the fever with symptoms like low muttering delirium, inability to speak, teeth loaded with black sores, skin covered with spots, flying blisters. He died the following morning."

In all, 247 Irish patients died and were buried on Deer Island between June and December 1847. Several physicians and at least one public official also died in that six-month period. Daniel Chandler,

Superintendent of Alien Passengers, died in mid-June, followed by Dr. Albert Upham, who was noted as "a young man of much promise." Two physicians in Rhode Island—Dr. Alfred Knight in Cumberland, and a Dr. Fletcher in Providence—died treating ship fever victims. In December Dr. Moriarty himself died of typhus, leaving behind a wife and three children.

Moriarty was replaced by his own brother, John, who continued the extraordinary work of saving immigrants. By December 1848 panic about an epidemic had abated, and the quarantine station was closed down. The city transferred to Deer Island the inmates of the House of Industry, formerly called the Bridewell, where able-bodied paupers and petty criminals were put to work while incarcerated. Dr. John Moriarty continued to treat patients at the hospital into the 1850s. The other physicians had distinguished careers in Boston, particularly Dr. Clark, who became a surgeon at Massachusetts General Hospital. Over the next quarter century, he weighed in on every public health issue in the city.

Although the threat of disease subsided, Bostonians became afflicted over the next few decades with another virulent epidemic, one that even the most dedicated of doctors were at a loss to cure. It was called Know Nothingism, and it spread through the Yankee working-class neighborhoods throughout the city. Its symptoms were hatred, intolerance, and brutality, and it evoked a mob mentality characterized by racist threats, bodily harm, and the destruction of property. It would become the typhus fever of the 1850s.

CHAPTER SIX

The Have-Nothings Meet the Know-Nothings (The 1850s)

O N THE VERY FIRST day of her job as a live-in maid, Irish immigrant Catherine Murphy stole an expensive silk dress from her employer's wardrobe and disappeared into the night.

It was May 4, 1853. That morning Murphy, a fresh-faced teenager, had been hired to clean house in the Fort Hill neighborhood, where sea captains and merchants had their stately homes. Murphy worked a full day in the house, dusting the furniture and putting away clothes, then retired to her room for the night. At some point she crept into the dressing room of her mistress and ran off with a brand-new silk dress.

The theft was discovered, and the aggrieved lady and her husband raced down the narrow streets of Boston, searching the Irish neighborhoods along the waterfront. They passed people begging on the streets or coming home from work muddy and tired from digging trenches for the new water lines. They saw children running around barefoot and a bagpiper playing on a street corner for spare change. Eventually they found young Catherine in one of the notorious dance cellars on Wharf Street. There she was, wrote the *Boston Herald,* "with the striped silk on her back, dancing merrily with the boys . . . in a dark place, in which about one hundred boys and girls were dancing to the music of a single fiddle." She was arrested.

Catherine Murphy was a teenager who yearned for nice things she couldn't afford. In normal times, her crime would have been viewed as a petty misdemeanor. But the 1850s in Boston were not normal times. To Bostonians, the teenager's action appeared to verify what many believed: The Irish could not be trusted. They didn't belong in this country. They shouldn't be taking jobs away from "real" Americans. They should go back to Ireland.

The suspicious, unforgiving nature of Bostonians was not new. But it reached an ugly nadir in the 1850s, as hundreds of thousands of immigrants streamed into the city. Discrimination and disdain, political opposition and mob violence rained upon the Irish. Having just barely survived the 1840s, one of the most dismal decades in Ireland's history, the Irish were about to be confronted by a new brand of discrimination 2,000 miles away from their tiny villages and farmlands.

Boston continued to be a favored destination for the Irish. By 1850, 46,000 Irish living in Boston comprised a third of the total population of 138,000. It was not uncommon to see articles in local papers presenting grim news with headlines like "More Foreign Paupers." This excerpt from the *Boston Herald* in April 1851 describes a typical scene:

> *One hundred and sixty-two foreign paupers arrived in Boston yester-*
> *day on the Worcester, Fall River and Boston and Maine Railroads.*
> *Of this number 71 were entirely destitute and 18 children from one*
> *poor house in Ireland were barefooted. A more miserable looking gang*
> *of human beings never were seen. They should be sent back at once to*
> *those who so unmercifully cast them away. In addition about 300*
> *Irish immigrants arrived in vessels at Quarantine Wednesday.*

The quarantine station on Deer Island had closed, but the hospital continued to treat Irish who were being shipped back to the island from Boston, where the unsanitary conditions of ghetto life afflicted the vulnerable just as the coffin ships had. One hundred and fifty-nine men, women, and children died and were buried on the island in 1850 alone. The youngest to die that year was Mary Aldrich, fifteen days old; the oldest was James Hurley, aged sixty-three. Donahues, Finns, Cronins, Harrigans, Kelleys, Gallaghers, Donovans, Shanahans, and McCanns were among those who died on Deer Island in 1850, a microcosm of the Irish Diaspora.

Edward Everett Hale, one of Boston's leading citizens of the day, described the Irish as "a horde of disappointed, starved, beaten men and women." They had become a burden to the taxpayers and a threat to Boston's health and welfare, not to mention its quality of life. "The healthy social and moral character we once enjoyed is liable to be lost forever," complained one public official. "Pauperism, crime, disease and death stare us in the face."

In fact, the immigrants were becoming indispensable to the city's expansion and industrialization during this time. Irish men were needed to work on backbreaking and dangerous public works projects like digging trenches for water pipes and railroad lines from Boston to the Great Lakes. The women were hired as mill workers, domestic servants, and nannies. The ubiquity of these immigrants in everyday life created an identity crisis for those Americans of English stock, who felt their lineage being diluted by "the fruitful invasion of barbarians," as well-known Bostonian Eliot Norton later put it.

Meanwhile, Irish immigrants in Boston were searching desperately to find families, friends, and neighbors from whom they were separated during the Great Exodus from Ireland. The *Boston Pilot,* which had been running a Missing Friends column since the 1830s, ran ads each week from Irish immigrants trying to restore the social connectedness that had defined their communities. The *Pilot* was also an early advocate of the Irish Emigrant Society, which formed to help Irish in need. The Society's real goal, though, was to take the newly arrived Irish and send them right out to "the fertile Western States, where the resources of a country are ready for the hands that shall cultivate them." Unlike the Germans, Scandinavians, and other northern European groups, the Irish decided to stay in the eastern cities, and by 1856 the Irish Emigrant Society had closed its doors.

Old-line Bostonians formed numerous relief agencies to help the Irish. The Boston Society for the Prevention of Pauperism, headed by Moses Grant, sought to find work for immigrants as housekeepers, servants, farmers, laboring men, coachmen, waiters, clerks, and mechanics. The Society was sincere in wanting to help, but its righteous pontifications against drinking and its interest in converting boys and girls to Protestantism turned many immigrants away from its services. One of its accomplishments was to rail against the practice of lumping together "under one roof the aged, the infirm, the sick and the virtuous poor" with "common street walkers, drunkards and vagabonds" at the facilities on Deer Island.

Dancing in the Dark

When rounding up the Irish during the 1850s, the police focused on the North End, today the city's celebrated Italian neighborhood of restaurants, cafes, and summer festivals honoring patron saints. In the mid-nineteenth century, the waterfront neighborhood where Paul Revere once lived was a bustling bowery of cheap saloons, flophouses, gambling dens, and dance halls. Jewish peddlers set up a cornucopia of imported goods and fresh fruit and vegetables that they hawked in open market stalls. Sailors came off their ships to let off steam, and travelers were constantly arriving on boat routes from New York or Nova Scotia. When the Irish began coming during the Famine years, landlords had converted dozens of warehouse buildings into hundreds of tiny apartments where dozens of people shared tiny rooms with no running water or sanitary facilities. In 1849 as an Asiatic cholera outbreak was killing more than 5,000 people, many of them Irish immigrants, the city's health inspector Lemuel Shattuck reckoned the life expectancy of Irish in Boston to be just fourteen years.

The North End became like the Avenue of Broken Dreams and Fleeting Pleasures for the Irish. The most vulnerable ones, traumatized by the famine they had escaped and the deaths of their loved ones, succumbed to the temptations of alcohol and vice. And as they had often done under British rule in Ireland, the Irish created a flourishing underground economy outside of authority. Naturally, authorities couldn't stand for that.

In April 1851 the Boston police made a series of famous raids along Ann Street, rounding up vagabonds, gamblers, prostitutes, and musicians who had created a Mardi Gras atmosphere in one of America's most conservative cities. One evening the police raided the gambling dens, rounding up eighty-six people and parading them before the press. Another night the police raided the "dance cellars," arresting more than 200 people, including "40 males and the rest females of the lowest class found in the city," reported the *Boston Herald*.

"There were persons taken of all ages and of every color known to the human race—varying in hue from the purest white to the most shiny black," noted the *Boston Herald*. Musicians and pipers were arrested and charged with disturbing the peace. One judge took pity on Michael McLaughlin, charged with being a common fiddler. The Court ruled that McLaughlin "could not see what company he kept" and was set free. One musician's wife tried to "soften the heart of the judge by stating that she had seven children, mostly of a tender age." The judge wasn't softened, and the husband went to jail.

Many of the women arrested were prostitutes, and several were brothel madams, charged with keeping houses of ill repute. In a gesture that can only be described as extraordinary for the time, the court arranged for many of these women to have their sentences suspended and instead put them to work as domestic servants to local families.

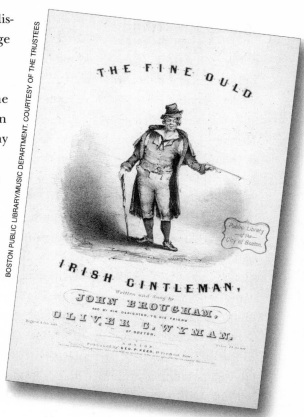

Parodies of the Irish—"The Fine Ould Irish Gintleman" is an example—were common in the mid-nineteenth century.

Could Catherine Murphy have been one of the women rounded up in the dance cellars? It's hard to know. She could just as easily have mended her ways and joined the majority of Irish who were hardworking, honest, intelligent, and ultimately good citizens. Most Irish had already begun putting down roots, creating a stable family environment for their progeny. In a pattern that stretched over several generations, the Irish saved money and sent it back to Ireland so their families could eventually follow them to Boston.

Rural Irish peasants suddenly cast into a thriving urban center like Boston were often overwhelmed by their new surroundings. For many of them, the timeless traditions of storytelling, poetry, song, and dance helped sustain them. Most Irish were encouraged to play an instrument, dance, tell a story, or sing, and they carried those skills with them to Boston. Several dance masters like Patrick Sullivan and M. H. Keenan began teaching Irish-American youngsters the jigs and reels of Ireland as well as the quadrilles and waltzes favored in New England. M. J. Mooney gave lessons on the organ and pianoforte to immigrant children and formed a Juvenile Drum Corps that played at Irish occasions. Jeremiah Cohan, father of George M. Cohan, the toast of Broadway in the 1920s and '30s and an influential entertainer, learned Irish step dancing and later transformed those skills to the minstrel and vaudeville stage. Irish dance steps had already been influential in creating a hybrid American dance known as tap dancing. Immigrant musicians like Edward Ryan and Patrick Gilmore transferred their skills onto the American scene and made their mark there. Many musicians joined temperance society and military bands.

In 1853 the Boston Irish formed a Thomas Moore Club dedicated to the music of Ireland's famous bard. The group met monthly and convened a dinner each May that drew more than 200 people, including poet Washington Irving and Bishop John Hughes from New York City. On Ruggles Street in Roxbury, Edward White from Galway opened a music shop in 1854 where he repaired Irish and Scottish bagpipes, gave lessons to children, and offered to play at functions around the city. Known as the Dandy Piper because he wore a tall black stovepipe hat when he went out, White eventually opened a successful dance hall in Roxbury in the years leading up to the Civil War and helped the complex art of uilleann piping take root in Boston.

In 1850, two musical concerts were held in celebration of St. Patrick's Day. By the end of the decade more than a dozen such events were offered. Mooney had formed a choir with Irish orphans of Boston, and they performed at Tremont Temple. The Irish Temperance Societies held a concert in Cambridge. The Charitable Irish Society held its soiree at the famous Parker House, using the Shaw and Weitz Quadrille Band, and Patrick Gilmore was heading up the prestigious Boston Brass Band. Even the Irish Protestant Mutual Relief Society offered its version of Irish music. At its annual dinner in April 1853, its musical list included "God Save the Queen," "Croppies Lie Down," and "The Protestant Boys."

At the same time, traveling minstrel and burlesque shows came through Boston regularly, offering a raw, sarcastic depiction of Irish, Blacks, Germans, Chinese, and others. Sadly, some of the most popular performers of the day were themselves Irish actors like John Broughton and Barney Williams. In an effort to give the public what it wanted, these actors depicted the Irish as the white equivalent of the Black Sambo, another caricature popular in the days leading up to the Civil War. Indeed, the mirroring of Paddy and Sambo in the work of cartoonists like Thomas Nast later in the century found its inspiration in these shows.

Other Irish immigrants like Dion Boucicault from Dublin, whose play *Andy Blake the Irish Diamond* made its American debut at the Boston Theater in November 1854, portrayed the Irish as heroic figures. Boucicault understood the importance of defining the Irish persona in a positive way, and he helped to keep alive nationalist sentiments of the Irish living in America, which would prove to be a powerful political force in the future. In 1865 Boucicault wrote the lyrics to the Irish anthem, "Wearin' o' the Green" for his play *Arrah na Pogue,* reminding the Boston Irish just how bad things had been in Ireland:

> *O Paddy dear and did you hear the news that's going round,*
> *The Shamrock is forbid by law to grow on Irish ground . . .*
> *She's the most distressful country that ever you have seen,*
> *They're hanging men and women there for wearin' of the green.*

The Rise and Decline of the Know-Nothings

As long as the police arrested the troublemakers and the Irish helped support their own, nativist Bostonians were appeased. But when the Irish started to demand a voice in political affairs and a vote in local elections, the nativists' antagonism toward the immigrants grew. Fearing that the emerging Irish political bloc would "vote down intelligent, honest native citizens" and take over local politics, nativists began organizing a political opposition. In 1854 they established an anti-Irish, anti-Catholic group known as the American Party, which preferred to be clandestine when promoting their mission. Party members were called the Know-Nothings, because they feigned ignorance of the party's activities when questioned by outsiders. The party adopted its constitution on June 17, 1854—the anniversary of the Battle of Bunker Hill. Ironically, hundreds of Irish soldiers had died in that battle, fighting valiantly alongside the grandfathers of the nativists who now opposed the Irish.

Nativists started a campaign to "Americanize America" by harassing Irish immigrants at every opportunity. Storekeepers were urged not to sell them goods. City officials tried to shut down the Catholic cemetery in South Boston. State legislators tried to lengthen the waiting time for immigrants to become naturalized citizens. And police cracked down on the Irish ghettoes in a manner that was harsh and unyielding. In one year, 14,000 of the 17,000 people arrested in Boston were Irish, charged mostly with petty crimes, public disturbances, and vagrancy.

The notorious NO IRISH NEED APPLY phrase began to work its way into the job marketplace, appearing in advertisements like this one from the August, 19, 1853, edition of the *Boston Traveler:*

> *Wanted—an experienced COOK, who is a good Washer and Ironer.*
> *Also, a Chambermaid who is a good seamstress and fond of children.*
> *Apply at 117 Harrison Avenue, between the hours of 11 A.M. and 1*
> *P.M. Protestants preferred, and no Irish person need apply.*

That same month, a gentleman named Ira Martin at the Livery Stable on Cambridge Street ran a NO IRISH NEED APPLY ad in the *Boston Evening Transcript* twenty-one days in a row! These ads were still turning up two decades later.

In 1871 the *Boston Herald* ran a NO IRISH NEED APPLY ad in its April 15 edition for an upholsterer job in Waltham. An offended reader sent the clipping into the *Pilot,* which reprinted the ad, along with some doggerel about the subject:

> *The phrase no Irish need apply*
> *By English bigots was the cry.*
> *But this was of a former date*
> *It now becomes quite obsolete*
> *As Irish talent, merit, fame*
> *Annihilates this crusty theme.*
> *Now harsh to freedom's ears the cry*

No Irish Paddys need apply
And he that would such slang maintain
Must be, indeed, a chaffy Beau.

The most vile and racist tract on the subject appeared on July 25, 1868, in *Every Saturday,* a weekly magazine distributed in Boston by Ticknor and Fields Publishers. The 1,200-word article by F. P. Cobbe, entitled "No Irish Need Apply," was filled with a hatred and malice that shocked decent people and made the ads seem paltry by comparison. The *Irish-American Weekly* responded, "the article puts into condensed form, double distilled and concentrated, the venomous essence of that bigotry which exists in certain quarters among us, to a much greater extent that we are sometimes apt to imagine."

In the mid-1850s, the Know-Nothing mobs wreaked havoc on Irish neighborhoods in Boston and in surrounding towns. One Irish immigrant, Patrick Collins, recalled a childhood incident involving this mob that seared his memory forever. It was 1854; ten-year-old Collins had come to Boston six years earlier with his widowed mother from County Cork. They were living in an Irish neighborhood in Chelsea on the outskirts of Boston. The *Boston Daily Globe* picks up the story from here:

> One afternoon after Sunday school some of the teachers and nearly all the children, went up on a high hill . . . just to see the country and bask in the sun. They saw toward East Boston a long winding serpent of people coming. It was the "Angel Gabriel" [a sectarian fanatic whose real name was Orr] and some two thousand in his train . . . . The crowd marched to the Catholic Church and a number of them mounted the roof and tore the cross off the apex and threw it into the crowd. [They] marched through the Catholic section of town and smashed with stones the windows and doors of all the houses in which Catholics lived. The fury lasted for weeks. Every Irish house was a fortification. Trunks and furniture barred every front window; some one was on guard every night in every dwelling.

Despite a broken forearm and a few bruises, young Collins survived the attack. He would eventually graduate from Harvard Law School, be elected a U.S. congressman, and be appointed as the U.S.

ambassador to England. He would also serve two terms as mayor of Boston from 1902–05, only the second Irishman to hold the post up to that time.

Later in his career, Collins articulated the way that his generation felt about being Irish in America:

Those of us who were born in Ireland or who spring from the Irish race are here to stay. [But] in American politics, we are Americans, pure and simple. We ask nothing on account of our race or creed, and we submit to no slight or injury on account of either. All we ask is equality for us and ours.

Patrick Collins was Boston's second Irish-born mayor.

By 1858 the Irish were not just asking for equality, they were demanding it. When the state legislature tried to extend the waiting time for immigrants seeking to become citizens, the Irish teamed up with German immigrants to fight the proposal. On March 14, 1859, Thomas Whall, an eleven-year-old Catholic student at the Eliot school, refused to pray from the Protestant Bible, and he was severely punished. The entire Irish community rallied behind him and sparked a nationwide protest against the local school officials, who relented.

The *Boston Pilot,* which led the fight for young Whall, was flexing its editorial muscles. In 1859 it noted the eighty-third anniversary of the British leaving Boston on March 17, 1776, and posed the rhetorical question as to why proper Bostonians hadn't yet celebrated Evacuation Day. Everyone knew the reason: Evacuation Day happened to fall on Saint Patrick's Day. The Yankees didn't want to give the Irish an opportunity to blend American patriotism with Irish pride. As if to underscore its point, the *Pilot* wrote:

The expulsion of the battalion of England from Boston was not a Know Nothing achievement; nor would the sentiments of those who accomplished it harmonize with the sentiments of that party.

The Pride of the Famine Generation

From the anguish and defeat caused by the Irish Famine, an extraordinary generation of Irish immigrants emerged in Boston. Liberated from the poverty, unrest, and social restraints caused by British rule, they discovered their own talents in America, the land of opportunity.

Thomas Ryan of Cork, a clarinetist, arrived in 1845, formed the Mendellson Quintette, and was a founding member of the Boston Symphony Orchestra.

Jeremiah Cohan was born in 1847 to Irish parents on Blackstone Street, was a leading vaudeville performer, and was the father of the great song-and-dance man George M. Cohan.

Augustus Saint-Gaudens arrived from Dublin in 1848, became the leading sculptor of his generation, and was the creator of the Shaw Memorial in Boston.

Patrick Collins arrived from Cork in 1848 and became the city's second Irish-born mayor, elected in 1902.

Bridget Murphy and **Patrick Kennedy** both arrived around 1848, married in Boston in 1856, and begat the nation's first family of politics.

Patrick Gilmore arrived from Galway in 1849 and wrote the Civil War anthem, "When Johnny Comes Marching Home."

Martin Milmore arrived from County Sligo in 1851 and created dozens of Civil War memorials throughout New England, including the Soldiers and Sailors Memorial on Boston Commons.

Louis Sullivan was born in Boston's South End in 1856 to an Irish father and Swiss mother and was famed as the Father of Modern Architecture and mentor to Frank Lloyd Wright.

John L. Sullivan was born 1858 to Irish immigrant parents and became the world's heavyweight boxing champion.

By 1861 the Irish wouldn't need Evacuation Day to display their patriotism: The American Civil War was looming. The Irish community was split about the pending war and the issue of slavery. Daniel O'Connell, known as the Great Liberator in Ireland, supported an anti-slavery petition back in 1840 and befriended the Black leader Frederick Douglass. But during the 1850s, many Irish didn't take warmly to the

Evacuation Day

Why is Saint Patrick's Day sometimes referred to as Evacuation Day around Boston? During the Revolutionary War, General Washington was struggling to outmaneuver British General Gage, whose troops had occupied Boston since 1768. On the night of March 17, 1776, Washington's troops, led by General John Sullivan of Maine, made a daring move to gain control of Dorchester Heights in South Boston, which overlooked Boston Harbor and the entire British fleet. Colonel Henry Knox's colonial troops transported cannons they had captured from Fort Ticonderoga in New York and pushed them all the way to Boston. On the morning of March 17, the British awoke to find the cannons aimed straight at them. When the British evacuated their perch a few days later, it was a turning point in the war. March 17 became known as Evacuation Day and was celebrated formally starting in 1876. In 1941 state representatives Thomas Coyne and Michael Cusik managed to make it a legal holiday in Suffolk County, which includes Boston, Chelsea, Revere, and Winthrop. By joyous coincidence, March 17 is also Saint Patrick's Day, when Ireland's patron saint is honored, and the two celebrations have blended together. On the morning of the Saint Patrick's Day parade, a solemn ceremony takes place at the **Dorchester Heights Memorial,** operated by the National Park Service, on G Street in South Boston. Then, as it has done since 1901, South Boston hosts its annual **Saint Patrick's Day Parade,** a public festival that draws hundreds of marching bands and hundreds of thousands of spectators.

abolitionists, who proclaimed the rights of African Americans in the south while doing little for the struggling Irish in their midst.

Even non-Irish leaders tackled Boston's hypocrisy head on. Among these leaders was Edward Everett Hale, who, in 1852, wrote a pamphlet entitled "Letters on Irish Emigration." "Here in Massachusetts we writhe and struggle, really with one heart, lest we return one fugitive who can possibly be saved to Southern slavery," Hale wrote. He continued that when it comes to the Irish, however, "we tax them first and neglect them afterwards, and provide by statute, and take care, in fact, to send them back to Ireland at the public expense, poor creatures who are as entirely fugitives from a grinding slavery as if their flight had been north instead of west."

The *Boston Pilot*, which faltered on the issue of abolishing slavery, ended its opposition in April 1861 when Fort Sumter in South Carolina was attacked by Confederate forces and it became clear that the Civil War could very well divide the country. The *Pilot,* which "honored Southerners for their chivalry but condemned them for their cause," backed the Union's side of the war effort enthusiastically, for it offered the Irish the ultimate chance to demonstrate their courage, valor, and patriotism for the world to see.

CHAPTER SEVEN

The Irish Come Marching Home Again (The 1860s)

T HAT SPLENDID summer morning of June 26, 1861, when soldiers from the Ninth Regiment of Massachusetts Volunteers paraded from Long Wharf to Boston Common for a final muster before heading off to fight in the Civil War, you can be sure the Milmore brothers scrambled to get the best view possible. The four brothers from County Sligo had many friends and neighbors in the Fighting Ninth, a regiment composed almost entirely of Irish immigrants.

The regiment was commanded by forty-year-old Colonel Thomas Cass, a native of Queen's County (now County Laois) and a Bostonian since 1829. When the unit formed earlier that spring, heeding the call of Governor John Andrew, more than 1,000 Irish had signed on for three years' service. They came from Boston and the nearby towns of Salem, Milford, Marlboro, and Stoughton. *Pilot* publisher Patrick Donahoe had raised the money to outfit and train the Irish, who were stationed in barracks near Faneuil Hall. They spent their final weeks on Long Island in Boston Harbor, which had been converted to a training center for many of the state's fighting battalions.

Now the regiment was coming to Boston for one last time before heading off to fight. That morning they had taken a boat over to Long Wharf and were greeted by a crowd of 800 men and women from various Irish organizations, who followed them up to the Common. Leading the procession from the wharf up State Street was Galway's own Patrick S. Gilmore, leader of the city's most famous military band. The Juvenile Drum Corps of music teacher M. J. Mooney was also marching in step, creating a heartbeat of excitement on their bass and snare drums. Gilmore's Band had played "Hail Columbia" and "St. Patrick's Day," the unofficial twin anthems of the American Irish.

Martin Milmore, who aspired to be a great cornet player like Gilmore himself, would have paid special attention to the tunes that brightened the day. In fact, his family changed its name from Milmoe to Milmore after settling in Boston, at the suggestion of a school teacher who thought it would be advantageous for the young brothers to have a name similar to Gilmore, the city's most popular band leader.

Most likely all of the Milmore brothers—Charles, Joseph, Martin, and James—climbed to the top of Frog Pond Hill so they could see the panorama of this military pageantry: 1,023 Irish soldiers in strict formation, proud and determined, ready to defend the union of a country some had been living in only for a few months. From up atop Frog Pond Hill, the Milmore boys could have turned to see Colonel Cass march his troops up to the Massachusetts State House for the formal review by Governor Andrew who offered a heartfelt thanks to Cass and his soldiers as thousands of state and city officials and well-wishers looked on:

I understand, sir, that like yourself, a majority . . . of your command, derive their origin, either by birth or directly by descent, from another

The Glorious 9th!

IRISHMEN

To the Rescue!

Irish Americans of Massachusetts!

The City of Boston has voted a

Bounty of $100!

FLAG OF IRELAND!

The Stars and Stripes!

GREEN FLAG!

A CHAPLAIN OF THE OLD FAITH

The Sum of $138.00!

REGIMENT to its full quota.

Headquarters, 112 Washington Street, Boston,
Over Little & Brown's Bookstore, to
Capt. B. S. TREANOR,
OR HIS AUTHORIZED AGENTS.

J. E. Farwell & Co., Steam Job Printers, 37 Congress Street, Boston.

This Civil War recruitment poster called men to the Irish Ninth Regiment.

country than this," the governor said, handing Cass the
Massachusetts and American flags. "When you look on the Stars and
Stripes you can remember that you are American citizens; when you
look on this venerable ensign, you can remember your wives and
families in Massachusetts.

Colonel Cass accepted the flags from Governor Andrew. Then the Ninth Regiment proudly unfurled its own regiment flag, made of green silk and inscribed on the front with gold scroll: "Thy sons by adoption; thy firm supporters and defenders from duty, affection and choice." The center of the flag showed an American coat of arms with an eagle and shield. The reverse side contained the Irish harp, with the motto, "The Union must and shall be preserved."

This Ninth Regiment Irish flag is on display at the Massachusetts State House.

COURTESY COMMONWEALTH OF MASSACHUSETTS

Marching bands, waving flags, cheering crowds, spotless uniforms: such was the memory of going off to war, a far cry from the muddy trenches and battlefields of broken limbs and broken hearts the soldiers encountered. More than 10,000 Irish from Massachusetts joined the war, fighting in the Ninth as well as the Twenty-eighth and Twenty-ninth, First and Third, and the Fifty-fifth regiments. More than 200 men were killed in the Fighting Ninth, including Cass, who was buried with honors at Mount Auburn Cemetery in Cambridge. Cass's successor, Patrick Guiney from Tipperary, had his eye blown away at the Battle of the Wilderness on May 5, 1864.

Sixteen years and three months after the Irish mustered on the Boston Common, on September 17, 1877, a crowd of 26,000 people gathered again on Frog Pond Hill, now renamed Flagstaff Hill. They had come to unveil the Soldiers and Sailors Memorial, Boston's tribute

to the valiant soldiers who had fought to preserve the Union. According
to the Boston Art Commission, "Civil War veterans marched . . . over a
route of six miles long. Peter Nolan of Post 75 marched the entire
route on crutches, having lost a leg at the second Battle of Bull Run."

The Memorial, which took six years to complete, included various
allegorical figures representing History, Peace, and the Genius of
America. Instead of praising generals and admirals, the memorial paid
tribute to the foot soldier and the sailor, ushering in a new era of art
that was more democratic in its sensibility about war. Standing next to
the war masterpiece on its installation day were the sculptors, Martin
and Joseph Milmore.

Monumental Irish-American Patriotism

When the Irish soldiers mustered on the Boston Common that day in
1861, the Milmore brothers had been in the country less than a decade.
Their widowed mother, Sara (nee Hart), and her eldest son, Charles,
had come from Killmorgan, Sligo, to Boston in 1851 and then sent for
the other boys to join them. One of the brothers, Patrick, had died a
few years after arriving, but the other four were enrolled in school. All
of them showed an artistic inclination, and after their schooling they
began apprenticeships in local studios. Joseph Milmore was carving
marble for Irishman John Foote and was already considered one of the
best craftsmen in Boston. Martin Milmore, who had given up his musical ambitions, was sweeping the floors in the studio of Thomas Ball, a
well-known artist who was then working on the equestrian statue of
George Washington for the Public Garden.

The Irish had few opportunities in the mid-nineteenth century to
prove they were on an equal par with native Bostonians. Being a soldier
was the most expedient path, which many Irish chose when the Civil
War started. Being an artist was a less likely path, since it required a
period of study and apprenticeship that most Irish could not afford or
would not be invited to join. But America gave the Irish a freedom of
expression that Ireland hadn't offered, especially to those of modest
background and education. As art historian and sculptor Lorado Taft
noted in his 1903 masterwork *The History of American Sculpture,* "The

versatile Irish have found in America a favorable field for artistic development; transplanted to this spacious land, not a few of the race have revealed an unusual gift for sculptural expression."

Martin Milmore had a glorious but short-lived career. His first war statue was the Roxbury Civil War soldier at Forest Hills Cemetery in Jamaica Plain, completed in 1868, followed by the Charlestown soldier in 1871. Editor John Boyle O'Reilly understood the significance of that occasion. Writing in the *Pilot*, he noted, "In the list of those whose death the statue commemorates, will be found a full representation of Celtic names. This pillar will be the common tombstone of Irish and American, telling us, by their union in death, to walk in union while living. And it is even more than this to us, for the artist who designed the splendid column, Martin Milmore, is one of our race and creed."

The Milmores opened a studio on Harrison Avenue in the South End and produced dozens of Civil War statues that stand in town commons across New England. Sculptor Daniel French once described Martin as "a picturesque figure, with long dark hair and large dark eyes . . . wearing a broad-brimmed soft black hat and a cloak. His appearance was striking and he knew it." Joseph was "eccentric in some respects," but also a man of "warm and generous impulses," who had married poet Henry Longfellow's sister and retired to Geneva, Switzerland. Martin Milmore died suddenly at age thirty-nine from liver complications; in his will he instructed Daniel French to create a fitting memorial for him and his brothers at Forest Hills Cemetery. French's masterpiece, entitled *Death and the Sculptor*, is considered one of the finest public sculptures in all of Boston.

But another Irish-born sculptor would surpass Martin Milmore as the greatest figurative sculptor of the nineteenth century. Son of a French father and an Irish mother, Mary McGuiness, Augustus Saint-Gaudens was born in Dublin on March 1, 1848. According to his son Homer Saint-Gaudens, Augustus Saint-Gaudens "was not destined to remain long in Ireland." For when he was but six months old, "red headed, whopper-jawed, and hopeful," as he often explained, "the famine in Ireland compelled his parents to emigrate with him to America, setting out from Liverpool, in the sailing ship *Desdemona*."

The family landed in Boston in September 1848, but finding no

The Shaw Memorial was created by Dublin-born Augustus Saint-Gaudens.

suitable situation, the father went down to New York City, found a job and an apartment, and sent for mother and child. Augustus's brother, Louis, was born there in 1854. Augustus apprenticed in New York as a cameo cutter and as a teenager moved to Rome and Paris to study classical sculpture. In Rome, Augustus met Augusta Homer of Roxbury and married her in 1877. His first commission, of Civil War Admiral David Farragut, was unveiled at Madison Square Garden in 1881, and from that point on, Saint-Gaudens remained busy as an artist until his death in 1907.

His most notable sculptures—of Abraham Lincoln and General William Sherman—satisfied the American public's yearning for larger than life heroes in the late nineteenth century. Saint-Gaudens himself was larger than life in many ways: Classical in appearance, with a long beard and quick wit, he later moved to Cornish, New Hampshire, and set up a vibrant artists' colony there. His son Homer described his "unfailing sense of humor and his dislike of morbid introspection."

Saint-Gaudens's most famous work of art is the Colonel Robert Gould

Shaw Memorial, which depicts the Fifty-fourth Black Infantry Regiment of Boston. He spent fourteen years in the creation of the memorial, and he took great care to carve individual features for the sixteen Black soldiers in the piece. The 1897 unveiling was attended by such luminaries as Booker T. Washington and philosopher William James.

Augustus's son Homer provided an interested insight into his father's viewpoint of Boston during the time. He noted, "His anxiety was increased by the fact that they were to go to Boston, a city which he regarded with ingrown hyper-criticism." This may account for the four-teen years he took to complete the Shaw Memorial and why he never completed the exterior sculptures at the Boston Public Library, which had been commissioned to him and his brother Louis. Louis created the majestic twin marble lions that straddle the grand stairway in the McKim Building of the Boston Public Library, a memorial that is dedi-cated to the Second and Twentieth regiments.

Other Irish-American sculptors contributed to the development of American sculpture through both war memorials and classical figures. Launt Thompson, who moved from County Laois to Albany with his widowed mother in 1847, created the Civil War Memorial in Pittsfield. Thomas Crawford, born of Irish parents in New York City, built the Soldiers and Sailors Memorial in Peabody, Massachusetts, as well as the *Armed Freedom* statue sitting atop the United States Capitol Building in Washington, D.C. Stephen O'Kelley of Dublin, who lived in Boston for many years, built memorials to the New York and Pennsylvania infantry regiments, though he is best known locally for his statue of Miles Standish, which stands in Duxbury, Massachusetts.

Why did this group of immigrant and first-generation sculptors excel in war memorials? Most likely they were inclined to demonstrate their patriotism to their new country, a litmus test of loyalty that all immigrants faced. Their sensibilities may have been shaped by their own culture of war, steeped as they were in a centuries-long conflict with England. The Irish were particularly sensitive to the notions of valor, honor, horror, pain, and loss associated with war. While their work captured the power and glory inherent in battle, it also revealed the humanity of those who did the actual fighting and an attention to detail that is the foundation of great art. To produce the carefully

Civil War Monuments in Massachusetts

Statues and memorial tablets and monuments created by Boston sculptors dot the landscapes of towns and cities throughout the nation. A great number of these honored the fallen soldiers as well as the political and military heroes of the Civil War period. Among them are these notable public monuments in Massachusetts:

Thomas Cass Memorial in Boston's Public Garden on Boylston Street commemorates the fallen leader of the Irish Ninth Regiment.

Soldiers and Sailors Memorial on Flagstaff Hill in Boston Common, the **Roxbury Civil War Soldier** and the **Charlestown Civil War Soldier** were created by the Milmore Brothers.

The Robert Shaw Memorial on Beacon Hill facing the State House and the **Civil War Soldier** on Cambridge Common were created by Dublin-born sculptor Augustus Saint-Gaudens.

Twin marble lions in the Boston Public Library McKim Building to commemorate the Twenty-second Regiment were created by Louis Saint-Gaudens.

Soldiers and Sailors Memorial in Peabody was created by Irish-American Thomas Crawford.

Civil War Memorial in Pittsfield was created by Irish-born sculptor Launt Thompson.

Civil War buffs may also enjoy visits to two other Boston landmarks:

The **Boston Public Library** has some rare photographs by Civil War photographer Matthew Brady, who studied briefly in Boston. The **Irish Flags Display** at the State House on Beacon Hill shows the banners that were carried into battle by the Ninth and Twenty-eighth regiments.

etched portraits of the infantrymen in the Shaw Memorial, Saint-Gaudens enlisted forty Black men to model so he could carve out individual features for the sixteen foot soldiers represented on the monument. In his work, Martin Milmore carved young, introspective soldiers and sailors to portray the common-man aspirations of American democracy.

The Irish were also shaped by the recent Famine, which was indelible in the minds of everyone affected by the catastrophe. The trauma of boarding a boat to flee one's country, leaving behind death, suffering, and anguish, rippled through the survivors and helped to shape a particular Irish-American ethos for decades afterward. The Famine experience, or the memory of it, unleashed a remarkable period of energy and ambition in the Boston Irish, of which artistic expression, along with political organizing, were its creative and practical outcomes.

When Johnny Comes Marching Home

In the years leading up to the Civil War, the best-known Irishman in Boston was Patrick Sarsfield Gilmore. In terms of creating a positive image in the eyes of Bostonians toward the Irish, no one did it better than Gilmore. The dapper, handsome native of Ballygar, Galway, arrived here in 1849 at age nineteen, a talented and ambitious musician who excelled on the cornet. His first job, thanks to *Boston Pilot* editor Patrick Donahoe's letter of introduction, was at Ordway's Music Store near the Old South Meeting House, where he was put in charge of the Band Instrument Department. While there he organized a troupe of local performers called Ordway's Minstrels.

This was an era when brass bands and military bands were the main source of musical entertainment, and many towns had their own band which competed to be the best around. Gilmore spent a few years as the leader of bands in Charlestown, Suffolk County, and Salem. In 1858 he was selected to head the Boston Brass Band, which quickly became known simply as Gilmore's Band. He played at President Buchanan's inauguration in 1857 and in 1860 at both national conventions—the Democratic in Charleston and the Republican in Chicago—the year Abraham Lincoln won the Republican nomination and the election. Gilmore organized Boston's first Fourth of July concert on the Boston Common, a musical tradition that continues today at the Boston Esplanade along the Charles River. Later, in New York, Gilmore started the New Year's Eve countdown in Times Square that flourishes still.

According to Michael Cummings of Milton, Massachusetts, founder of the Patrick S. Gilmore Society, young Gilmore penned a number of wartime anthems popular with both the troops and the public, including "God Save the Union," "Coming Home to Abraham," and "Good News From Home." His tune "John Brown's Body," written for the slain civil rights leader of the 1860s, became the most famous marching song of the Civil War. But the song that people still sing today is the famous anthem he composed in 1863: "When Johnny Comes Marching Home." It was inspired by the ragged soldiers returning home from the front, on foot, by ambulance, or in coffins. The song debuted at Tremont

Temple on September 26, 1863, in a concert conducted by Gilmore. The tune, inspired by an Irish marching song called "Johnny We Hardly Knew Ye," was played by both Union and Confederate bands and became wildly popular during the 1898 Spanish-American War. It has since entered the pantheon of American patriotic songs and was reportedly the favorite song of President John F. Kennedy.

> *When Johnny comes marching home again*
> > *Hurrah! Hurrah!*
> *We'll give him a hearty welcome then*
> > *Hurrah! Hurrah!*
> *The men will cheer and the boys will shout*
> > *The ladies they will all turn out*
> *And we'll all feel gay*
> > *When Johnny comes marching home.*

Gilmore and his Band enlisted in the Massachusetts Twenty-fourth Regiment of Volunteers and spent several years playing music around the country, for soldiers on the front and for their families back home. He became the Bandmaster of the Union Army and spent a few years in New Orleans.

After the war, Gilmore was inspired to create a Peace Jubilee that would be the largest musical concert in the world's history. Against all odds, he raised the capital to build a temporary Coliseum, 500 feet by 300 feet, in the Back Bay, just west of where Copley Square and the Fairmont Copley Plaza sit today. On June 15, 1869, Gilmore opened the five-day concert, which featured 1,000 musicians and 10,000 singers. President

Patrick S. Gilmore was a Galway native and music impresario.

Ulysses S. Grant arrived in Boston to attend the concert on June 16, and more than 100,000 people attended. He followed the feat in June 1872 with an International Peace Jubilee, which marked the end of the Franco-Prussian War. This occasion featured 2,000 musicians and 20,000 singers. One of the highlights of the week was a performance of Giuseppe Verdi's "Anvil Chorus," during which one hundred Boston firemen banged anvils in unison with the tune. It also marked the American debut of Austrian waltz king Johann Strauss, who in the nineteenth century had the status of a modern-day pop star.

Gilmore spent the last twenty years of his life traveling the world with his orchestra, basing himself in New York City, where his concert venue, Madison Square Garden, was often called Gilmore's Garden. He continued to produce patriotic music that spoke to the hearts of both Americans and Irish. He provided the music for such major Irish-American occasions as the Centenary of Irish bard Thomas Moore in 1879 and the American visit of Land League organizer Michael Davitt of Mayo, who spoke before 10,000 people in New York in January 1887. On that occasion, Gilmore's sixty-five-piece orchestra played "Minstrel Boy," "The Rocky Road to Dublin," and "A Day with the Irish Brigade." Gilmore died in 1892 while playing a concert in St. Louis. He had come a long way from Ballygar, County Galway.

The Irish Reconstruction

During the Civil War the Irish community continued to gain confidence and strength. On March 17, 1862, Irish Bostonians established the city's first St. Patrick's Day parade. It began on the Boston Common at 8:00 A.M., proceeded through the North End, over to Charlestown, then to East Cambridge, then went back to Boston and over to South Boston and the South End, and finally ended back at the Common. Not a single neighborhood was missed as the marchers raised the spirits of all of Irish Boston.

The Civil War ended in 1865 and the United States entered the Reconstruction phase of reuniting the nation. The Boston Irish were buoyed by their success in the war, having ably demonstrated their patriotism to America. The heroes of the Irish regiments returning from the war settled back into civilian life. Families were reunited, wounds were healed, and people tried to get on with their lives.

One group of Irish soldiers, however, was not finished fighting. The Irish Republican Brotherhood (IRB), founded on March 17, 1858, in New York City, included a feisty bunch of Irish expatriates whose sole mission was to win Ireland back from England. Thousands of its members, known as Fenians, had enlisted in the War, hoping to gain an alliance with the United States against Britain as well as firsthand experience in military fighting that could one day be directed against Britain.

One of the leading Fenians in Boston was Timothy Deasy, whose family landed in the city in 1847 from Clontakilty, Cork, then settled in the city of Lawrence just north of Boston. Deasy and his brother Cornelius were among the first to enlist in the Fighting Ninth on June 11, 1861, and both were wounded in May 1864.

Deasy became part of a fantastic and foolish scheme to invade part of Britain's commonwealth, namely Canada. The mission was to create "a provisional Irish government and a base from which they could liberate Ireland," according to Deasy's great-grandnephew Robert J. Bateman. Canadian authorities got wind of the attack and dispatched armed troops along the border while U.S. gunboats patrolled the St. Lawrence River and Lake Erie. On the night of May 31, Colonel John O'Neill and his company of Fenians crossed over to Fort Erie, took down the British flag, and hoisted the Irish flag. They won a small scrimmage near the village of Ridgeway and seemed poised to continue. But ultimately O'Neill was forced to surrender when the United States Army cut off their supplies and reinforcements.

By June 1870 the Fenians had reorganized and again prepared to invade Canada, with O'Neill still in command. The *Pilot* sent a rookie reporter named John Boyle O'Reilly to cover the war effort.

O'Reilly's dispatch from the front read, in part:

> *At six o'clock on the morning of June 25 I arrived in St. Albans,*
> *Vermont. There were about 60 Fenians on the train—forty from*
> *Boston under the command of Major Hugh McGuinness, and about*
> *20 who were taken in at various stations . . . . We proceeded to the*

*front . . . and at about 10 o'clock we arrived in Franklin [near the
Vermont/Canadian border]. For the first time, we saw the uniformed
Fenians here in very considerable numbers. The uniform was a capital one for service and most attractive—a green cavalry jacket, faced
with yellow, army blue pantaloons, and a blue cap with green band.*

*At eleven o'clock General George P. Foster, United States Marshall
for Vermont, arrived at the encampment. He formally ordered O'Neill
to desist from his "unlawful proceeding." The order was coolly
received by General O'Neill, [who] ordered the men to fall in . . . . As
soon as the column had reached the border, and before the company
could deploy, the Canadians opened a heavy fire upon them. Almost
at the first discharge, Private John Rowe of Burlington was shot
through the head, and fell dead in the center of the road.*

After a few hours of fighting, the Fenians fell back, and O'Neill was
arrested by the U.S. Marshall. As he was being led away, O'Neill turned
the command over to O'Reilly, who was then arrested and detained
overnight. The Fenians fought for a few more days, but "were utterly
demoralized and disheartened" against overwhelming forces. The men
disbanded and drifted back to their old lives. Some continued the struggle back in Ireland. O'Reilly returned to Boston, intent on starting a
new phase of his adventurous life.

CHAPTER EIGHT

Poets and Patriots of the Gilded Age (1870–1900)

A NOVELIST COULD hardly have invented a more fantastic tale than the life story of John Boyle O'Reilly. A fictionalized synopsis of O'Reilly's life might read something like this:

> Serving life imprisonment in Australia for sedition against the British Crown, the dashing Irish-born hero makes a daring escape through the Australian jungles and boards a New Bedford whaler, which smuggles him to America. He makes his way to Boston and becomes the leader of the Irish community and eventually a national spokesman. He works his way from reporter to editor to owner of the nation's foremost Catholic newspaper. Writers like Oscar Wilde, Fanny Parnell, and William Butler Yeats send him their poems for publication. He publishes several volumes of his own verse and is selected as the poet laureate of Massachusetts. Boston Brahmins like Oliver Wendell Holmes and Wendell Phillips befriend him for his intellect and wit and invite him to their literary salons. Blacks, American Indians, and Chinese and Jewish immigrants praise him for espousing their rights to equality. He eventually hatches a plot to return to Australia to release his fellow Irish prisoners from the British penal colony—and amazingly pulls it off. And the tragic dénouement: he can never return to his native Ireland, to which he has devoted his life, because the British are eagerly waiting to lock him up again, despite his great accomplishments and universal acclaim.

The story is no fiction, however. The life of O'Reilly—poet, publisher, and patriot—was all of that and more. A powerful orator and a gifted sportsman, he was a devoted husband and the father of four daughters who adored him, as the entire community did. His biographer, James Roche, described his character as "unvarying heroism,

John Boyle O'Reilly was a poet and a patriot.

tenderness and beauty." Edwin Walker, a Black Bostonian, said at O'Reilly's funeral, "As long as Mr. O'Reilly lived and spoke, we felt that we had at least, outside of our own people, one true, vigilant, brave and self-sacrificing friend who . . . claimed for us just what he claimed for himself."

Born in Drogheda, County Meath, O'Reilly was twenty-six years old when he escaped from the Australian penal colony and made his way to America. He arrived in Boston in 1870, penniless but impassioned by the potential of American democracy, which protected the freedoms and liberties he had been denied.

After covering the Fenian invasion of Canada, O'Reilly was hired full time at the *Pilot,* where he quickly established the paper as a forum for espousing his viewpoints.

One of the first controversies he tackled was the "Stage Irishman." Within a year of landing in Boston, O'Reilly took aim at a group called the Hibernian Minstrels, who were portraying the Irish as comic buffoons. O'Reilly wrote:

> *The stage Irishmen [invented by the English] seems to be accepted by the Irish people, who not only laugh at and applaud his vagaries, but even become more English than the English themselves in performing them . . . . This exaggeration by our own people is unworthy. No wonder people who do not know us should judge us harshly and wrongly.*

O'Reilly advised his readers, "If we want to see the truth let us do it ourselves and do it truthfully." For the rest of his career, he set about doing that, using the *Pilot* as a bully pulpit to speak out on politics in Ireland and in the United States. His candor was bolstered by truth. He

John Boyle O'Reilly Memorial

When John Boyle O'Reilly, newspaper publisher and staunch defender of the Irish, died suddenly on August 10, 1890, his family and friends were shocked and saddened. His supporters quickly raised $22,000 to build a fitting memorial, selecting Daniel Chester French as the artist. **The John Boyle O'Reilly Memorial** at Boylston and Fenway Streets in the Fens was officially unveiled on June 20, 1896. The memorial features a bust of O'Reilly encircled by a Celtic design. On the reverse side are three bronze figures representing Ireland (the female figure) and poetry (the male figures).

O'Reilly's summer home is today the Hull Public Library, located at Main and Spring Streets. O'Reilly's residence at 34 Winthrop Street in Charlestown is a private home. In 1988 Charlestown unveiled an O'Reilly plaque at Thompson Square, near the corner of Main and Austin Streets. Sculptor John Donoghue's bust of O'Reilly is in the Fine Arts Reading room of the Boston Public Library, with a facsimile at the John J. Burns Library at Boston College. O'Reilly is buried at Holyhood Cemetery in Brookline. Each June the Ancient Order of Hibernians holds a special ceremony at his gravesite. For more information, visit the Web site www.irishheritagetrail.com.

admonished Yankee leaders for not doing enough to create a pluralistic society; he praised them when they did. He chastised Irish-Americans not only for acting like Stage Irishmen but for their petty squabbling, such as the intractable rioting between nationalists and Orangemen that they carried with them from Belfast to New York City. He praised them for becoming good American citizens while staying connected to their own culture. He encouraged freed slaves to demand their rights as citizens. As the state's poet laureate, he created poetry celebrating some of New England's most cherished moments in history. Among his work were pieces on the Mayflower's landing at Plymouth Rock, the Pilgrim Fathers, and the Boston Massacre.

It was O'Reilly who first brought national and international notoriety to Boston as a distinctly Irish city, and he helped to spawn an Irish cultural renaissance in the city that lasted about three decades. He hosted dozens of visitors, from poet Oscar Wilde to rebel John Devoy, and he helped organize fund-raising rallies for Ireland's home rule leader Charles Stuart Parnell and Michael Davitt, founder of Ireland's Land League movement. He served as a mentor to the young Chicago sculptor John Donoghue, who created the masterpiece *Young Sophocles,* now owned by the Isabella Gardner Museum in Boston. He supported the young poet Fanny Parnell, who headed up the Ladies Land League and published regularly in the *Boston Pilot.*

When O'Reilly died suddenly on August 10, 1890, at the age of forty-six, Boston lost one of its greatest citizens. The impact he made during his twenty years here was felt not only by the Irish community but by the Yankees, Chinese, Jews, American Indians, and African Americans.

Edwin Walker, a leader in Boston's African-American community, said at the funeral, "As long as Mr. O'Reilly lived and spoke, we felt that we had at least, outside of our own people, one true, vigilant, brave and self-sacrificing friend who . . . claimed for us just what he claimed for himself."

Publishing the Irish

As the Irish community grew between 1830 and 1880, nativist Bostonians continued to snipe at the Irish, especially in the newspapers. No Irish Need Apply ads were seen in print along with a steady stream of racist jokes known as Irish Bull. These latter insults portrayed Paddy as unintelligent, belligerent, cunning, or immoral, depending on the punch line. A more odious stream of criticism arose when legitimate issues (such as the matter of parochial school versus public school education or the process of becoming a voting citizen) became points of contention between the Irish and the Know-Nothings.

The most public defender of the Boston Irish had long been the *Pilot* newspaper, the official standard bearer of Irish and Catholic causes. Other sympathetic papers like the *Boston Vindicator* and *Irish Illustrator* had appeared briefly, but it was the *Pilot,* under Patrick Donahoe and then O'Reilly, that for five decades had challenged the remnants of the parochial Puritan mind-set reluctant to accept a world outside of itself.

The 1880s saw a burst of Irish publishing activity that would complement the efforts of the *Pilot.* In 1882 Patrick J. Maguire, a native of County Monahan, founded the *Republic* newspaper, a feisty, graphically attractive paper whose mission was to "intelligently give shape to the desires and aspirations" of the Boston Irish while disproving James Russell Lowell's view that "it is impossible for a man to be an Irishman and an American at the same time." The weekly paper, whose circulation quickly jumped to 35,000 copies, became a forceful platform for the Democratic Party, since Maguire was, as historian John T. Galvin noted, an influential "back-room operator" and possibly "the only city-wide boss Boston ever had."

The issue of whether an immigrant could be a good American while remaining a true Irishman was at the very heart of the Irish struggle to gain acceptance in nineteenth-century Boston. O'Reilly, Maguire, and others knew that it was possible to balance love of one's native land with loyalty to one's adopted country, but the difficult task was to present such largesse to the skeptics of Boston. This Irish genera-

> ## Celtic Studies at Harvard
>
> Fred Norris Robinson, a Chaucer scholar, taught the first Gaelic course at Harvard University in 1896. The **Celtic Languages and Literatures Department** (Warren House, 12 Quincy Street, Cambridge, MA 02138) was eventually established in 1940 by Henry Lee Shattuck, a descendant of famous privateer Patrick Tracy. He contributed $51,000 to launch the program. Charles Dunn headed the department from 1962 to 1984, and John V. Kelleher held the first Chair of Irish Studies. Patrick Ford heads the department today. The department awards advanced degrees in Celtic Studies and offers introductory courses to the public through the University Extension program. The Friends of Harvard Celtic Studies group, headed by Phil Haughey, raises funds so graduate students can conduct research in the Celtic countries. For more information, call (617) 495–1206 or visit the Web site www.fas.harvard.edu/~celt_fcs/.

tion sought to blend the two urges together by creating a singular Boston Irish persona.

When the Irish of the 1830s realized they could openly practice their Catholic faith in Boston, despite the often brutal objections of the nativists, that breakthrough served as an epiphany for the entire community. A similar epiphany occurred in the 1880s when the Irish realized they could be, in the best sense of the hyphenated word, Irish-Americans. They could enter the world of local politics as Americans, putting Irish immigrant Hugh O'Brien in office as the city's first Irish mayor in 1885 and gaining numerous spots on the Boston Common Council and School Committee. They could retain their Irish roots by supporting Ireland's continued struggle for independence. And they could create their own cultural revival right in Boston, passing on to the younger generation the language, music, dance, literature, and sports of ancient Ireland.

Maguire's newspaper focused on the political life of the Boston Irish. The *Republic* was a forceful proponent of Ireland's Land League movement, and it gave zealous updates of League meetings in East and South Boston, Charlestown, Roxbury, Dorchester, Brighton, Chelsea, Belmont, Watertown, Brookline, and Somerville. In June 1882 the paper announced a Grand Irish Celebration featuring Michael Davitt of Mayo, founder of the Land League, and predicted 75,000 people would attend. The actual figure was closer to 7,000, but that didn't dampen the paper's enthusiasm for the Land League and other Irish movements. On the American political front, it was Maguire who coordinated Irish and Yankee leaders to nominate the city's first Irish-born mayor, Hugh O'Brien, who served from 1885 to 1889. Maguire also helped launch the political career of Patrick A. Collins, who became the city's second Irish-born mayor from 1902 to 1905.

Representing the cultural life of the Boston Irish was the newspaper the *Irish Echo,* created in 1886. The *Echo* (no relation to the New York paper started in 1928) was a bilingual newspaper in Irish and English issued by members of the Philo-Celtic Society, a group formed in 1874 to promote the Irish language and Gaelic culture in Boston. Its leader was P. J. Daly, an energetic, committed individual who helped create dozens of Irish language schools in greater Boston that lasted well into the twentieth century. The Society displayed a middle-class gentility to which many Irish aspired. Beneath the veneer, however, was a forceful and earnest mission, as described in the first issue of the *Echo:* "to aid and assist in the vindication of the character of the Irish race from the foul slanders of centuries by English writers."

That slander gained an official bully pulpit in Boston when the *British American Citizen* newspaper was launched on October 29, 1887. The *Citizen* attempted to unify British-Americans in New England by attacking Irish-Americans who appeared to be on the rise. "Ignorant, Narrow-minded and Boorish," screamed one headline about the Irish Home Rule movement. "When will Boston be delivered from this . . .

THE IRISH ECHO.

"Devoted to Matters of General and Popular Information."

Devoted to the Interests of the Language, Literature, History of Ireland and Autonomy, and to "Matters of General and Popular Information."
"No People will look forward to Posterity who do not often look back to their Ancestors."

PRICE FIVE CENTS

BOSTON, MASS., APRIL, 1887.

No. 16.

GREEN ERIN,
GRADH MO CHROIDHE.

[Written for the IRISH ECHO.]

BY MICHAEL C. O'SHEA.

The heart in pain cannot refrain,
From a sigh or a song of grief,
To ease the smart in that aching heart,
By a transient and relief,
This overflow of the cup of woe,
Relaxes awhile the strain
On the anguish'd breast, and a seeming rest,
Affords from the goad of pain;
Thus bursts this song, from a bosom long,
Inured to a gloomy fate,
On a foreign soil from its native isle,
Exiled by a tyrant's hate,
To its early home no more to come,
By the stern unjust decree
Of the cruel foe that laid thee low,
Green Erin, gradh mo chroidhe.

That home where each mount, and crystal fount,
Lent a joy to the morn of life,
Ere the pride of man through each veinlet ran,
Inciting to freedom's strife,
With the foe that long by a course wrong,
Inhuman in thought and deed,
Caused a wail of woe on the gale to go,
And a nation to groan and bleed;
That home whose scene of emerald green,
Reflected the sunbeams' light,
In a flood that rolled its green and gold,
O'er a landscape bol i and bright,
O'er the towering hills and the gleaming rills,
O'er the slopes to the foaming sea,
Which the exile bore from his native shore,
Green Erin, gradh mo chroidhe.

How sad to find that the manly mind
That urges to deeds of fame
In country's cause by a tyrant's laws,
Can win but the weeds of shame
In dungeon cell with the vile to dwell,
A race of crime who dies,
And on scaffold high to stand and die
For the sake of the rights of man,
And thou to feel that thousands kneel
In bold worship low,
Of those who in pride o'er mankind ride,
Rejoicing in human woe,
In famine graves of shackled slaves,
Whom death at last set free
From serfdom's chain 'neath the tyrant's reign,
O'er Erin, gradh mo chroidhe.

But a morn will rise on the eastern skies,
To drive and dispel the gloom,
From each heart and face of the Irish race,
And commence better days to come,
When the banner bright shall aloft be seen,
O'er Erin's marshalled bands,
Arrayed to hold by efforts bold,
Their own and their fathers' lands;
United! no more let might,
Of descend foil each hope,
The foroe remains a battle plains,
With modern Danes to cope,
We've sail to say, discord away,
Henceforth ye shall agree,
And not a foe shall seat this low,
Green Erin, Gradh mo chroidhe.

"Gradh Mo Chroidhe (love of my heart)
pronounced "Graw mo-chree."

COME TO THE

14th ANNIVERSARY

—OF THE—

PHILO-CELTIC SOCIETY

OF BOSTON,

which will be celebrated in

NEW ERA HALL,

176 Tremont Street,

Thursday Evening, May 5th, 1887.

Following is the Programme of Exercises for the occasion :

1. Address in Irish and English, by the President, Michael C. O'Shea.

2. A song, in Irish, "O'Domhnaill A Pu" (in chorus with "harp" accompaniment, by members of the Irish school.

3. Recitation in English, "An Incident of '98," by Martin F. Curley.

4. A duet, in Irish, "An Deoraidhe o Erin" (The Exile of Erin), with harp accompaniment, by Miss Maggie O'Reilly and P. J. Sullivan.

5. A song, in English, "Call Me Back Again Caithileen," by Miss Lizzie Doherty.

6. A song, in Irish, "Eibhlin a Ruin," with harp accompaniment, by John Fitzgerald Murphy.

7. Recitation, in English, "The Celtic Tongue," by John Hickey.

8. A song, in Irish, "Ros Deighanach an t-Samhraidh (The Last Rose of Summer), with harp accompaniment, by Miss Nellie T. Hart.

9. Recitation, in English, "Morning on the Irish Coast," by P. J. Conlon.

10. Recitation, in Irish, "Aotha Sheanduin" (Ay-ho Handhoo-in), Bells of Shandon, by Miss Nellie T. Hart.

11. A song, in English, "Caithileen mo Mhairnin," by Mr. Wm. Ryan.

12. A duet, in Irish, "An Cliruit do Scaip, etc.,' (The Harp That Once, etc.,) with harp accompaniment, by Miss Mary Ni Hynes and Miss Bridget Ni Ryan.

13. A Duet in English, "The Pilot," by Curley and Fitzgerald.

14. Recitation, Irish and English, by the President.

15. Presentation of prizes by the President.

The above programme will commence prompt at 8 o'clock, and will be over at 10 o'clock, or soon after, at which time dancing will commence and continue to 2 o'clock a.m. Doors will open at 7.30.
Admission—Gentlemen 50 cents, ladies 25 cents.

---

threatened to strike it down
staff, that it fell towards the
face having been turned
which was in a southeastern
and that the impression of
was found on its left side
had never left the hand of the
God. The 12 smaller idols w
buried up to their necks in th
St. Patrick erected a churc
Domhnach Mor, (Downach M
the immediate vicinity of
In commemoration of this de
of idolatry, it is thought that
Sunday in summer is called
nach Crom Duibh (Duly
Sunday of the Black Crom.
[To be continued.]

IRISH GENEALO

Heber Fionn's Poster

[NOTE.—In the Genealogic
K. M. stand for King of Mu
L. for King of Leinster; K
King of Connaught; K.U.
of Ulster, and M.I. for Mo
Ireland. The information
these tables are from differen
sources, mainly from Dr. Kea

THE PEDIGREES OF
"MAC CARTHY MORE,"

(Continued from No. 1

32. Aengus, K. M. Tha
the first King of Man that
Christian. He had twenty
and twenty-four daughters
of whom (of both sexes)
to the service of God, Oh
tized by St. Patrick, the
Crozier of the Saint
pierced his foot by mean
be lost much blood, bu
that it was a part of the ce
baptism, he patiently bor
the ceremony was over H
in A.D. 464. son o
33. Nadfraech (New-fraeh
son of, Core, (Kurk) K. M
had a son named Cas Mac
whom have sprung the follo
namely : O'Donoghue Mo
branched O'Donoghue Mo
and O'Mahony Fionn
Roe, O'Mahony of Carbery
O'Mullane and O'Croubh
From Cairbre (Kair-th
otherwise Cairbre the

---

which is now dried up, but its site is rank of the subjects by different
the same in Irish and colors in their dress as

ignorant and superstitious multitude who are permitted to rule the capital of New England?" another article asked.

The foremost mission of Boston Irish newspapers in the nineteenth
century was to speak for the Irish community, not simply about it. The
strong editorial stance of the *Pilot, Republic,* and *Echo* prevented the Irish
community from becoming languid and disinterested, as it would later
in the twentieth century. The constant flow of opinion, news, and activities made the Irish community take a stance in its own affairs.

Irish writers became active participants in an era of increased publishing growth in the United States. Technological advances in the printing process and the growing popularity of sheet music and inexpensive
books allowed the Irish to create their own literature rather than allow
their detractors to tell the story.

The *Pilot* had long dabbled with publishing and distribution. In the
1830s Patrick Donahoe had printed a book on temperance, and in the
1850s he began distributing copies of *Moore's Melodies* and similar Irish
books. O'Reilly continued that tradition, publishing the poems of
Fanny Parnell, the prolific and passionate poet who spoke around the
country with her sister Anna in support of the Land League. Blending a
growing women's consciousness in political affairs with Irish nationalist
concerns, Parnell's poem "To My Fellow Women," published in the
Boston Pilot in 1880, called upon middle-class women to support Irish
activism:

> *The sisters whose palms ye would scarcely touch,*
> *Whose palms are rugged in toil,*
> *From penury's story they have given like queens*
> *And poured out the wine and the oil.*
> *The hot Irish heart, is it dead in the breasts of you*
> *Who have gold and power?*
> *Can never a* lady *of all put on the* women *again for an hour?*

O'Reilly himself was widely published during his twenty years in
Boston. He published four volumes of poetry and two prose collections.
Upon his death, his friend and protégé James Jeffrey Roche wrote
O'Reilly's biography, entitled *Life of John Boyle O'Reilly, Together with his
Complete Poems and Speeches,* published in 1891.

Irish Women Writers

Starting in the late nineteenth century Boston Irish women began to emerge as poets, journalists, novelists, and authors of nonfiction and children's literature. These women published frequently in the *Pilot, Donahue's Magazine,* and *Republic* as well as the *Atlantic Monthly,* and the daily Boston papers.

Louise Imogen Guiney (1861–1920) first published her poems under the initials P.O.L., and everyone assumed she was "a bright Harvard boy."

Born in Dungarvin, County Waterford, **Mary McGrath Blake** (1840–1907) was the mother of eleven children and published several poetry and travel books.

Katherine E. Conway (1853–1927) served as the only woman editor of the *Boston Pilot,* between 1905 and 1908. A published poet, Conway organized the O'Reilly Reading Circle for young women, in memory of her mentor, John Boyle O'Reilly.

Louise Imogen Guiney was a popular Boston poet whose earliest poetry collections were published in the 1880s.

Fanny Parnell (1848–1882) was frequently published in the *Pilot,* which compiled her poems into a booklet when she died.

Katharine M. O'Keeffe O'Mahoney (1852–1918), immigrated with her family from Kilkenney to Lawrence when she was ten months old. She taught poetry to Robert Frost at Lawrence High School and wrote *Catholicity in Lawrence, Famous Irishwomen, An Evening with Longfellow,* and *Moore's Birthday: A Musical Allegory.*

Annie Sullivan (1866–1936) was not only a persistent and brilliant teacher, she was also a lucid writer. Starting in 1887, Sullivan provided regular reports on her teaching methods for Helen Keller to the Perkins School for the Blind in South Boston. These reports are included in Keller's best-selling autobiography, *The Story of My Life.* They reveal Sullivan to possess a sure grasp of language, style, and structure.

The Boston Irish publishing scene was further enhanced in 1889 by *The Irish in Boston: Biographical Sketches of Representative Men and Noted Women,* compiled and edited by James B. Cullen. The 444-page book took the reader on a fascinating journey that started in the 1620s and wound its way through the tumultuous odyssey of the Irish throughout Boston history. A historical narrative, which takes up a third of the book, was written by William Taylor Jr., while Cullen himself wrote nearly 400 profiles of individuals, including forty-seven distinguished men of history. He wrote thumbnail sketches of fifty-nine lawyers, twenty-four doctors, sixty-three journalists, and 189 politicians. It demonstrated the road to respectability the Irish had taken in the latter half of the nineteenth century.

Becoming Irish Yankees

As the Irish moved into the ranks of respectability, they often tried to duplicate the trappings of comfort and influence enjoyed by the Yankees, coveting and then re-creating the old Brahmin institutions to which they had long been denied access. In April 1882 the *Republic* announced the need for an Irish American Club, "such as the Union and St. Botolph clubs . . . which shall be first class in every respect and a credit to the race in the city." A year later Thomas Riley created the Clover Club of Boston, a men's association whose "object shall be the social enjoyment of its members." Most of the members were Irish natives or Irish-Americans, and they seemed to relish the opportunity to be frivolous in a bourgeois sort of way. Still, it was a good-natured gathering where wit was the supreme arbitrator. O'Reilly himself was a member, even though he had been invited into some of Boston's old-line gentleman's clubs. In 1900 the Clover Club was making a grand occasion out of the fact they had a Ladies Night each year where the wives and girlfriends were invited to join the merrymaking in the strictly male club.

The Irish were keen to be part of the city's civil and cultural life. When playwright Oscar Wilde visited Boston in 1882, O'Reilly took him to see Henry Longfellow, Wendell Phillips, Oliver Wendell Holmes, and Julia Ward Howe, author of the "Battle Hymn of the Republic." When Hugh O'Brien was mayor in 1888, he laid the cornerstone for the new

Boston Public Library, which had been created in 1848 to educate the immigrants. The Irish were proud when Henry Doogue, an Irish immigrant, became the city's chief horticulturalist and turned the Public Garden into a nationally acclaimed botanical garden. When sculptor John Donoghue from Chicago had an exhibit at Horticultural Hall, O'Reilly praised his work and suggested that Donoghue should be considered an American master. The Irish were always delighted when a Yankee acknowledged their positive characteristics, as in 1896 when Mayor Josiah Quincy told a Charitable Irish Society gathering, "I feel that the members of your race . . . set an example which the members of other nationalities upon this continent may emulate. No one can look around Boston today and [not] note the progress which the Irish race has made in Boston."

The Boston Irish were also gaining national attention. In 1893 several notable Boston Irish participated in the Columbian Exposition in Chicago, celebrating Christopher Columbus's visit to America in 1492. More than 25 million visitors attended this world's fair, and every nation had its own pavilion. Augustus Saint-Gaudens, along with Daniel Chester French, was brought in early to help promote the Expo and to help design the American pavilions. Saint-Gaudens recommended that one of his students, Frederick MacMonnies, whose parents were Scottish, be brought in to design the Columbian Fountain, one of the centerpieces of the show. Louis Sullivan, by now an established architect in Chicago, designed the massive Transportation Building in the American exhibit. And finally, Patsy Touhey, the uilleann piper from South Boston, played his exciting style of music at the Irish pavilion.

With a firm footing in the city's political, business, and social circles, Irish-American leaders turned their attention to history. Irish leaders were long miffed at the way Anglo-American historians had minimized the Irish contribution in America. Even the Irish who had come from Ulster in the eighteenth century and made such a contribution to this country were now being called Scots-Irish to distinguish them from the hordes of Irish Catholics who had arrived since the 1840s. On January 20, 1897, a group of forty distinguished Boston Irish convened a meeting at the Revere House to form the American-Irish Historical Society, which set out "to correct the erroneous, distorted and false views of history in relation to the Irish race in America; to encourage and assist in the formation of local societies; and to promote and foster an honorable national spirit of patriotism." It was to be influenced "by no religious or political divisions, for with us the race stands first, its qualifying incidents afterwards."

The Society swiftly became a national organization, with hundreds of members subscribing from more than a dozen states. The early roster of members was impressive: writer Thomas J. Gargan; James J. Roche, editor of the *Pilot;* Thomas Hamilton Murray, editor of the *Lowell Daily Sun;* Thomas Lawlor of the publishing house Ginn & Company; and Augustus Saint-Gaudens were just some of the Boston names. Its most distinguished member, though, was Theodore Roosevelt, who claimed Irish roots on his mother's side of the family.

The Society held numerous meetings and published a journal that uncovered some fascinating genealogical and historical material on the American Irish in the seventeenth and eighteenth centuries. Michael J. O'Brien from Fermoy, County Cork, emerged as the Society's leading Irish-American historian. For more than sixty years, O'Brien patiently waded through libraries, archives, court records, genealogy papers, and military records to track down early Irish settlers in North America dating back to the seventeenth century. His book *The Irish at Bunker Hill,* published after his death in 1960, determined that hundreds of Irish and Scots-Irish were involved in that famous fight, a sharp retort to historians who insisted it was an Anglo-American occasion. O'Brien was certainly intense about his work, and he openly quarreled with those who put forth the Scots-Irish as a way of minimizing the role of the Irish in America. Having proven conclusively that the Irish were involved in many significant episodes throughout American history, the Society tried to avoid being vainglorious and self-laudable. The evidence spoke for itself.

CHAPTER NINE

Sporting Paddy (1890–1920)

I
T WAS A LONG WAY from South Boston to Athens, Greece, but that didn't faze James Brendan Connolly. When he learned that French nobleman Pierre de Coubertin was planning to revive the Olympic Games in April 1896, after having been dormant for almost 1,500 years, the pride of Southie knew that he must find a way to make the journey. "I thought of the land of Homer . . . and made up my mind that I would make that trip," Connolly later told the *Boston Sunday Post.*

Thirty-year-old Connolly was already leading an adventurous life when he was bitten by the Olympic bug. He had left school in the fifth grade to help support his family, and as a teenager had begun working with his uncle Jim O'Donnell on the fishing boats out of Gloucester and Boston. He spent a few years down in Savannah, working alongside his brother Michael with the Army Corps of Engineers, where he became a surveyor. He returned to Boston in 1895 to attend Harvard University and was awarded an engineering scholarship given to children of immigrants. He was studying the classics as a freshman when he heard about the Olympic Games.

Connolly was one of twelve children (including eight boys in a row), the son of immigrant parents John and Ann (O'Donnell) from Inis Mor, Arans Islands, off the coast of Galway. Like many young men and women growing up in Boston in the late nineteenth century, Connolly was steeped in a sports culture that placed a high premium on athletic skills and competition. Groups like the Irish Athletic Club, the Irish American Club of South Boston, and the Columbian Rowing Association flourished with the full support of political, church, and community leaders. South Boston was a sportsman's haven, with miles of coastline and dozens of parks and playing fields for children.

s the national champion in the hop, skip, and jump, as the triple
p was then known, Connolly was eligible to compete in the
Olympics. The American team was made up almost entirely of athletes
from Harvard, Princeton, and the Boston Athletic Club. Harvard would
not allow Connolly a leave of absence, so he quit the school. With his
life savings of $700, plus funds the parishioners raised for him at Saint
Augustine's, Connolly made his way down to Hoboken, New Jersey,
where he boarded a Greek freighter, the SS *Fulda*, and headed for the
Olympics.

Connolly's athletic career blossomed just as individual athleticism
and team sports were becoming popular American pastimes. The swift
growth of cities throughout America in the late nineteenth century
spawned a remarkable parks and playground movement that had
Boston roots. Frederick Law Olmsted designed the city's Emerald
Necklace, a string of parks that included 527-acre Franklin Park, with
playing fields, running paths, and tennis courts widely enjoyed by the
Irish community. Joseph Lee, known as the Father of the American
Playground, theorized that children in tenement housing needed
playgrounds to grow, and sports became a legitimate venue for poor
children.

In later years, Connolly looked back with pride on how his own
childhood involvement in sports shaped his later career as a writer and
public figure. "I would rather be born in South Boston than any other
place I know," he wrote, citing the "mental, physical and spiritual" bene-
fits of the neighborhood.

Years of practice and preparation served Connolly well in Athens in
1896, where an international cast, mainly of European athletes, had
come together. The field was relatively small, with 285 men competing
in forty-two events. After a few preliminary heats in the running events,
and in front of 140,000 spectators, Connolly stepped up to compete in
the hop, skip, and jump. Beverly Cronin of the *Boston Herald* reported
the scene: "[Connolly] walked up to the line, and with Prince George of
England and Prince George of Greece as judges, yelled in a burst of
emotion, 'Here's one for the honor of County Galway.'" Connolly then
jumped 44 feet, 11¾ inches and won the first medal of the Modern
Olympic Games.

According to Ellery H. Clark, his teammate from Harvard, Connolly had beaten the nearest competitor by almost 6 feet, causing the crowd to chant his name and yell, "Nike! Nike!"—the Greek word for victory. To further cement his status as a world-class athlete, Connolly placed second in the high jump, clearing 5 feet, 5 inches, and third place in the long jump, leaping 20 feet and ½ inch. (Clark won first place in both of those jumps.)

Upon returning to Boston, Connolly was feted at an elaborate ceremony at Faneuil Hall, followed by a boisterous parade on the streets of South Boston where he remained a popular figure throughout his life. He continued to train and returned to the next Olympics, held in Paris in 1900, taking second place in the triple jump. The *Herald*'s Cronin reported, "In typical Connolly fashion, he walked the seven miles to Paris Stadium before that competition because he couldn't afford the taxi fare."

Connolly stayed active in athletics long after his career ended, emerging as a critic of the commercialization of amateur sports. He wrote a scathing article about the 1908 Olympic Games in London, titled "The English as Poor Losers," where he accused the organizers of cheating. He turned his hand to writing and had a successful career, writing twenty-five books and dozens of short stories about the sea. In 1898 he covered the Spanish-American War, enlisting in the Fighting Ninth Irish Regiment, commanded by South Boston's Lawrence J. Logan, an immigrant from Ballygar, Galway. They saw action in Santiago, and Connolly sent back dispatches to the *Boston Globe* under the heading Letters from the Front in Cuba. During World War I he traveled with the U.S. Navy and wrote articles on the war effort. In 1921 he covered the Black and Tan War in Ireland and wrote a series of articles titled "Tortured Ireland: The Black and Tan Warfare in Ireland," published in the *Boston American.*

Perhaps his greatest compliment came from President Theodore Roosevelt, who told interviewer Frank Sheridan, "My ideal of an all around man is James Connolly of Boston. . . . Connolly is what I think a man should be. If my boy Theodore turns out to be as good a man I will be satisfied. Connolly has strength, agility, and perseverance. He loves outdoor, healthful life, and he is clean through and through. I want my boy to be as good a man as Connolly."

At Play in the Old Country

Growing up to be like Jim Connolly was a common goal in sports-crazed South Boston, where love of athletic competition was part of a culture that immigrants brought from Ireland. Most nineteenth-century Irish immigrants came from rural backgrounds, where people married late in life because of the shortage of land and economic possibilities. A widely accepted bachelor subculture emerged in Ireland, according to sports historian Steven A. Reiss, with groups of single men often whiling away their free time engaged in sports, betting, and drinking. That subculture was transferred to Boston, where numerous sports clubs flourished in Irish neighborhoods.

Irish groups such as the Ancient Order of Hibernians, along with trade unions and church groups, frequently held outdoor picnics and field days where sports competitions were common, along with music and dancing, oratory contests, and other pleasantries, historian Dennis Ryan noted in his book *Beyond the Ballot Box*.

"Most of the older people were of high blood still keen for the field sports of the old country," Connolly once wrote. "You could find old men unable to read or write [who] could argue keenly, intelligently on any outdoor sport whatsoever. . . . Many had been themselves athletes of fame: hurlers, bowlers, wrestlers . . . . Children growing up healthy, rugged just naturally had a taste for athletics."

The Irish had a particular passion for hurling, which had taken root in America. The *Republic* newspaper published regular notices about hurling matches in the Boston area, and matches between the South Boston Athletic Club and the Worchester Hurling Club were held as early as 1882.

The City of Boston Archives has records of hurling matches on Boston Common every Fourth of July, starting in 1884 and continuing through the 1890s. Teams included the Shamrock Hurling Club, the William O'Brien Hurling Club, and the Boston Hurling Club, who played for a prize of $100. In July 1893 team captain John W. Flynn wrote a letter to parks official Hillard Smith, complaining that the Shamrocks had been given the prize money even though they "walked off the field before the match was decided."

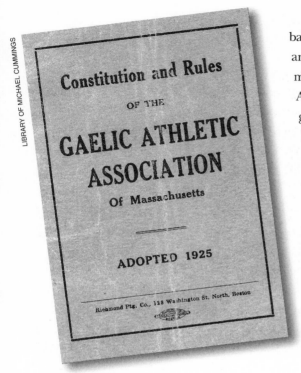

Irish immigrants brought their love of sports with them to Boston.

Hurling, along ball and camogie, ancient Irish spor moted by the Gaelic Athletic Association (GAA), a sports group that formed in Ireland in 1884 and quickly spread to the United States. As part of a burgeoning nationalistic fervor in Ireland, sports became a way for the Irish to connect with their ancient traditions. This movement went hand in hand with a broader cultural renaissance taking place in both Ireland and the United States.

The Boston Irish also excelled in competitive rowing during this time. Local Irish clubs like the Columbian Rowing Association, Shawmut Rowing Club, and West End Boat club competed along the Charles River and in Boston Harbor. The most famous rower in the Irish community was Bill Caffrey, champion oarsman from Lawrence. Competing for the Lawrence Canoe Club and the Columbian Boat Club in Boston, the 5-foot, 8-inch, 145-pound sculler worked his way up the local ranks, winning the New England single-scull championship in 1890 at age twenty-three. Later that year he stunned a field of prominent champions across the United States and Canada by winning the national rowing championships, a feat he repeated in 1891. Caffrey later became a policeman and a pillar of the Lawrence community.

Distance walking and running were also popular pastimes for the Boston Irish. Michael J. McEttrick of Roxbury entered long-distance competitions of 100 miles, winning the American Championship crown

Irish Runners Honored

The Boston Irish have always shown great enthusiasm for their athletes, and three public installations pay special homage to their heroes in running and in track and field. In 1987 the people of Boston honored **James Brendan Connolly** by erecting a statue at Columbus Park (now called Moakley Park) that depicts his winning Olympic jump in 1896. The park is on the hillside next to the stadium along Old Colony Boulevard. Connolly's extensive papers are kept at Colby College in Maine. In 1996 the Boston Athletic Association placed a bronze medallion at Copley Square Park to celebrate the centenary of the Boston Marathon. Irishman **John J. McDermott** won that first race. The medallion was created by Robert Shure, sculptor of the Boston Irish Famine Memorial. In 1997 the Boston Athletic Association honored marathon runner and two-time winner **Johnny Kelley** with a statue on Commonwealth Avenue.

in 1868, which he held for a number of years. In 1882 John Meagher of Lawrence and D. A. Driscoll of Lynn competed against each other in the 100-mile heel-and-toe walk, which ended at mile 51 when Driscoll admitted defeat, noting graciously that Meagher was "the best 100 mile walker in the country."

In the 1890s the Irish began to dominate running. Thomas E. Burke of the West End, whose father was an undertaker at Saint Joseph's Church, was a track star at English High School and later Boston University. In 1896 he was on the Olympic team that went to Athens, where he won two first-place medals in the 100 meters and the 400 meters. Burke later went to Harvard Law School, worked as a sports reporter for a time, and became the oldest pilot to serve in World War I.

Burke served as the official race starter at the first Boston Marathon, staged by the Boston Athletic Association in April 1897. It was won by John J. McDermott, an Irish-born lithographer from New York, in two hours, fifty-five minutes, and ten seconds. McDermott beat a field of fifteen runners, which included a Maguire, two Sullivans, and a Harrigan. John Caffrey, son of Irish immigrants from Ontario, won in 1900 and 1901, wearing the St. Patrick's Athletic Association shirt with a shamrock emblazed on the front.

The most famous Irish-American athlete ever to participate in the Boston Marathon was, of course, Johnny Kelley, later called "Johnny the

Elder" when another runner by the same name started competing in the world's best-known marathon race. Kelley did not finish his first two marathons, in 1928 and 1932, but then he finished every Boston Marathon from 1933 to 1992! He finished in the top ten eighteen times, taking first place in 1935 and 1945. His best time was two hours and thirty minutes, posted in 1943. When asked by the *Boston Globe* about his Irish connections, he replied, "My people left Wexford to go to Australia. The boat stopped in Boston and they never left."

The Perfect Pugilist of Modern Times

None of the athletes, not even James Connolly or Johnny Kelley, could compete in stature and notoriety with the most famous Irish-American athlete ever to come out of Boston. John L. Sullivan was his name, and like Connolly, he was the son of Irish immigrants. His father, Mike, came from Kerry and his mother, Katherine Kelly, from Galway. He was born in 1858 on East Concord Street, growing up just a few miles from Connolly over the Broadway Bridge in the South End. The Boston Strong Boy, as Sullivan was proudly called, had his first boxing success in 1878 at the Dudley Opera House, where Jack Scannell was challenging all the local boys to take a round in the ring. Sullivan's punch knocked Scannell out of the ring, and his career was under way. Four years later, Sullivan startled the sports world by winning the heavyweight boxing title at age twenty-six and holding the title for a full decade. His brash confidence and often outrageous displays of drinking, gambling, and womanizing, combined with his sense of humor and charm, endeared him to the Boston Irish.

A number of Irish-Americans opposed the art of pugilism, including Patrick Donahoe, who refused to cover the sport in *Donahoe's* Magazine. John Boyle O'Reilly, on the other hand, was an enthusiastic sportsman who had written a book called the *Ethics of Boxing and Manly Sports* and had sung the praises of a sculpture of Sullivan that had been created by John Donoghue and exhibited at Horticultural Hall in 1888. He wrote:

> *This statue stands for nineteenth century boxing for all time. It is the statue of a magnificent athlete, worthy of ancient Athens, and*

> *distinctly and proudly true of modern Boston. It is a personification*
> *of the power, will, grace, beauty, brutality and majesty of the perfect*
> *pugilist of modern times.*

Sullivan's trip to Ireland in 1887 was widely reported in the press
and followed eagerly by Boston's Irish community. Feted and praised
every step of the way by huge crowds, the larger-than-life champion
defeated every fighter who dared to step into the ring. University of
Limerick lecturer Jack Anderson wrote that Sullivan was greeted in
Dublin to the musical strains of Handel's "Hail the Conquering Hero,"
followed by "Yankee Doodle." He gave several boxing exhibits while in
Ireland and even weighed in on the topic of Home Rule for Ireland,
which he of course endorsed.

The biggest journalism scoop of the day was when Sullivan returned
from Ireland. John S. Taylor, sporting editor of the *Boston Globe,* waited
in a tugboat near the Boston Lighthouse for two days for Sullivan's ship
to come in and snagged an exclusive interview with Sullivan. He had
already filed the story while the other reporters waited at Commercial
Wharf to meet the boxer, according to James B. Cullen, author of *The
Story of the Irish in Boston.*

Upon his return to Boston, Sullivan was awarded a championship
belt studded with diamonds and other stones. (The *British American
Citizen*'s snide headline read "Diamond Belt to Rum-Selling Pugilist.")
He continued to amass victories, defending his title against worthy
opponents or offering $50 or more to anyone who could stay with him
in the ring for three rounds. In September 1892 the sporting world was
shocked, and the Boston Irish were in mourning, when their Strong
Boy was defeated by a more nimble Jim Corbett in a famous match in
New Orleans. Sullivan continued to fight until 1905, when he hung up
the gloves forever and, a few months later, quit the booze. He spent
years on the temperance circuit, warning anyone who would listen
about the evils of whiskey. He once told reporter Jerome W. Power,
"Whiskey is the only fighter who ever licked John L. Sullivan."

Sullivan remained a popular figure, first on the temperance circuit and finally as a vaudeville performer. Everywhere he went, up to
his death in 1918, he attracted crowds of admirers. Political power-

Boxing champ John L. Sullivan sits in the Red Sox dugout with player-coach Jimmy Collins in 1904.

house James M. Curley enlisted him on the campaign trail, and the Boston Red Sox used to invite him into the dugout during ball games.

He became a living legend in Boston long after his death. "What other man," wrote James Brendan Connolly about Sullivan, "being waked out of his sleep and finding two burglars in his room—what other man in the world would lock the door, give the two burglars a beating, and then order them up a good breakfast, and turn them loose with a sermon on the error of their ways?"

The Irish Pilgrims Play the Olde Ball Game

Early efforts to name baseball teams in Boston were not so successful. In 1901 the team was nicknamed the Boston Somersets, after team owner Charles Somers. But that name conjured up unfortunate reminders of the city's exclusive gentleman's club, called the Somerset, which had been formed in 1851 as a way for the old Brahmins to escape the Irish masses in the comfort and privacy of a stiff brandy and a Cuban cigar. A full century later John F. Kennedy complained to a friend, "Do you know it's impossible for an Irish Catholic to get into the Somerset Club? If I moved back to Boston even after being president, it would make no difference."

Some fans started calling the team the Pilgrims, and then the Puritans. Not too many Pilgrims or Puritans, however, were apparent on a team that sported a roster with Jimmy Collins, Bill Dinneen, Patsy Dougherty, Duke Farrell, Tommy Hughes, and Jackie O'Brien, with German-American Cy Young thrown in for good measure. Finally, the Taylor family who owned the team renamed it the Boston Red Sox after the 1907 season, and the rest is history.

The first baseball teams in America formed in the 1850s as a pastime for middle-class young men, but immigrants and blue-collar athletes soon took over, forming leagues united by their trade, neighborhood, or religious affiliations. Baseball easily supplanted cricket, which had made some headway in America but was essentially viewed as an elitist sport. Baseball seemed to embody something so democratic that it ultimately became the national pastime, and the Irish, enthusiastic about anything that was both patriotic and enjoyable, quickly filled the ranks. By the 1880s Irish players dominated the game of baseball, accounting for more than one third of the league.

The ball players were matched in the local sports pages by a crop of Irish-American reporters. Timothy Hayes Murnane started the respected sports paper *Referee* in 1886 and later covered sports for the *Boston Globe* and *Sporting News*. Eugene Buckley published the Baseball Record; and Peter Kelly, a journalist from South Boston, was chosen as secretary of the Boston National baseball team in 1910.

Journalist Ron Kaplan, writing in *Irish America Magazine*, claims that the first superstar of baseball was first-generation Irish-American Mike "King" Kelly, who was sold by Chicago to the Boston Braves in 1887 for $10,000, and in 1890 became the team's player/manager. Kelly once stole six bases in a single game, a feat memorialized in a popular song called "Slide, Kelly, Slide."

The most famous baseball coach to come out of Massachusetts was Connie Mack, born Cornelius McGillicuddy, in East Brookfield. In 1914

Mack's team, the Philadelphia Athletics, lost four straight games to the Boston Braves in the World Series Championship. Jimmy Collins, regarded as the greatest third-baseman ever to play, coached Boston to the World Series title in 1903 against the Pittsburgh Pirates. Joe Cronin, who played his last ten years with the Red Sox, had a .301 batting average, including 1,424 runs batted in. Rough Carrigan, from Lewiston, Maine, led the Sox to two consecutive World Series in 1915 and 1916. He was "the greatest manager I ever played for," said Babe Ruth. "He taught me how to be a big league pitcher."

Speaking of Ruth, the player who brought him to Boston was none other than Patsy Donovan, who was born in Cork but at age three emigrated to Lawrence, a mill city of Irish immigrants north of Boston. Donovan broke into professional baseball in 1886 when he was twenty-one, playing in the New England League. He spent seventeen years as a player and manager, coaching the Boston Red Sox in 1910 and 1911. He had 2,263 hits as a player and a lifetime batting average of .313.

According to his son Charles M. Donovan, Patsy was in Baltimore scouting some players when he ran into a priest he knew who was working at St. Mary's Industrial School in Baltimore. The priest suggested that Patsy take a look at Herman Ruth, then playing for the Baltimore Orioles. As journalist Arthur Daley recounted in the *New York Times,* "The instant he saw him work he fell in love with a huge softpaw pitcher of obvious skills, Babe Ruth. He rushed helter-skelter back to owner Joe Lannin with the demand that the Red Sox buy Ruth from the Orioles regardless of price. Ten minutes later Lannin had closed the deal over the phone." Daley called it "the greatest bargain buy in baseball history."

Patsy's name was on the original 1936 Hall of Fame ballot and was recently reentered for consideration by his surviving children, Charles M. Donovan and Ellenora O'Brien. "He was well spoken, quiet, positive, never crude," their application stated. "He was not only an outstanding athlete and major league figure but a warm and caring human being with strong values and impeccable integrity . . . . He was good for baseball; he does deserve to join the Hall of Fame for his performance, courage, and inspiration—even to this day."

Apparently one of Donovan's former players agreed. In 2001 the

Baseball Hall of Fame received a letter from former President George Herbert Walker Bush, whom Donovan had coached at Phillips Academy in Andover, Massachusetts. "I write this as an admirer of Patrick J. Donovan," President Bush wrote to the committee. "I understand that Mr. Donovan has been nominated to the Baseball Hall of Fame, and I enthusiastically second the motion."

CHAPTER TEN

The World's Greatest Irish City (1900–1930)

MAUDE GONNE, known as Ireland's Joan of Arc, helped to usher in the Boston Irish Century in style. The raven-haired beauty arrived in the city on Sunday afternoon, February 17, 1900, as part of a national tour to tell Americans about British atrocities in the Boer War. She was greeted at South Station by a delegation of fifty men and women from the local Irish societies, who then escorted her to the Vendome on Commonwealth Avenue, the city's fanciest hotel. Dr. P. J. Timmons spoke for the entire delegation when he praised her "noble efforts" to rail against British imperialism in South Africa and in Ireland, "our suffering motherland."

The tall, slender Englishwoman-turned-Irish rebel had captured the world's imagination. She was the muse of poet William Butler Yeats, and local Boston writers seemed smitten with her too. *Republic* newspaper editor Patrick Maguire remembered her "wealth of wavy hair and eyes that flash at will when she becomes animated in discussing the cause of Ireland." The *Boston Globe* wrote that she looked "picturesque in a black velvet gown with a silver girdle at the waist . . . her splendid voice extremely musical."

When she arrived at the Tremont Temple on Monday to speak before 2,000 cheering supporters, the stage was ablaze with colorful bunting and the flags of the United States, Ireland, and the Boer Transvaal. Gonne wasted no time blasting the British for "the greatest crimes in the world" and invoking a time-honored belief among many Irish nationalists. "From an Irish point of view, it matters not whether it be right or wrong, the nation that is the enemy of England is a friend and ally of Ireland." Many Bostonians, mindful of Britain's opposing role in the Revolutionary War, the War of 1812, and the Confederacy during the Civil War, agreed with that assessment.

Gonne's visit was just the kickoff to a flurry of Irish activities taking place in Boston in the first year of the new century. Composer and singer Chauncy Olcott brought his new play *A Romance in Athlone* to Boston Theatre, featuring the hit song "My Wild Irish Rose." The Gaelic League of America held its national convention here, and so did the Ancient Order of Hibernians, the country's largest Irish-American group. South Boston's star athlete James Connolly went to the Olympic Games in Paris and came in second in the triple jump. And James Michael Curley launched a half-century political career as an elected official on the seventy-five-member Boston Common Council.

By 1900 an air of cockiness infused the spirit of the Boston Irish. Ascending in all directions, the Irish were ready to put their distinctive stamp on a city that had initially banned them from even entering the town. True, some nasty attempts were made by the American Protection Association and nativists like Henry Cabot Lodge to slow them down, but the Irish were having none of it. Trying unsuccessfully not to gloat, John "Honey" Fitzgerald, grandfather of a future president, would announce, "The Celt has replaced the Puritan" in dear old Boston. In 1906, the year that Fitzgerald became the city's third Irish mayor, journalist Herb Classon would take that sentiment one step further, declaring in *Munsey's Magazine,* "Boston, not Dublin or Belfast, is now the greatest Irish city in the world."

Many old-line Bostonians weren't happy about that, but what could they do? By 1900 sixteen percent of Boston residents had been born in Ireland, and another 25 percent of the residents claimed some sort of Irish connection. They had grown in confidence and stature under the political leadership of O'Reilly, Collins, and O'Brien. Gilmore and Cohan had become household names in the entertainment world. Sullivan and Connolly were spreading fame around the world as sports stars. Labor leaders like Mary Kenny O'Sullivan and Margaret Lilian Foley had emerged as labor organizers for women working in factories. The Catholic Church, which had only one church and two priests in 1800, had 260 churches and 635 priests in 1900, according to a Boston almanac entitled *Our Church, Her Children and Institutions.* The Irish had taken over South Boston, Charlestown, and Roxbury, towns that had once rejected them.

John F. Fitzgerald, mayor of Boston and grandfather to President John F. Kennedy, promenades through the streets of Boston.

But the opening decade of the twentieth century also marked a changing of the guard for the Boston Irish. The incredible generation of leaders who helped beleaguered Irish immigrants weather their considerable tribulations in the nineteenth century was passing. Newspaper publisher and poet O'Reilly had died young in 1890 at age forty-six. Hugh O'Brien, the city's first Irish mayor, died in 1894. Patrick Donahoe, philanthropist and publisher of the Boston *Pilot*, died in 1901. Mayor Patrick Collins died in office at the height of his popularity in 1905. James Jeffrey Roche, *Pilot* editor and biographer of O'Reilly, died in 1908.

These were the immigrants who laid the groundwork for the Boston Irish Century and made it the world's greatest Irish city. They restored a social cohesion that had been stripped away during the great migration from Ireland, implanting a powerful sense of ethnic identity in the city's Irish community. They laid claim to a hyphenated Irish-American identity that offered the best of both worlds to the Irish community. From that dual identity a special brand of Irish-American patriotism emerged, wrapped around the American flag while waving the Irish tricolor. It was a patriotism celebrated by George M. Cohan,

The Independent Irish

July Fourth, when American colonists declared their independence from Great Britain, has long been a holiday that inspired the Irish in America. In the early 1930s, the *Irish World* newspaper published this poem, which sentimentalized the dual patriotic feelings of the Irish in America.

A Poem Dedicated to All Men of Irish Blood on July 4

Unfurl old Erin's banner
Fling its green folds to the breeze
In this, the greater Ireland
Our home o'er the seas.

And in many a well fought battlefield
On the mountains, vale or glen
Did the Redcoats cry with terror
"There's that damn green flag again."

Let us show the cursed Briton
How we glory in the pride
Of the countless line of heroes
Who for freedom's cause have died.

Wear the glorious Stars and Stripes then
With the green entwined in one
With the memory of the Irish brave
Who fought with Washington.

Men of Erin! Men of Erin!
You may well feel proud that day
For the Irish troops fought bravely
In grim battle's fierce array.

Then bear yourselves right proudly
And hold your heads on high
In this, our adopted country
On the Fourth Day of July!

politicized by James Michael Curley, and implemented by the thousands of Irish-Americans from South Boston, Charlestown, Dorchester, and other Irish neighborhoods who enlisted in the American military throughout the century.

Boston's Branch of Irish Independence

The city's distinctive Irish persona made Boston a headquarters for Ireland's political exiles, aspirants, agitators, and leaders between the 1880s and the 1920s, a critical time in the history of Ireland. By the late nineteenth century, Ireland's politics were roughly divided between constitutional nationalists, who sought to win Home Rule from Britain through political pressure and negotiation, and militant nationalists, who held that the British would only leave Ireland when kicked out by physical force. A third category of Unionists insisted on allegiance to Britain, but their leaders rarely ventured to Boston to state their case.

The nationalists did come to Boston—frequently. Charles Stuart Parnell, Fanny Parnell, John Redmond, John Devoy, John Dillon, and Michael Davitt all journeyed to the city with three goals in mind: to muster political support, to raise money, and to create publicity for their various causes.

Maude Gonne set the standard in 1900, accomplishing all three goals with relative ease. When she left Massachusetts, she had spoken in Boston as well as in Fall River and Lowell. She had raised more than $50,000 in pledges and had achieved front-page news coverage in the major papers. Others followed, with varying degrees of success, and each with their own particular agenda. Home Rule advocate Joseph Dillon came in 1903 on behalf of the United Irish League and raised $10,000 at a meeting at Faneuil Hall. In December 1904 Douglas Hyde, founder of the Irish language movement, visited Boston to promote cultural nationalism. (He was introduced by Fred Norris Robinson, an Irish language enthusiast who initiated the Celtic Studies program at Harvard University.) Francis Sheehy-Skiffington, a militant pacifist who espoused women's rights, vegetarianism, and Irish independence came to Worcester and Boston in 1915. James Larkin, the trade union leader from Belfast, spoke at the Tremont Temple in February 1915, during which he was described as "more of a poet and idealist than a red-handed agitator."

Groups like the Ancient Order of Hibernians, Clan na Gael, and the Irish Progressive League had chapters in Boston, supporting an emerging physical force movement. The United Irish League of America seemed to attract more middle-class, respectable Irish Americans who were worried by the worldwide advance of socialism and other radical solutions. In Charlestown a Parnell Literary Club kept the Home Rule leader's memory alive. Despite the various shadings of political activism, it looked to casual observers like the Irish were coming together at last. Even the headlines of the *Boston Globe* commented on the development:

> *TORY ALARM At the Uprising of the Irish People*
> *Celtic Race United in a Most Surprising Manner*

Irish Rebels and Irish Yankees

The outbreak of World War I in August 1914 interrupted the momentum that the Home Rule Movement had gained in Ireland, setting up a quandary for the young men of Ireland. Would they join the British Army and fight against Germany, with hopes that Britain would look kindly upon the Irish when the war ended? Or would they heed Maude Gonne's slogan from her Tremont Temple speech: Any Enemy of England Is a Friend of the Irish. They did some of both: 60,000 Irish enlisted in the British Army during World War I, and thousands more did not.

The issue of allegiance became more complicated in April 1916 when a group of Irish rebels—an assortment of poets, labor leaders, schoolteachers, and soldiers—tried to take over Dublin on Easter Monday and proclaim an Irish Republic. The uprising was quelled within a week and would have likely become another footnote in the annals of Irish history. But British General John Maxwell changed all that when he decided to execute fifteen of the rebels as a lesson to future insurgents. In doing so he elevated them to martyrs.

Across America thousands of Irish held "indignation gatherings" to protest the action. Twenty thousand people gathered at the Parkman Bandstand on Boston Common to hear Congressman Joe O'Connell of Dorchester lambaste the British execution of the Irish rebels.

According to Lenahan O'Connell and James W. Ryan, in their book *The O'Connell Family of Massachusetts,* the congressman tried to steer President Woodrow Wilson away from entering the war, believing it would jeopardize Ireland's chances of independence. The congress-man's instincts were correct, the authors continue, because when the United States entered the war on April 6, 1917, the Irish question "was placed on a back burner until after the fighting ended."

Once America entered the war, most Irish-American feelings of ambiguity toward fighting alongside Britain were put to rest. Senator David I. Walsh, who had been elected the state's first Catholic governor in 1914 and then became the state's first Catholic senator in 1919, put it best when he said, "Let every man of Irish blood face his duty as an American citizen in passing judgment on national and international questions. Let us remember to be Americans first."

That's exactly what Boston's Irish community did. Colonel Edward L. Logan of South Boston, after whom Logan International Airport is named, led the city's famous Irish Ninth Regiment, which had been reorganized into the 101st regiment of the Yankee Division. Logan and his men went to the front lines in France and fought at Argonne Forest and other battles. One of his men, Mickey Perkins from South Boston, single-handedly took over a German machine gun nest and captured the twenty-five soldiers inside, according to Curt Norris of the *Quincy Patriot Ledger*.

Not surprisingly, it was Irish-American George M. Cohan, born on the Fourth of July, who best gave musical expression to American patriotism during World War I. Cohan's father Jeremiah was born to Irish immigrants on Blackstone Street in Boston in 1848; his mother was Nellie Costigan. Along with his sister Josephine, George and his parents toured the minstrel and vaudeville circuit for two decades before they made it in New York, where George was to become the toast of Broadway.

A trilogy of Cohan compositions became America's theme songs during World War I. The first was "Yankee Doodle Dandy," which Cohan wrote in 1904 for his play *Little Johnny Jones*, appropriating an old jingle that British troops had sung to lampoon the ragtag colonial army at Lexington and Concord in 1775. According to Cohan biographer John McCabe, "The audience was electrified. They had never heard a song like this—patriotically stirring, yet funny." The second tune, "You're a Grand Old Flag," was written in 1906, after Cohan met a Civil War veteran at a funeral who reminisced about his love of America and inspired the song. Cohan completed the trilogy with a song that became the American anthem during the war. He named it "Over There." Two days after "President Woodrow Wilson declared war on Germany on April 6, 1917, Cohan had written the song and performed it for his wife and children on a Sunday morning," writes McCabe.

Hungering for the Truth

When the war came to an end on November 11, 1918, Irish leaders in Boston turned their attention again to Ireland. Riding the coattails of Irish-American valor and patriotism during the war, they created an advertising campaign to promote an Irish Victory Drive for Freedom of Ireland:

> *Let us pay our debt! Remember what you owe to Ireland. As you*
> *honor the Irish blood shed for American liberty, help the cause of*
> *liberty—NOW!*

The Irish managed to tie in the Ireland issue with the post-war negotiations taking place in Europe thanks to the astute leadership of Eamon De Valera. The New York-born son of a Spanish father and Irish mother, the Irish patriot, politician, and statesman would become the dominant figure in twentieth century Ireland. He visited Boston numerous times over a period of nearly five decades and received without doubt the most enthusiastic welcomes ever accorded a foreign leader, Irish or otherwise.

In 1919 De Valera, whom the British had imprisoned on a trumped-up "German Plot" charge toward the end of the war, escaped from jail, smuggled himself aboard a ship, and made his way to America, where he spent the next nineteen months raising funds and lobbying for Ireland's independence. He arrived in Boston on Saturday, June 28, 1919, and was greeted by more than 20,000 people at South Station. The *Irish World* reported:

> *The crowd was so dense and so demonstrative that the automobile in*
> *which the Irish leader was conveyed from the station to Copley Plaza*
> *Hotel had great difficulty in getting through. The difficulty was*
> *solved by the crowd itself, forming into a procession behind the car,*
> *every man and every woman carrying the Stars and Stripes and the*
> *Irish Republican flag.*

At the banquet that evening, De Valera called upon America to "take up the responsibility for the moral leadership of the world" by ensuring the rights of all nations, particularly small ones. Referring to Boston's own colonial history, De Valera told his rapt audience, "Your fathers fought and broke the chains that bound you to George III. We ask you, their sons, to assist us in breaking the chains that bind Ireland to George V."

The next day De Valera spoke at Fenway Park before a crowd esti-

At the end of World War I, Irish activists hoped to turn American attention toward Ireland's drive for independence.

mated at 50,000 to 60,000 people. It was the largest gathering for a foreign politician in Boston's history, surpassing even the visit of Lafayette in 1825. Governor Calvin Coolidge sent a letter "expressing strong support with Ireland's Cause." Boston Mayor Andrew Peters and Mayor Edward Quinn of Cambridge gave rousing speeches, and Senator David I. Walsh, who would become close friends with De Valera, gave what the *Boston Post* called "the best speech of his life," comparing De Valera with Abraham Lincoln and predicting he would be as successful.

Irish leader Eamon De Valera (in glasses) always drew a large crowd when visiting Boston.

De Valera addressed his comments directly at President Wilson: "Let America and America's President take the fortunes that fate clearly indicates for them—emancipate and save the world . . . . Let [America] lead—true democracy will organize itself the world over to press on to salvation and happiness behind her."

The *Boston Herald* cited De Valera's "passionate sincerity and utmost simplicity" as his outstanding characteristics, which "burned their way into the consciousness of everyone who sees and hears him."

De Valera returned to Ireland in December 1920 and continued negotiating with the British. On December 5, 1921, one of the most startling breakdowns in diplomacy occurred when De Valera's hand-picked envoys, led by Michael Collins, were pressured into signing a treaty that partitioned the island into two. Six counties in Ulster would become Northern Ireland, and twenty-six counties would be the Irish Free State. De Valera rejected the treaty, and an Irish civil war ensued between supporters of De Valera and Collins. It lasted until May 1923 when De Valera called a halt to the struggle. On September 10, 1923, Ireland was recognized as a Free State and was accepted into the League of Nations. DeValera, reduced to opposition leader, stood on the sidelines.

By 1926 De Valera had created a new party, Fianna Fail (Soldiers of Destiny), and the following March he returned to the United States. He visited Boston three times that year, each time strengthening his record as the most popular foreign leader ever to visit the city. His first visit on March 20, 1927, was a triumph. James T. Sullivan of the *Boston Globe* wrote, "It was undoubtedly the greatest reception any Irish leader ever got in Boston for an indoor meeting."

De Valera was speaking at Boston Symphony Hall, the famous concert hall renowned for its acoustic brilliance. By 7:00 P.M. 5,000 people had already crowded into the hall, and police shut the doors. Another 20,000 people surrounded Symphony Hall, in the snow and rain, on "one of those mean and miserable nights when people have to be strongly tempted to leave the comforts of their own homes," wrote the *Irish World*. The organist hired to lead the crowd in patriotic songs had to be escorted to the building by police, forty-five minutes late for her gig. De Valera was not able to speak until nearly 11:00 P.M., and first had to quell the noise outside the Hall by addressing the crowd waiting in the snow. When he finally walked onto the stage, the *Irish World* reported,

> Men and women rose and cheered again and again. There were old men there too, men who have followed the fortunes of Ireland through many a weary length of years. And there were white haired old women who gazed up at the tall, spare figure of the man with tears in their eyes, their lips quivering as they called to him and blessed him and prayed that he must lead their nation to the so long deferred victory. . . . All through his speech . . . the people listened to every word with an almost painful intensity. They were hungry for the truth.

After touring the United States, De Valera again returned to Boston where his ship, the *Republic,* was sailing to Ireland. There he received another joyous and frenzied welcome. He addressed a farewell banquet hosted by the chamber of commerce, invoking America's history:

*Instead of getting its liberty, Ireland has been partitioned and muti-
lated. Lincoln fought a great civil war in this country to prevent the
partition of the United States and that is just what we are opposing
today in Ireland.*

On April 30, the day of his departure, De Valera spoke at the
Parkman Bandstand on Boston Common before thousands of
Bostonians, who were "clutching at his coat and struggling with each
other to shake him by the hand." The Saint Ambrose Fife and Drum
Corps led a procession to Commonwealth Pier, where the *Republic* was
docked. At the pier De Valera's car was closed in by thousands of sup-
porters, "many of them with children held high in their arms to give
them an opportunity to shake hands with the leader," wrote the *Irish
World*. He stood up in the car and spoke to the crowd in Gaelic and
English, and they finally let him board the ship, which sailed out of
Boston Harbor "to the skirling of the bagpipe music of the Irish
Republican Band playing the *Soldiers Song.*"

CHAPTER ELEVEN

Musical Stages: Symphony Hall and Hibernian Hall (1900–1940)

W HEN IRISH TENOR John McCormack burst onto the music scene in the early 1900s, the Boston Irish rejoiced. Here at last was a worthy purveyor of the ancient melodies of Ireland, and he could also sing opera! After winning the Dublin *Feis Ceol* (music festival) in 1903 at age twenty, the Athlone-born singer embarked on a forty-two year career that placed him in the pantheon of the world's greatest singers. Novelist James Joyce, a fair tenor himself, wrote that McCormack had "a voice from beyond the world." Even Italy's great tenor Enrico Caruso considered McCormack the best tenor alive, which he told the young Irishman to his face when they met by chance in the lobby of the Copley Plaza Hotel.

The Boston Irish agreed wholeheartedly with Joyce and Caruso. The *Republic* newspaper noted McCormack's "superb presence, magnetic personality and rare voice," hailing him as "about as potent an influence for the conservation of what is distinctly Irish . . . as any that has appeared in our time. He makes people glad they are Irish."

McCormack made his first Boston appearance in April 1910, performing at the Boston Theatre in the Manhattan Company's production of *La Traviata*. The following year, on February 5, 1911, he made his debut at Boston Symphony Hall, one of the great concert venues of the world. Between 1911 and 1936 he performed there sixty-seven times, more than any other singer.

McCormack's arrival on the music scene was timely, since the Irish influence on America's songbook was beginning to wane. Ireland's ancient melodies had been retrieved during the Celtic Revival of the 1880s, but they were being overshadowed by what author Mark Sullivan has called "melting pot songs," as discussed in his popular American history book, *Our Times: 1900–1925*. These songs were usually written by

Irish Tenor John McCormack burst onto the music scene in the early 1900s.

Americans about newcomers—or greenhorns—whether they were Irish, German, or Italian. They fed into the stereotypes of each group with "a sophisticated air of humorous condescension," Sullivan wrote. Songs about the Irish, predictably, often involved drinking, fighting, thick-headedness, and parochialism. In the 1900s the mass production of sheet music and the emergence of the recording industry flooded the marketplace with these songs.

John McCormack temporarily reversed this trend by restoring a genuine reverence and respect for Irish melodies. He also added credibility to Irish-American songsters like Chauncy Olcott and Ernest Ball, who cowrote McCormack's first hit "Mother Machree," in 1910. Of McCormack's rendition of "Mother Machree," Sullivan thus observed, "true Irish songs enabled a singer to be sentimental without causing shivers to the discriminating listener."

The Boston Irish loved McCormack's ability to enthrall mainstream audiences, since they themselves were moving into mainstream society at a time when other immigrant groups—Italians, Poles, and Lithuanians—were being considered the greenhorns of America. His vast repertoire combined the old Irish songs he had learned as a boy with the classical arias of Italy, France, and Germany. He favored the melodies of Thomas Moore, Ireland's great nineteenth century bard and poet, and relied upon the arrangements of fellow Irishman Herbert Hughes. Hughes described Irish songs as having "the rarest beauty and distinction, with more variety of mood than can be found in any other European language" in his two-volume set *Irish Country Songs*, published in 1909. H. Earle Johnson's book, *Symphony Hall, Boston,* notes that McCormack "often went to the Public Library in Copley Square" hunting for new songs and "came away with the prizes of research."

McCormack also developed a distinct patriotism toward America that was in tune with an overall Irish-American sensibility at that time. Like Patrick S. Gilmore and George M. Cohan, McCormack was unabashed about his admiration for what America offered to him and his family. During World War I he did a musical tour for the American Red Cross and recorded songs like "God Be With Our Boys Tonight," earning him popularity with the troops in Europe. In 1914 he took out papers to become an American citizen, further endearing him to his American audience.

During his visits to Boston, McCormack got to know many well-known artists of international stature, such as Enrico Caruso and Dr. Karl Muck, the Boston Symphony Orchestra's celebrated conductor. In April 1925 he met painter John Singer Sargent, the prolific artist whose murals grace the Boston Public Library and the Museum of Fine Arts. The two artists hit it off at once, recalls McCormack's wife Lily in her charming memoir *I Hear You Calling Me*. Sargent told Lily he would paint McCormack's "magnificent head and sensitive mouth" later that fall, but Sargent died in London before that work got under way.

A devout Catholic, whose "inner life was built upon his faith," McCormack was befriended by William Cardinal O'Connell and devoted time to various Catholic causes in Boston, doing benefit concerts for the Knights of Columbus War Fund, Emmanuel College, and Saint Mary's Infant Asylum in Dorchester.

McCormack's final Symphony Hall concert in 1936 was a benefit for the Guild of Saint Elizabeth's on Dudley Street in Roxbury, which did "benevolent work among children," according to the program book. "There was a poignant realization in those brief hours," H. Earle Johnson writes, "that he was standing on hallowed ground, as it were, for the last time. He seemed to linger with the audience, and people applauded when they would rather have wept."

Dancing on Dudley Street

Roxbury was a fitting place for McCormack to direct his charitable donations, since it had become the center of Boston's Irish-American community. Saint Patrick's Church was established there in 1836, followed by Saint Francis de La Sales and the Mission Church, which became anchors for the Irish community moving out of inner city Boston in the nineteenth century. The Sisters of Notre Dame moved to Roxbury in 1853, followed by the Carmelite nuns and the Sisters of Charity.

In 1913, the Ancient Order of Hibernians, the largest Irish fraternal group in the country, firmly added to the area's Irish flavor when they announced plans to build a new AOH headquarters at 184 Dudley Street. The $100,000 project would accommodate close to two dozen AOH chapters in the area. It would be designed by architect Edward T. P. Graham, who would create one of the city's largest dance halls on the third floor of the building. Organizers envisioned Hibernian Hall to be the "finest building owned by the AOH in the United States," wrote the *Boston Sunday Post*.

When the builders decided to lay the cornerstone for Hibernian Hall on May 30, 1913, they asked themselves, who better to place the stone than the local Irish political maestro himself—James Michael Curley?

Indeed, there was no one better than the up-and-coming politician who had already been mayor and was currently serving as the U.S. Congressman for Boston. Curley was a native son of Roxbury, having been born on Northampton Street in 1874, and he and his wife Mary (nee Herlihy) still lived on Mount Pleasant Street. He was a proud member of the Ancient Order of Hibernians, the organization that was building the new Hall to serve as a headquarters for 10,000 Boston members. Rumor was that Curley had planned his Niagara Falls honeymoon in 1906 so he could swing by the national AOH convention at Saratoga Springs on the way back to Boston.

The crowd of 5,000 Irish-Americans cheered and waved tiny American flags as Congressman Curley laid the stone with a silver trowel. Patrick J. Larkin, head of the Hibernian Building Association, placed a copper box inside the stone with "a copy of the deed, pictures, newspapers, and other things . . . of interest in the future." Local papers reported that Curley launched into an impassioned oratory about the Irish community, and what it meant to Roxbury, to Boston, and to the nation.

"Congressman Curley said the Irishman today stands for liberty and progress and his daily life is the most highly developed form of American citizenship," reported the *Roxbury Gazette*. "He spoke of the character, purity and honesty of the Irish, who came here at the time of the thirteen colonies and made such a republic possible. He told of the Irish in the Civil War."

An Ancient Order for the Irish

Established in 1857 by Edward Riley, Boston's **Ancient Order of Hibernians** remains a vibrant, active group in Massachusetts, with more than 2,500 members. The group works closely in the local community, raising funds for local food banks and hosting a variety of cultural activities throughout the year. It provides educational outreach on historical topics like the 1798 Uprising, the Irish Famine, and the Troubles. For example, it supports the *Jeanie Johnston* project, a foundation that created a replica of the famine ship *Jeanie Johnston,* which sailed to North America in 2003. The AOH supports various Irish causes, including the Special Olympics and the Green Cross, which assists the families of political prisoners in Northern Ireland. It has actively supported the Irish Peace Process and educates local officials on political developments in Northern Ireland. Its motto is Friendship, Unity, and Christian Charity. For more information, visit the Web site www.massaoh.org.

Hibernian Hall Revival

The beloved landmark Hibernian Hall, designed by architect Edward T. P. Graham and located at 184 Dudley Street in Roxbury, fell into disrepair in the middle decades of the twentieth century. It was nearly torn down in the 1990s to make way for new construction. In fact, a group of musicians who had played there in the 1950s returned in 1998 for a final set of tunes before, they thought, the building would be demolished. But the Massachusetts Historical Commission designated the building a historical property, and it was spared. The Roxbury Consortium of Arts, Culture and Trade (ACT), along with the Madison Park Development Corp., are turning the building into a multi-arts facility for residents of the Dudley Square area. ACT director Candelaria Silvia and her staff have researched the building's Irish history and plan to keep an exhibit honoring the building's illustrious Irish past. For more information, call (617) 541–3900 or visit the Web site www.actroxbury.org

It was vintage Curley: preaching to the converted, laying another Irish brick atop the cobblestoned city of Puritans, extolling Irish virtues while wrapping himself around his own Americanism. How fortunate for a guy like Curley that he had come of age at the very beginning of the Boston Irish Century, when his ethnicity, religion, politics, and worldview seemed perfectly suited for taking the city from a stifled seaport town of Puritans to a vibrant Celtic city where men roared through life with a vengeance and built a future their recent ancestors had been denied. The quid pro quo of promising favors for votes became the formula for Curley and others to maintain their post atop the city on a hill, and ceremonies like the Hibernian Hall event was a perfect backdrop to promote this trade-off.

The notion of using local government to help friends, neighbors, and relatives certainly gave the Irish a leg up in the early days, when they needed it. But by the time they were fully in control and an Irish ethos dominated Boston government, the motto All Politics Are Local had become a thinly veiled ruse for patronage, nepotism, and cronyism. In the end, it was a feeding trough for political appointees, coat holders, and sign holders who ultimately detracted from rather than contributed to the Boston Irish persona that O'Brien, O'Reilly, and Collins envisioned back in the 1880s.

Politics and popular culture intersected frequently in Boston during the twentieth century, as politicians trolling for votes went looking for voters looking for favors. The often uproarious theater of Boston Irish

THE BOSTON SUNDAY GLOBE—FEBRUARY 25, 1900.

ST VINCENT'S FAIR MUSICIANS.

ST VINCENT'S YOUNG LADIES' BANJO, MANDOLIN AND GUITAR CLUB OF SOUTH BOSTON.

*By the turn of the twentieth century, there were dozens of musical groups in
Boston's Irish neighborhoods.*

politicians recalls Curley biographer Jack Beatty's observation of the
Irish tendency to "see life in a comic light." So it would have been
charming and all in good fun to see John "Honey Fitz" Fitzgerald standing on a chair to sing "Sweet Adeline" in his mellifluous voice, or James
Curley puffing into a set of highland bagpipes or donning elaborate
Indian headgear for the photographer. Even nonelected officials like
Richard Cardinal Cushing took a go at the Scottish bagpipes or played a
few tunes on the button accordion at Blinstrub's in South Boston while
a couple of old-timers danced the Kerry set. Fitzgerald later recalled in
the *Eire Society Bulletin,* "When I was mayor of Boston, I learned that
everywhere a mayor went, he had to make a speech, and no one really
wanted to hear a speech every time, so I sang."

There were plenty of places to sing thanks to the expansion of Irish
organizations in Boston between 1900 and 1920. At the Gaelic League
of America convention in 1900, local musicians presented *Feis Ceoil Agus
Shanachus* (Festival of Irish Minstrelsy, Song, and Story), featuring
"Gaelic folk songs, gems of Irish opera, Irish harp, and bagpipe music"

at the Hollis Street Theatre. County club functions often drew 1,200 people or more and featured both modern American dance music and traditional Irish music. On January 11, 1910, a group launched the Boston Irish Pipers club with a concert at Wells Auditorium. Joining Touhey and the local pipers were Sean O'Nolan, originally from Wexford and now a recording star with Columbia Records, and Sergeant William Early, a Chicago cop who had formed a piper's club in the Windy City.

Traditional Irish dance music was wildly popularly among the Irish. It had had a terrific boost in the 1890s when brothers Michael and William Hanafin emigrated from County Kerry to Boston, bringing a rich repertoire of Irish tunes that had been passed down orally for centuries. Here they met up with Patsy Touhey, the uilleann piper from South Boston whose exceptional playing brought him to national platforms like the Chicago Exposition in 1894 and the St. Louis World's Fair in 1902. The Hanafins' brand of dance music—jigs, reels, hornpipes, quadrilles, and polkas—was popular with middle-class Irish Americans seeking authenticity and with newly arrived Irish immigrants from a rural background familiar with the repertoire.

The Boston Irish were constantly on guard against the Stage Irishman, who was still winding his way across the American landscape. Local Irish papers proudly reported that the Stage Irishman was hounded out of Butte, Montana, in 1905 for portraying the Irish as baboons.

In a larger context, Irish music appeared to be losing ground to America's changing tastes in music. Jazz and swing swept through the nation in the 1920s, offering rhythms, tempos, and improvisations that broke free of traditional music idioms. The new sound centered on urban black music that drew from such influences as Creole roots, brass band, minstrelsy, jigs, blues, and ballads. It arrived during a decade in which postwar angst and Prohibition drove people to excess.

But excessive behavior was exactly what made leaders in the Irish community fear for their flocks. As in Ireland, local politicians and clergy had become vigilant about protecting the Irish from themselves when it came to music, dancing, and cultural expression that might have immoral consequences. When Dublin's Abbey Theatre came to

Boston in 1911 with the production of J. M. Synge's *Playboy of the Western World*, rumblings came from some Irish that the play was too risqué. In 1929 Eugene O'Neill's play *Strange Interlude* was banned in Boston. This kind of censorship prompted Methodist Reverend Frank Case to smirk in 1925, "The Irish make good Puritans."

The jazz movement put some Irish music lovers on the defensive. Reverend Francis P. Donnelly, S.J., a Boston College professor and song composer, gave a lecture on Irish music in all its glory. He concluded that "it is degradation for America to pass by this rich Irish inheritance and to adopt the monstrosities of China, Japan, of Hottentot and Hawaiian and American savages. Let us drive out, therefore, these vaudeville reversals to barbarism and bring up your children in the music of civilization and of art, in the folk music of Ireland."

Perhaps he hoped the Irish institutions and gathering places of Boston would be the great bastions of the culture he so loved. But immigration reform dashed those dreams for most of the 1930s. The Great Depression had virtually stopped Irish emigration to Boston, while Prohibition, which lasted until 1934, inhibited public gatherings. With money tight, many Irish resorted to house parties or kitchen rackets, wherein a few musicians would simply play on a more intimate scale in someone's home.

By the late 1930s a new surge of Irish immigration brought a renewed Irish community. With Irish county clubs leading the shift, Dudley Street became the Irish Mecca in Boston. In January 1938 the Fermanagh, Mayo, Cork Ladies, Saint Brendan's, Roscommon, and Sligo associations all held events at Hibernian Hall, with only the Tyrone Association opting for the Veterans Hall in Central Square, Cambridge. The Central Council of Irish Clubs held its Saint Patrick's Day dance at Hibernian Hall. As the social scene picked up, other venues along Dudley Street, including Intercolonial Hall, Dudley Street Opera House, Winslow Hall, Palladio Hall, Deacon Hall, and Rose Croix Hall, also began hosting Irish activities.

From 1940 to 1943 the *Irish World*, a national Irish-American paper based in New York, hired three columnists to report from Boston. Dan Horgan, who later ran a Celtic cigar shop in front of Hibernian Hall and coached a women's camogie team, covered the downtown and

Dudley Street scene; M. J. Upton reported as the Cambridge Traveler; and accordion player Eva Connors, known as the Irish Rambler, had free rein to report on whatever she wished. A typical edition of the *World* in the early forties devoted five to seven thousand words of Boston coverage.

The columnists were diligent in reporting every single aspect of the Boston Irish community. They covered the county clubs, concerts, lectures, and the Gaelic classes, along with weddings, funerals, births, and baptisms. The *Irish World*'s Boston pages became the village square for the sprawling Irish community, providing a steady stream of gossip, news, schedules, and activities that provided a continuity and definition to the Irish from the 1940s through the early 1960s.

Even as Irish music remained secondary to mainstream American tastes, the caliber of Irish music in Boston was extremely high in the 1940s. Dozens of talented local musicians emerged, including Joe Derrane, Billy Caples, Tom Senier and his sons, Jack Storer and his sons, Joe Joyce, Jack Concannon, Johnny Powell, Johnny Bresnahan, and Virginia Doherty. After the war they were joined by immigrant musicians like Larry Reynolds, Brendan Tonra, Mike Landers, and

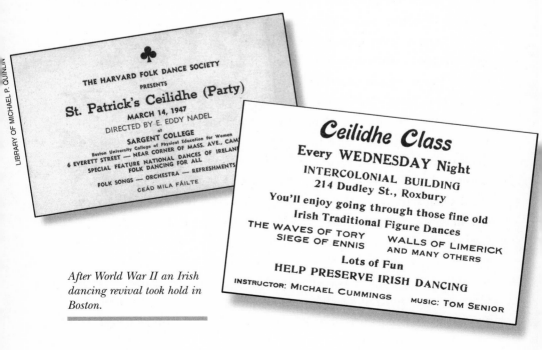

After World War II an Irish dancing revival took hold in Boston.

Mayor James Michael Curley dons a set of warpipes at an Irish gathering in Boston.

Paddy Cronin. These musicians presided over a fabulous era in which it wasn't unusual for thousands of people to converge on Dudley Street on any given night, going from one hall to the next, standing out in the street as crowds of dancers streamed down from Dudley Street station.

The scene was further elevated when Justus O'Byrne DeWitt started a small recording label called Copley Records and began publishing local musicians. Irish radio programs on WBOS, WHDH, and WTAO featured such stars as singer Terry O'Toole and Myles O'Malley, a talented saxophonist and clarinetist in the 1940s who was popular live and on the radio, especially when he played a few novelty tunes on the tin whistle. O'Malley spent four years in the Navy and in 1947 returned to Boston. Decca Records gave him a contract, and soon the Tin Whistle King was playing jazz nightly while setting aside Thursdays as Irish night.

Pianist Dick Senier recalled that many Irish musicians, including his father Tom, were comfortable playing in various musical styles, from traditional Irish and Scottish to swing and jazz. Saxophones, trumpets, and drum sets were regularly used in Irish ensembles, and most Irish-American sidemen were able to play the popular tunes of the day.

Not all Irish-Americans, of course, gravitated toward the Dudley Street scene during this time. Connolly's Tavern at 1184 Tremont Street, for instance, featured local jazz musicians and was later nick-named Boston's Black Cheers Pub, where everyone knew each other. In the 1950s Norman J. O'Connor, chaplain at Boston University, was board member of the first Newport Jazz Festival and became known as the jazz priest. According to his 2003 obituary in the *New York Times,* O'Connor saw "nothing wrong with using jazz in religious services," though he apparently encountered criticism from "lay Catholics who viewed the music as disreputable."

The Irish were probably among O'Connor's critics, since many of them preferred Irish melodies to anything else. When Connie Foley, a traditional singer from County Kerry living in Worcester, recorded "The Wild Colonial Boy" for Copley Records, "letters evaluating the tenor's performance—both pro and con—rolled in," according to a 1951 pro-file in *Newsweek* magazine. One of Foley's fans was quoted as saying, "Let those who don't enjoy Connie turn to the old English stations for their jazz and silly songs."

Ironically, the preservation of Irish traditional music in Boston dur-ing the 1950s was somewhat compromised by a new musical fad coming out of Ireland. Called "show bands," these groups of musicians played a hybrid of rock 'n' roll, Irish, and country-western tunes that captured the growing Americanization of music worldwide. They began arriving in Boston in the late 1950s with their horn sections and gyrations imita-tive of Elvis Presley. Before long, the Irish crowds followed the show bands from Dudley Street to the New State Ballroom on Massachusetts Avenue in Back Bay. By then popular music was being changed funda-mentally by folk music and ultimately by rock 'n' roll. With the Dudley Scene in demise, it would be nearly two decades before Irish traditional music returned to its former glory in Boston.

CHAPTER TWELVE

The Camelot Era
(1945–1965)

MICHAEL CUMMINGS from Ballygar, County Galway, got his shot at the American Dream when he was just twenty-two years old. The 6-foot, 1-inch football star arrived in Boston in June 1947 to play in the season's final game for Boston's Galway football team, a match it handily won. The following season Cummings was elected team captain and led his squad to five successive championships between 1948 and 1952 at Dilboy Field in Somerville.

The end of World War II launched an exciting phase of the Boston Irish experience, as thousands of Irish-American soldiers returned home from their duty and a wave of new immigrants from Ireland settled in Boston. Newcomers like Mike Cummings waded into the future with optimism and resolve. He settled in Dorchester and took a job with Boston Consolidated Gas, remaining a leader in the Irish community. In 1956 he married the beautiful Noreen McSweeney from Saint Gregory's parish and started a family, eventually moving to nearby Milton to raise their two boys and two girls.

Like so many Bostonians of that generation, Cummings became, in some measure, a part of history, having come of age during the Camelot Era, a phrase of obvious significance to the world at large, but on a more local scale an apt description of the Boston Irish experience at its pinnacle.

Not since the 1880s had there been such an Irish revival in Boston as the one that took place between 1945 and 1965. Dudley Street, full of music and dancing and socializing, was just part of the revival. Third- and fourth-generation Irish-Americans became interested in knowing more about Ireland, and they created groups like the Eire Society as a way of reestablishing their roots. Local institutions like Harvard University, the Museum of Fine Arts, and the Boston Symphony

Orchestra all became involved in Irish projects in the 1950s, and even Jordan Marsh, Boston's main department store, ran some highly publicized marketing campaigns to promote Irish goods.

Part of the enthusiasm had to do with Ireland finally becoming an independent nation. Eamon De Valera, who served as Ireland's prime minister from 1933 through 1948, had remained forceful in calling for the unification of Ireland and for breaking away from the British Commonwealth. De Valera got part of his wish in December 1948 when the Irish Parliament passed the Republic of Ireland Act, in tandem with the British Nationality Bill, declaring that "People born in Eire in the future will be Eire subjects and not British subjects." On April 18, 1949, Ireland officially became the Republic of Ireland and severed its ties to the British Commonwealth. Northern Ireland chose its right to remain with Great Britain, cementing the partition of Ireland that remains to the present day.

The new Irish Republic was ably represented in the United States by two officials in particular, Sean MacBride and Sean Lemass. The son of Captain John MacBride and Irish rebel Maude Gonne, Sean MacBride understood that gaining worldwide sympathy for the new Ireland was more than a political venture; it was a public relations exercise too. In a speech to the Eire Society in Boston in 1950, MacBride, minister of external affairs for Ireland, said, "Whether it be in the field of international politics, foreign trade, or tourism, one of the first tasks to be achieved is to make the people of other countries interested in our island and to make them feel kindly to us."

One of the ways the Irish chose to court Irish-Americans was to export Irish culture to the United States. In 1950 Ireland's Cultural Relations Committee sent an Irish photo exhibit to Boston as part of department store Jordan Marsh's 100th anniversary. The following year an exhibit of paintings by Jack Yeats, brother of the poet W. B. Yeats, opened at the Institute of Contemporary Art on Newbury Street.

Meanwhile, Sean Lemass, minister of commerce, was working on the business front to open up investment and travel opportunities. Irish journalist Seamus Malin wrote in the *Boston Globe* that it took Lemass ten years to bring to fruition a transatlantic air route that connected Shannon Airport to Boston and New York. It finally happened on

October 5, 1958, when the first Aer Lingus flight left Boston's Logan International Airport, filled with Irish-Americans like Robert Murphy, the state's Lieutenant Governor; John Hynes, Mayor of Boston; and Reverend Timothy O'Leary, superintendent of Catholic schools. On the return flight, Lemass and Robert Briscoe, Dublin's Lord Mayor, came to Boston to further develop the Boston-Irish connection. Aer Lingus offered two flights each week from Logan Airport, on Thursdays and Sundays, with return flights from Ireland on Mondays and Fridays.

Groups like the Eire Society, the Irish Social Club, and the Gaelic Athletic Association were all enthusiastic about promoting tours to Ireland, and Boston quickly joined the publicity campaign on behalf of the old country. "The delights of visiting, sightseeing, shopping, and sharing the warm friendliness of the dear Emerald Isle are now but a few hours from Boston," noted the *Eire Society Bulletin*.

The new wave of immigrants helped to reinvigorate Irish clubs that had been the staple of Boston's Irish community since the turn of the century. Mary Concannon and Nora Hart founded the Irish Social Club to provide cultural activities in a family setting. Every Sunday evening at Hibernian Hall the Social Club hosted a dance that featured a junior ceili band of budding future musical stars like Joe Derrane.

It wasn't just Dudley Street where people were dancing to Irish music. Across the Charles River in Cambridge, accordionist Tom Senier taught Irish dances to the Harvard Folk Club. Cummings, along with Walter Norris and Walter O'Regan, gave dance instruction to Eire Society members along Commonwealth Avenue.

In the summer of 1950 the Central Council Irish Clubs presented an Irish feis, or festival, at Malden Municipal Stadium, modeled on popular gatherings in Ireland. More than 500 entrants registered to compete in seventy-five areas, including uileann pipes, the fiddle, the accordion, dancing, oratory, Gaelic singing, storytelling, and sports. The feis, which attracted thousands of people, flourished throughout the decade. The inaugural program book was printed in Irish and English. The dedication page read:

> *Cuis athais duinn indhiu an Doctuir D. deHide (an Craoibhinn Aoibhinn) comoradh san chead Feis seo I m Boston. (We proudly*

*dedicate this greater Boston Feis to the memory of the late Dr. Douglas
Hyde, co-founder of the Gaelic League and later president of Ireland.)*

The dedication continued:

> *Dr. Hyde awakened a slumbering, almost defeated people, to a con-
> sciousness of the power and beauty of their language and their
> ancient culture; he opened up new vistas of freedom of thought from
> which again developed fresh concepts of political freedom. . . . May
> this Feis be worthy of the name of Dr. Douglas Hyde.*

The vitality of Boston's Irish community attracted national attention, and in 1956 the NBC television series *Wide Wide World* arrived to
film an Irish field day at Dilboy Field. The crew interviewed the versatile
Cummings on the fine points of set dancing and football. It filmed a
joint performance by the Kevin Barry Pipe Band and the Saint Joseph's
All-Girl Pipe band, which featured nearly three dozen pipers and drum-
mers playing at once! Also filmed for American viewers were a hurling
match and some "Irish-American colleens" dancing the Kerry set in full

The rise in Irish immigration strengthened the local Gaelic football teams in Boston.

traditional costume. The program even documented a display of imported products from Ireland, organized by Florence Garrity of the Eire Society.

The most inventive and ambitious proponent of Irish culture in Boston was the Eire Society, an enthusiastic group of mostly white-collar teachers, lawyers, academics, and artists. In 1947 the *Eire Society* commissioned composer Leroy Anderson to write the Eire Suite, which was performed and later recorded by Arthur Fiedler and the Boston Pops. In 1953 the Society partnered with Harvard University to raise funds to microfilm the National Library of Ireland's collection of rare manuscripts and scholarly material.

At a time when the Irish-American newspapers were covering almost exclusively the social scene, the *Eire Society Bulletin* offered insightful snippets about Irish culture, education, theater, and the emerging bond between Irish Americans and the Irish. Contributors to the *Bulletin* featured some of Boston's most intrepid researchers, such as Dr. Regina Madden, James J. Ford, and George E. Ryan.

The Society held its meetings and dinners downtown, at the Copley Plaza Hotel, creating an environment for the area's sprawling middle-class Irish-Americans who had moved away from the dance halls in the old neighborhoods.

A lively literary scene also sprouted up during this era. In November 1951 the Dublin Players had a two-week run at John

The Eire Society

Founded in 1937, the Eire Society of Boston has become one of New England's leading supporters of Irish cultural expression. The Society provides funds that preserve Irish arts and historical documents in the collections of such institutions as the Museum of Fine Arts, Harvard University, and Boston College. It also hosts lectures, forums, and performing arts programs that showcase Irish artists, writers, statesmen, and others. Among its social gatherings are an annual Christmas party and a tea at the Ritz Carlton each spring. It also presents an annual Gold Medal award to recipients who have dedicated themselves to the study and preservation of Irish arts or to the betterment of Ireland itself in varied charitable causes. Among these Gold Medal winners are scholars and historians such as Eoin McKiernan, Dr. Margaret MacCurtain, O. P., and Helen Landreth. Among the honored writers are Mary Lavin, poet Seamus Heaney, and athlete/writer James Brendan Connolly. Filmmaker John Ford, politician John F. Kennedy, architect Charles Maginnis, and actress Siobhan McKenna are also in the impressive list of Gold Medalists. For more details, visit the Web site www.eiresociety.org.

Hancock Hall, where they performed plays by Michael MacLiammoir, Lennox Robinson, and Paul Vincent Carroll. Molly Manning Howe, a Dublin-born novelist and playwright who taught drama at Radcliffe College, founded the Poet's Theater in Cambridge to encourage young writers. In 1957 acclaimed Irish actress Siobhan McKenna performed in *The Rope Dancers* and was honored by the Eire Society. Around this time novelist Edwin O'Connor published his most famous book, *The Last Hurrah,* a fictionalized account of James Michael Curley, the legendary Boston politician whose reign in public office stretched from 1900 to 1950. The best-selling novel became a Book-of-the-Month selection and was later made into a movie staring Spencer Tracy.

From Last Hurrah to Camelot

When Curley stepped away from public life, or rather was ushered away by Boston voters (he served his fourth and final term as mayor from 1946 to 1949), pundits like O'Connor interpreted this changing of the guard as the Last Hurrah. Curley's demise, O'Connor concluded, marked the end of an era when cunning, ambitious, and often outlandish young men stormed out of Irish neighborhoods to dominate local politics through the first half of the twentieth century.

Voting "early and often," as Mayor Curley used to quip, was the rallying cry for those politicians, whose constant goal was to get reelected. They worked their way up the ladder, from school committee to city council to the mayor's office, and wherever else luck and ambition took them. The quid pro quo for the voters was a full expectation of being rewarded in some way, with a job, a stoplight, or a new ballpark down the street.

In addition to controlling the mayor's office for most of the first half of the twentieth century, Irish Americans served five terms as governor between 1914 and 1953: David Walsh, James Curley, Charles Hurley, Maurice Tobin, and Paul Dever. In the 1950s, South Boston's John McCormack, the consummate deal maker, and Thomas "Tip" O'Neill, the cigar-chomping storyteller from Cambridge, were in Washington, D.C., bringing home the bacon, as it were, to their constituents.

But the back-slapping, camera-mugging Irish politicians who once roamed the streets of Boston looking for handshakes or shakedowns had already begun to die out. By the 1950s, they were being replaced by a more sophisticated generation of public officials who sensed that the curtain was coming down on the Irish burlesque routine that Curley and his cronies had perfected. Mayors John B. Hynes and John Collins represented the new generation of Irish-American politicians who brought a sense of purpose and professionalism to local politics in the 1950s and 1960s.

JFK Seizes the Day

The star of this generation was John Fitzgerald Kennedy, the young war hero who had saved his crew members when his PT *109* was sunk in the Pacific Ocean. His father Joseph had been ambassador to Great Britain and was well-connected in Washington. JFK's maternal grandfather, John "Honey" Fitzgerald, had been mayor of Boston for six years and also had served as a United States congressman for six years. His paternal grandfather, Patrick Kennedy, was a state representative and senator but was better known as a successful businessman.

John Kennedy's first foray into politics came in 1946 when he ran for U.S. Congress. His demeanor had an impact on Eva Connors, the bubbling Boston correspondent for the *Irish World*. Connors wrote about Kennedy's visit to a bridal shower in June 1946. "John Kennedy, son of Ambassador Joseph Kennedy, stopped in during the evening to extend his congratulations to Kay Dowd," Connors wrote. "Mr. Kennedy is candidate for office of Congress." As JFK's career progressed, his mother and sisters hosted tea parties designed to capture the women's vote. He was elected to the United States Congress in 1946 and to the Senate in 1952.

Kennedy showed more than a casual regard for Ireland, according to Arthur Mitchell, whose book *JFK and His Irish Heritage* traces the president's youthful interests. Though educated in private, non-Catholic schools, Kennedy was aware of the Boston Irish plight, and he himself sensed anti-Irish feeling among some of his Harvard classmates, Mitchell writes. He made the first of his six trips to Ireland in 1939. In 1945, as the son of the American ambassador to Britain, JFK had had the opportunity to meet De Valera, forging a friendship that lasted through Kennedy's life.

Kennedy had interviewed De Valera during that trip and submitted a thoughtful piece titled "De Valera Aims to Unite Ireland" to the *New York Journal American* in July 1945, writing, "De Valera is fighting the same relentless battle fought in the field during the uprising of 1916, in the war of independence and later in the civil war. He feels everything Ireland has gained has been given grudgingly and at the end of a long and bitter struggle. Always, it has been too little too late."

When De Valera visited Boston in 1948 to promote Irish unification, Kennedy met him at Logan Airport, even though his flight arrived after midnight. Kennedy also cosigned a bill sponsored by Rhode Island Congressman John E. Fogarty in 1951 calling for Irish unification, and he supported a similar Senate resolution.

When Kennedy first won the Eighth Congressional seat in 1946 and the Senate seat in 1952, many hailed him as a new breed of Irish-American politician, unhindered by ward politics and backroom deals. Given the complex problems emerging in world politics with the rise of communism, voters were seeking leaders of the highest caliber. He was a war hero who rescued his crew members during the sinking of PT *109*. His wealth and political pedigree enabled him to travel the world, meet influential leaders, and observe firsthand the problems of other nations. He was well educated and had gained modest acclaim as a reporter and later as an author with his books *While England Slept* and *Profiles in Courage*. He was young, handsome, witty, and charming, and politics was in his blood.

Kennedy's run for president in 1960 raised the thorny issue of his religion, a cross that the Boston Irish had had to bear since the city was founded by the Puritans in 1630. The innuendo that a Catholic would somehow subvert the American system of government by paying allegiance to a foreign pope was as ludicrous in 1960 as it was in 1830, when preachers and plebeians fretted about a popish invasion. Kennedy handled the issue with a firm confidence and graciousness that silenced his critics, and no one objected when his friend Richard Cardinal Cushing officiated at Kennedy's inauguration on January 20, 1961.

Kennedy's religious background was quickly eclipsed by his cultural sophistication. As Louis M. Lyons later wrote, "The elevation of the tone of the national life may be John Kennedy's most enduring contribution

JOHN FITZGERALD KENNEDY LIBRARY, BOSTON

Newlywed Senator and Mrs. John F. Kennedy, escorted by ushers Charles Bartlett, Edward Kennedy, and Torbert MacDonald, were all smiles on their wedding day, September 12, 1953.

to his country." Along with his beautiful, stylish wife, Jacqueline Bouvier Kennedy, JFK brought a savoir faire to the White House that would be dubbed the Camelot Era. Both the president and his wife were lovers of the arts, and they surrounded themselves with singers, poets, dramatists, artists, and dancers. In a well-deserved nod to the power of poetry, Kennedy invited New England poet Robert Frost to read at his inauguration. Frost later told Kennedy, "You're something of Irish and something of Harvard. Let me advise you, be more Irish than Harvard."

On October 26, 1963, Kennedy gave a well-crafted, compelling address at Amherst College called "On Poetry and National Power," in which he laid out a vision of American life to which the Irish, the politician and the poet could relate.

> *When power leads man towards arrogance, poetry reminds him of his limitations. When power corrupts, poetry cleanses, for art establishes*

*the basic human truths which must serve as a touchstone for our
judgment. . . . I look forward to a great future for America—a future
in which our country will match its military strength with our moral
strength, its wealth with our wisdom, its power with our purpose. I
look forward to an America which will not be afraid of grace and
beauty. . . . And I look forward to an America which commands
respect throughout the world not only for its strength but for its civilization as well.*

The high point for the Boston Irish was the president's trip to
Ireland in June 1963. It not only captured the world's imagination but
shone a spotlight on the new Republic of Ireland. The visit was a triumphant, emotionally charged promenade in which the entire population of Ireland seemed to participate. Kennedy's motorcade passed
regally through the streets of Dublin, Cork, and Galway as thousands of
proud Irish cheered him with tears of joy in their eyes, and the twin
flags of Ireland and the United States waved madly for him. He also visited the modest town of New Ross, Wexford, which twenty-five-year-old
Patrick Kennedy had left in 1848 on a ship bound for Boston. Dozens

*Ireland's President Eamon De Valera signs the honorary degree conferred upon President
John F. Kennedy on June 28, 1963, at Dublin Castle in Ireland.*

of young men named Patrick never
made it past Deer Island that same
year—Patrick Casey, Patrick Walsh,
Patrick Mannin, and Patrick White all
died and were buried on the island.
There was even a seventeen-year-old
girl who died on Deer Island that
January named Bridget Murphy, the
same name as the girl Patrick Kennedy
would marry.

On June 29, 1963, in Limerick,
Ireland, Kennedy told the crowds of
cheering Irish, "This is not the land of
my birth, but it is the land for which I
hold the greatest affection, and I will
certainly come back in the springtime." It was a sentiment wrought with
love, promise, friendship, and possibil-
ity, and it was almost unbearable to
recall when the president was assassi-
nated in Dallas on November 22, 1963.

Like the entire world for years to

JFK Library and Museum

The **John F. Kennedy Library and Museum** at Columbia Point in Boston is the official library of the nation's thirty-fifth president. The president's 1,000 days in office are recreated in the exhibits revealing the legacy of Kennedy's short but historically signifi-cant administration. Among the chang-ing exhibitions have been Kennedy's wedding to Jacqueline Bouvier Kennedy, the Cuban Missile Crisis, and the presi-dent's trip to Ireland in 1963. The Library/Museum welcomes leading speakers from around the world to speak on the pressing topics of the day, and it also hosts annual events like the Profiles in Courage Award. The Library/Museum is open from 9:00 A.M. to 5:00 P.M. daily. For more information, call (617) 514–1600 or visit the Web site www.jfklibrary.org.

come, the Boston Irish community was stunned by the staggering
tragedy of Kennedy's death. The Boston Irish followed the president's
visit to Ireland with immense pride, reveling in how he had turned the
world's attention to their small island off the coast of Europe. Kennedy
had expressed an abiding love for Ireland that would have grown over
time, as it did for his other siblings, had not his promising life been
taken. The Irish in Boston knew that he had grown up in a different
society, one of privilege and wealth. But they considered him to be one
of them. To that postwar generation in particular, John F. Kennedy
would always be one of them.

Shortly after his death the Kennedy family took up the task of creating a presidential library. In January 1964 they formed a committee to
raise funds for the project. A group was formed called the Irish
American Committee for the John F. Kennedy Memorial Fund in

Boston, led by Cornelius O'Connor and Humphrey Mahoney of the
Central Counties committee. Cummings was on the advisory board and
did much of the writing. Its motto was Modest Donations by Many
Rather Than Large Endowments of a Wealthy Few. As they had done
for generations, the Boston Irish envisioned that the library would be
built by the small cash donations of thousands of ordinary believers, the
same way they had built their churches, parish schools, and colleges.
The committee held a fund-raiser at the New State Ballroom on
Massachusetts Avenue on May 17, 1964, and proudly donated $6,550.20
to the Kennedy Library Fund.

Numerous delays developed with the Cambridge site originally designated to be the home of the library, and finally in 1975 the committee
selected a different patch of land on Columbia Point peninsula in
Dorchester, overlooking Boston Harbor as well as Boston's skyline. The
Library and Museum, designed by architect I. M. Pei, was formally dedicated on October 20, 1979, before 7,000 people. Heading the list of dignitaries was President Jimmy Carter, who said:

> President Kennedy understood the past and respected its shaping of
> the future. [He] entered the White House convinced that racial and
> religious discrimination was morally indefensible. He never failed to
> uphold liberty and condemn tyranny. . . . The essence of President
> Kennedy's message—the appeal for unselfish dedication to the com-
> mon good—is more urgent than ever. The spirit he evoked—the spirit
> of sacrifice, of patriotism, of unstinting dedication—is the same spirit
> that will bring us safely through the adversities we face.

The podium that day was crowded with President Kennedy's loved
ones: former First Lady Jacqueline Kennedy and her children John Jr.
and Caroline; his brothers and sisters, nephews and nieces, cousins and
in-laws. Any of them could have glanced out at Boston Harbor settling
their gaze on Deer Island, the last island separating the United States
from Ireland. This is where their ancestors—the Kennedys, Fitzgeralds,
Murphys, and Coxes—would have been stopped at the quarantine station before they were allowed to enter Boston, where history could then
take its course.

CHAPTER THIRTEEN

The Irish on the Run
(1965–1985)

L
ONG-HAIRED, bearded Francis McCann, the blanketman, didn't
expect to find himself on the run in Boston the morning of
September 23, 1980, as he was holding a press conference at the
Massachusetts State House. True, the twenty-seven-year-old activist had
entered the United States illegally. But he had a story to tell. As a political prisoner in Northern Ireland's Long Kesh prison who refused to
wear standard-issue prison clothing assigned to ordinary criminals,
McCann had survived for forty-two months with only a blanket wrapped
around him. He had gone "on the blanket."

Boston Globe reporter Eileen McNamara wrote that McCann was in
the middle of the press conference, chatting amiably with Governor
Edward J. King and Senate President William M. Bulger when he suddenly disappeared "through the basement corridors of the State House."
Authorities were racing up Beacon Street to arrest him for entering the
country illegally. McCann sprinted through the State House's maze of
corridors, then climbed out of a basement window, escaping into the
American heartland. He eventually ended up back in Belfast.

An Irishman on the run was certainly nothing new in history. In
fact, the McCann episode recalled an incident nearly 250 years earlier
when indentured Irishman Hugh McCan escaped from the Bridewell
Prison in Boston, situated, as coincidence would have it, on the State
House grounds. That prison had on its staff a whipper who was "constantly in attendance."

The modern-day equivalent of Bridewell was surely Long Kesh, a
prison where suspected Irish rebels were thrown in with common criminals during the political unrest in Northern Ireland during the 1970s.
The blanket protest, as it was called, lasted for almost five years and
involved more than 350 men. When British officials refused to meet the

COURTESY OF MARIE HOWE

State Representative Marie Howe, Irish activist Bernadette Devlin McAliskey, and activist Mel King join together in Boston.

prisoners' five demands, including the right to wear civilian clothing, the protesters began a hunger strike in 1981 to force the issue. Ten inmates, led by Bobby Sands, began a hunger strike and starved themselves to death as the whole world watched in horror.

The Troubles in Northern Ireland ushered in a new chapter of political theater in Boston. The drama was often directed by Marie Howe of Somerville, an elected state representative whose father had immigrated to Boston from Cork in 1929. She and her allies—Leo and Ann Cooney, Marion McCarthy, Ann Murphy, and Charlie Doyle—were vocal about exposing human rights violations in Northern Ireland. They held state house press conferences to display the lethal plastic bullets that British paratroops shot to quell Irish gatherings. They picketed the British Consulate on Boylston Street, bringing young bearded men wrapped in blankets to illustrate Long Kesh prison conditions. On March 17, 1980, they joined with Irish-American governor Edward King in proclaiming Human Rights Day for Northern Ireland.

At the height of the Long Kesh hunger strike, which lasted eight months, Howe and other Bostonians issued a state house resolution:

*The people of Massachusetts, remembering the oppression of King
George III prior to the American Revolution and their break from the
tyrannical rule of the British Empire, view the present government of
Great Britain as unconscionable toward the enormous suffering of the
people of Ireland. . . . [We] insist that Prime Minister Margaret
Thatcher recall and withdraw its local emissary.*

That didn't happen, but the hunger strike was a public relations
nightmare for the British Consulate in Boston. It also galvanized the
Irish community to action. In 1981, for instance, Vincent O'Sullivan,
formerly of Kerry, started the *Boston Irish Press,* a weekly newspaper with
fiery editorials reminiscent of those in the *Republic* and the *Pilot* of the
1880s. A Boston-based distributor, Quinlin Campbell Publishers, helped
to educate American readers by importing more than 300 books, maga-
zines, and pamphlets on Northern Ireland, and then distributing them
to colleges, libraries, media, and Irish organizations around the country.

Labor leaders Marty Foley and Joe Faherty formed the Irish
American Labor Coalition and initiated a dialogue with Belfast trade
unionist Inez McCormack and others. In 1987 the Coalition and Eire
Society gave separate awards to Sean MacBride, son of executed Easter
Uprising rebel John MacBride and Maude Gonne. Father Sean
McManus in Washington, D.C., championed the MacBride Principles,
which urged American companies doing business in Northern Ireland
to abide by a nine-point fair employment agreement. On November 21,
1985, Massachusetts became the first state in the nation to pass the
MacBride Principles, and New Hampshire and Maine followed suit.

On the academic front, Padraig O'Malley and Catherine Shannon
organized a Symposium on Northern Ireland in 1982 and 1984 at the
University of Massachusetts' Boston campus. It brought together adver-
saries from the nationalist and unionist camps to talk out their problems. In 1983 Ruth Ann Harris of Northeastern University hosted the
Forum on Media and Northern Ireland, which explored the ways the
Troubles were being covered in the news. In 1986 Bernadette Devlin-
McAliskey, champion of the civil rights movement in Northern Ireland,
spoke at a "Black and Green" forum sponsored by *Forward Motion,* a
local progressive magazine. Aware of the fracture between Boston's Irish
and Black communities as a result of court-ordered school desegregation

in the 1970s, she urged the two groups to quit squabbling and become allies.

Throughout the 1980s a steady stream of Irish political advocates came to town. Sean Sands, younger brother of Bobby Sands, one of the hunger strikers, moved to the Boston area and helped to animate the grassroots movement in support of the Irish involved in the Troubles. The families of the Birmingham Six and Guildford Four came to publicize the plight of their sons and brothers, who were wrongly imprisoned for bombings in England. John Stalker, England's top cop who had exposed police brutality and cover-up in Northern Ireland, came to town promoting his new book *The Stalker Affair.* Irish prime ministers Charlie Haughey and Garrett Fitzgerald also stated their cases here, along with Ireland's Cardinal Tomas O'Fiach and a contingent of Protestant clergymen.

All of these visitors were welcomed earnestly by Mayor Ray Flynn, Congressman Joe Kennedy, state Senate President Bill Bulger, and various other officials. The climate was reminiscent of the early 1900s when Irish visitors Gonne, Hyde, Larkin, and De Valera turned Boston into a headquarters for political support, fund-raising, and publicity for the Irish cause.

Many British pundits were unhappy about Boston's interest in the Troubles. When Senator Ted Kennedy and Congressman Tip O'Neill suggested that the British reconsider their brutal response to civil unrest—which included torture, internment, and the suspension of habeas corpus—British press and politicians accused them of aiding terrorism. Kennedy and O'Neill eventually teamed up with John Hume, a respected peace advocate from Derry, Northern Ireland, to state their case for a peaceful resolution.

British visitors were not as well received by the Boston Irish as the Irish ones were. In 1986 Prince Charles gave the commencement speech at Harvard University, advising the graduates on moral education. He also paid a quick visit to the State House, where he was nimble enough to avoid Representative Howe and her picketers.

British golf writer Peter Dobereiner was not so lucky. That hapless gentleman arrived in Boston to cover the 1988 U.S. Open in Brookline for *Golf Digest,* a magazine owned by the *Boston Globe*'s parent company, the *New York Times.* Dobereiner's article was a tasteless and offensive

lampoon about the Irish he imagined he would meet here in Boston.
When the magazine hit the street, the city's Irish community went into
an uproar. *Globe* truck drivers refused to deliver the issue, which was to
be inserted into the daily paper. A group of activists led by Mayo-born
Kieran Staunton rented a boat and took hundreds of copies out into
Boston Harbor, and in a mock recreation of the Boston Tea Party, they
dumped the magazine overboard. Mayor Flynn demanded and received
a printed apology from the *Boston Globe, Golf Digest* and the *New York
Times.* The stunned journalist was at a loss for words and slipped out of
Boston in remorse, still baffled by the uproar he had caused.

More Irish on the Run

As the trouble in Northern Ireland percolated, an entirely different
group of Irish was on the run in Boston throughout the 1980s. Hiding
in the shadows, lurking on the margins of society, they were the illegal
Irish immigrants who had overstayed their visitor visas and gone underground. Their numbers were growing by the day, and so too was the
constant trepidation of getting caught and deported. Newspaper articles
on this subculture included only the first names—Hugh, Francis,
Bridget, or Colette—to carefully protect identities.

You could spot them on any Friday night at places like the Kinvara
Pub on Harvard Street in Allston. Irish-born painters, plasterers, and
carpenters from nearby construction sites stood three deep at the bar,
waiting to cash their checks, preferring cash in hand to the paper trail
of a bank account. It was like market day at the Ballinasloe Fair, with
local fiddlers Sean Reynolds and John Winston playing jigs and reels in
the corner and animated men and women talking about the football
scores or the news back home. After a round or two and a generous tip
to the bartender, the illegal Irish headed for home with cash from a
week's work stuffed in their pockets, enough to pay their bills and hopefully enough left over to tuck away for the uncertain future.

Under other circumstances, in other eras, this generation of Irish
would have come to Boston without worry. But the 1965 Immigration
Act passed by the U.S. Congress had eliminated the "national origins"
criteria that had favored Europeans for so long, substituting a "family

reunification" preference that favored people from Latin America, Asia, and Africa. Along with France, Germany, Italy, and other European nations, Ireland's annual allotment of visas to the United States dropped drastically. Between 1955 and 1965, 70,000 visas were issued to Ireland, an average of 7,000 per year. After 1965 the number dropped to 1,000 a year, and by 1985 the annual Irish allotment of visas was 515.

The Irish quickly discovered a loophole in the law. While permanent visas were scarce, the United States was issuing up to 50,000 holiday visas each year. Once the Irish made their way into the country on a 180-day visitors visa, they could disappear into the vast network of Irish enclaves from Boston to San Francisco to stay in America indefinitely. But they lived in constant fear of getting caught, and if they went home for a holiday, wedding, or funeral, they risked not being allowed back into the States. They were trapped in No Man's Land.

In 1985, when the media broke the story that 15,000 to 30,000 illegal Irish immigrants were living clandestinely in Boston, the public was shocked. This was America's most Irish city, where the Irish had been coming since the 1700s. This was the home of Kennedy and O'Neill, the headquarters of the newly formed American Ireland Fund, which was collecting millions of dollars to send back to Ireland. How could Boston have overlooked a generation of young Irish living a frightful existence, afraid to open a bank account, get a driver's license, or start a business for fear of getting deported?

In truth, Irish-American leaders, especially the successful ones who worked downtown and lived in the suburbs, had become disconnected from Irish immigrants living in Dorchester, Quincy, and Brighton. The Irish government, accused of using migration as a safety valve against high unemployment, was also mute on the issue. And the illegals themselves were silent, not wishing to draw attention to themselves at a time when Boston's construction industry was booming, with large-scale projects like the Boston Harbor cleanup and the "Big Dig"—a revamping of Boston's roadways—in full swing.

Grassroots leaders were the only group left to address the problem. Bill McGowan, a former Irish priest and Gaelic Athletic Association official whose small insurance company on Dorchester Avenue helped Irish immigrants, was hearing that Irish coming into Logan Airport were increasingly hassled, detained, or deported by immigration officers. Every day rumors swirled that the Immigration and Naturalization Service might raid a job site, a pub or an apartment and arrest illegal Irish. McGowan's office was getting constant calls for help. People were looking for advice.

McGowan contacted his congressman, Brian Donnelly, who had also been receiving similar reports about Irish being detained at Logan. Donnelly's four grandparents came from Roscommon and Galway, and his Eleventh Congressional District included Dorchester and Quincy, making it one of the most Irish districts in the country. As he told one reporter, "Of the 12 houses in my street, six have families who have emigrated directly from Ireland."

In May 1985 Donnelly submitted HR Bill 2606, "to make additional immigrant visas available" for Irish and other groups who had been shut out by the 1965 Immigration Act. Two months later, encouraged by Donnelly's proposal, McGowan convened a meeting at the Irish Social Club in West Roxbury, attended by sixty representatives of Irish groups in Boston, and announced a national effort to reform immigration laws.

The group, which became known as the Massachusetts Immigration Committee, set about amending the 1965 Immigration Act. Joining McGowan in the campaign were Mike Joyce, a Connemara man working at the state house, GAA official Joe Lydon, attorney Paul Kilgariff, and Mike Cummings, the Galway football star who had helped jump-start the Irish revival of the 1950s. Throughout 1986 the Committee contacted hundreds of elected officials across America by tapping into the national networks of the Gaelic Athletic Association and the Ancient Order of Hibernians. They established relations with Italian, Greek, Canadian, and German groups. They took out ads in the paper and set up hot lines for illegal aliens.

Cummings approached his close friend Thomas J. Flatley, a successful real estate developer, about getting involved in the campaign. Flatley agreed to match all funds raised by the Massachusetts Immigration Committee and began working with Donnelly's office. On July 26, 1986, Flatley and Cummings traveled to the nation's capital to testify in favor of the Donnelly Bill that was before the House subcommittee. Flatley testified for the Boston Irish community about the importance of the bill, reflecting on his own successful career as a Boston businessman:

> *In no other country in the world but America could I have realized*
> *my dream of pursuing the entrepreneurial spirit. It saddens me . . .*
> *[that] had I been born 25 years later, I too might not have been able*
> *to realize my dream.*

With great fanfare and relief, the Donnelly Bill passed in fall 1986 as part of the U.S. Immigration and Control Act. The Donnelly Visa program allocated 40,000 permanent visas to Europeans, of which 18,363 were given to Irish immigrants, including many who had been living illegally in the United States. But the allotment barely dented the number of illegal Irish who were already here, and besides, upward of 25,000 Irish were still coming into the country annually, using holiday visas to get here and then going underground when those temporary visas expired.

Michael Cummings and Thomas Flatley traveled to Washington, D.C., to lobby for immigration reform.

In response to the continuing illegal crisis, a group of Irish immigrants in New York City formed the Irish Immigration Reform Movement, and in the summer of 1987 they formed a Boston chapter, which started a renewed effort in the Irish visa campaign. Like the Massachusetts Immigration Committee, the IIRM became part of a broad alliance of Irish and Irish Americans trying to help the Irish stay in America.

This time the effort was led in Congress by Bruce Morrison of Connecticut, a Yale-educated attorney with Ulster Protestant roots. He had taken a genuine interest in Ireland during a 1987 fact-finding mission to Northern Ireland, according to *Irish Echo* writer Ray O'Hanlon, whose book *The New Irish Americans* provides a fascinating account of the Irish visa issue as it worked its way through Congress. As chair of the immigration subcommittee, Morrison steered the visa bill past countless obstacles, negotiating support with Asian and Hispanic lobby groups while keeping IIRM and other Irish groups in the loop.

In 1991 it appeared that the Morrison Bill, HR 4300, would languish in Congress, but Boston's Congressman Joe Moakley came to the rescue. A few years earlier Morrison had supported Moakley's congressional investigation into the murder of American nuns in El Salvador, O'Hanlon reported, and now Moakley would return the favor. As Chairman of the Rules Committee, Moakley was able to maneuver Morrison's bill for a final House and Senate vote, and it passed into law.

The Morrison Visa Bill was more ambitious than the Donnelly Bill, and the celebration was even more frenzied. The passage of the bill provided the Irish with 51,715 Morrison Visas in a three-year period, effectively solving the problem of Irish illegals in the 1990s. Morrison was feted in Boston by grateful Irish immigrants now able to get on with their lives, and, like Donnelly, was considered a genuine hero in the Irish community. So too were the hundreds of grassroots leaders who dedicated several years of their lives to securing a future in Boston for new Irish immigrants.

The Boston Irish now turned their attention to the considerable amount of paperwork and legal advice that Morrison Visa recipients needed to become legal in America, and two groups came to the fore. The first was the Irish Pastoral Center, formed in 1988 by Father Dan

Help for Newcomers

Formed in 1989, the **Irish Immigration Center** located at 59 Temple Street in Boston, is a year-round service agency that helps immigrants get settled in the Boston area. The staff provides assistance in such areas as legal status, green cards, driver's licenses, and other matters important to newcomers. It offers workshops for those wishing to become citizens and provides guidance counseling and other social services. The Center's cross-cultural program brings together immigrants from Ireland, Haiti, Cape Verde, and other parts of the world to share their cultures and to establish a common ground. Since 2001 the Center has been one of four groups in the United States to administer the Walsh Visa Program, which brings Unionists and Nationalists from Northern Ireland and Ireland to Boston where they work together and experience the pluralism of American society. For more information, call (617) 542–7654 or visit the Web site www.iicenter.org.

Finn and Sister Veronica Dobson, as part of the Boston Archdiocese. It offered the new Irish spiritual advice, marriage counseling, and information on health, housing, and jobs. Their offices were based in the Irish parishes around Boston—Saint Mark's in Dorchester and Saint Columbkille's in Brighton—and provided a familiar setting for anyone seeking a connection with the Catholic Church, long a steadfast anchor of Irish life.

The second group was initiated in 1989 by young immigrants operating out of a basement in Dorchester. Calling their organization the Irish Immigration Center, they offered a hotline for illegals worried about their status. Under the energetic leadership of Sister Lena Deevy, Patrick Riordan, and others, the Center set up workshops on citizenship and health care and offered counseling and other services the new Irish needed. As the Morrison Visa holders became acclimated to American society, the Center expanded its mission to help other immigrants. Deevy, who had worked in poor neighborhoods in Dublin, Belfast, and Glasgow, recognized the need to find a common ground among immigrants from other parts of the world as a way of resolving inner-city tensions. She initiated an annual event called Black and Green, which connected the Irish with Haitian, Cape Verdean, and other immigrants living in Dorchester. She knew, as Irish leaders in the past knew, that for this generation of Irish to settle into Boston in a fruitful way, they needed to learn to live in harmony with other Bostonians.

CHAPTER FOURTEEN

The Gaelic Roots Revival (1985–2000)

WHEN BOSTON COLLEGE hired fiddler Seamus Connolly in 1991 to head up an Irish music program, it was one of the best moves the college ever made on behalf of its growing Irish Studies program. The ten-time All-Ireland fiddle champion from County Clare had been a major presence on the local scene since his arrival in Boston back in 1976. His exquisite style helped to elevate the caliber of Irish music in the city, and along with Galway fiddler Larry Reynolds he helped to usher in a revival of traditional Irish music in the area. Now he was taking the fiddle to Boston's Irish commuter college where generations of Irish Americans had trudged across town to be educated.

Founded in 1863 by businessman Andrew Carney and Jesuit priest Reverend John McElroy, S.J., Boston College was originally located next to the Immaculate Conception Church on Harrison Avenue in the South End. The college was modest at first, supported by the pennies of Irish immigrants who put their dreams into their children's futures. When Boston College eventually purchased land in Chestnut Hill to build a full-sized campus, the marquee building was to have been called the Daniel O'Connell Memorial Hall and Irish Hall of Fame, a testament to Ireland's great leaders. Noted architects Charles Donagh Maginnis, an immigrant from Derry, Northern Ireland, and his partner Timothy Walsh from Cambridge had pulled together the plans, and Irish organizations enthusiastically began raising funds. That hall was never built, but Maginnis and Walsh created a masterpiece that was called Gasson Hall.

By 1980 the pennies of immigrants were replaced by endowments from wealthy Irish businessmen, prompting the college to form an Irish Studies Program. Cochaired by history professor Kevin O'Neill and

Gasson Hall at Boston College was created by architects Charles Maginnis and Timothy Walsh.

English professor Adele Dalsimer, the program swiftly became one of the finest in the United States. It established a junior-year-abroad program at Cork University and developed ties with Dublin's prestigious Abbey Theater. The John J. Burns Library, under the direction of Dr. Robert K. O'Neill, became a leading repository for important papers belonging to poet William Butler Yeats, novelist Samuel Beckett, singer John McCormack, athlete James Brendan Connolly, and many other Irish notables. In 1987 BC hosted the annual meeting of the American Conference of Irish Studies (ACIS), bringing a national spotlight to its program.

With academic credentials firmly in place, the program sought to connect with Boston's grassroots community.

By hiring Irish musician Seamus Connolly for its Irish Studies program, Boston College began attracting people who had never stepped foot on the campus before. Along with archivist Beth Sweeney he helped to jump-start the Irish Music Archives at the John J. Burns Library, soliciting old recordings from his friends across the country. He and musicologist Micheal O'Suillebhain from University College Cork staged a concert with sixteen of the world's best Irish fiddlers, recording on a compact disc called *My Love Is in America*. The concert was a tour de force, and Connolly quickly followed it with an impressive gathering of harpists and a convention of uileann pipers.

In 1993 Connolly launched a unique program called Gaelic Roots: A Music, Song and Dance Summer School and Festival. Noted music critic Earle Hitchner hailed it as an unprecedented and historic event. Indeed it was, growing stronger annually for the next decade. For a full week each June, the world's finest Celtic musicians, dancers, singers, and scholars came to Boston College, where they taught classes and gave concerts. Hundreds of students registered for the program, living in the dormitories and eating in the school cafeteria. Most importantly, they played together in both classes and casual music sessions in the quiet repose of the beautiful campus. The master musicians gave two evening concerts through the week, open to the general public. Students came from as far as Japan, Sweden, and Australia, and the classes typically filled six months in advance.

COURTESY OF HIGGINS & ROSS

Seamus Connolly was founder of the Gaelic Roots festival at Boston College.

Along with his wife Chrysandra Walter, Connolly developed Gaelic Roots into the best program of its kind in the Celtic world. It combined hands-on instruction and performances with lectures and research, while showcasing the school's vast collection of Irish materials and Irish Studies experts. It brought from Ireland old music masters from remote areas of Ireland who specialized in regional styles, while integrating Scottish, Cape Breton, and Appalachian musicians and dancers to underscore the roots of the music. In the finest Irish tradition, it encouraged adult students who always wanted to learn an instrument while inspiring a whole generation of young people to take up Irish music and dancing.

To the surprise and dismay of the Irish community at large, the college announced in June 2003 that it was scaling back Gaelic Roots, just as the program was celebrating its tenth anniversary. Budgetary constraints combined with the new difficulty of securing temporary visas for foreign artists caused school officials to terminate the weeklong summer school in favor of ongoing workshops, lectures, and concerts during the academic year.

An Irish Renaissance

Gaelic Roots was part of a larger Irish cultural revival taking place in Boston, a fact noted by *Boston Globe* music reporter Scott Alarik in his 1990 article, "Keeping Ancient Irish Culture Alive." Alarik described "an Irish renaissance in Boston, a resurgence not just of music, but of dance, language and lore." He pointed to the new popularity of Irish set and ceili dancing hosted by *Comhaltas Ceoltoiri Eireann* (Irish Musicians Association). He cited the popularity of a genealogy group, the Irish Ancestral Research Association, interest in the Irish language in local colleges, and the success of local storyteller Sharon Kennedy. A sidebar to the story praised new Irish businesses like Keltic Krust, an Irish bakery, and Cuchulainn's, an Irish restaurant in Dorchester's Field's Corner that served Irish breakfast, providing "an atmosphere similar to what you would find in Ireland," as owner Kieran Staunton explained.

Atmosphere, or more precisely authenticity, had become the cornerstone of the new revival. Irish immigrants and Irish Americans alike had become dismayed by how beer and greeting cards companies had hijacked the Irish identity in America, especially around Saint Patrick's Day. Green plastic derbies, shamrock-shaped beer coasters, and tacky tee-shirts were hawked by shameless hucksters cashing in on sentimental icons of Irish culture. The Irish wanted something real, and partly as a response to the stale and commercialized stereotyping of the Irish in America, they harkened back to the underpinnings of Irish culture: language, literature, music, and dance.

Irish groups such as Sugan Theatre injected a new vitality into Boston's community theater. Formed in 1992 by Carmel and Peter O'Reilly, the Sugan staged Irish and Scottish plays that fought the image of a romanticized Ireland by displaying an often disturbing reality of Irish society. They showcased actors like Billy Meleady and Brian Scanlon, while staging works by playwrights Aiden Parkinson, Ronan Noone, and others. The Huntington Theatre produced nationally

acclaimed productions by leading
Irish playwrights. The Irish Poet's
Theater in Cambridge, founded in
the 1950s by Irish actress Mary
Manning Howe, hosted poet
Seamus Heaney and novelist John
McGahern. And the City of Boston
itself teamed up with Waterstone
Books, led by Scotsman Bert
Wright, to create an Irish Writers
Series featuring novelists Peter
Quinn and James Carroll, scholar
Angela Bourke, and poets Nuala Ni
Dhomhnaill and John Montague.

At Stonehill College, President
Bartley MacPhaidin and Richard
Finnegan formed an Irish Studies
program that included a year-
abroad program at University
College Dublin. At the same time
they built a collection of Irish government documents valuable to
historians and students. Harvard's
Celtic Department celebrated its

Comhaltas Ceoltoiri Eireann

Comhaltas Ceoltoiri Eireann (Irish
Musicians Association) is an international group that promotes traditional
Irish music and dance in more than
twenty countries. The Boston chapter
was formed in 1975. Comhaltas holds
regular Irish ceilis (dances) on the first
and fourth Sunday afternoons of each
month (except in July and August). The
group also offers set dance instructions
on Tuesday nights at 7:00 P.M. These
events are held at the Canadian-
American Hall at 202 Arlington Street in
Watertown. Comhaltas also has a fine
year-round teaching program on fiddle,
flute, tin whistle, accordion, harp, and
other traditional instruments. Each
October an ensemble of the best
Comhaltas musicians and dancers from
Ireland hold a concert in Waltham.
For more information, call (781)
899–0911 or visit the Web site
www.cceboston.org.

centenary of Celtic studies in 1996, and Chairman Patrick Ford and
alumni Philip Haughey formed a Friends group to aid graduate students in their scholarly pursuits. Elizabeth Shannon convened conferences on women from Northern Ireland at Boston University. At
University of Massachusetts/Boston Padraig O'Malley brought in the
Northern Irish to discuss their troubles, while Thomas O'Grady brought
Irish poets to discuss their verse.

A literary ambience even showed up in the city's new wave of Irish
pubs. A generation of Irish bartenders, many of whom apprenticed at
the Black Rose, opened their own pubs, offering traditional music,
healthy food, a hip jukebox, and a friendly, intimate ambiance. It was
fashionable to christen these pubs with a literary or cultural name—The

Brendan Behan, Flann O'Brien's, Mr. Dooley's, and the Midnight Court as well as the Kells, Claddagh, and Druid. By the late 1980s these pubs, along with the Burren, O'Leary's, and the Green Briar, ushered in a robust era where the pubs became the cornerstone of Irish nightlife in the city.

The pub scene was the place that Irish music next took hold in Boston after the demise of the Dudley Street dance halls left a gap in the social scene. It started around 1976 when Phil Sweeney and Richard McHugh opened the Black Rose on State Street and George Crowley opened the Plough & Stars on Massachusetts Avenue. Both became hot spots for Irish music sessions, with Dublin musicians Shay Walker, Declan Hunt, Alan Loughnane, and Johnny Began leading the tunes. The Plough attracted a crowd of rugby players but quickly became a hangout for Irish poets Desmond O'Grady and Seamus Heaney and raconteur Peter O'Malley, who started *Ploughshares* magazine. The Black Rose brought in an eclectic but energetic mix of city hall types, tourists, and businessmen, as well as Irish artists such as David O'Docherty, whose murals adorn the walls.

Over in Brookline Village, Henry Varian opened the Village Coach House, where fiddlers Connolly and Reynolds held court at the Monday night sessions. The Coach House became a showcase for *Comhaltas Ceoltoiri Eireann,* which Reynolds and others had formed in 1975 to foster Irish music in the Boston area.

Comhaltas trained a whole generation of outstanding traditional players. In 1991 Connolly's prized student Brendan Bulger of South Boston won the All-Ireland fiddle championship. A few years later accordionist Colm Gannon of Dorchester, whose Connemara-born father and brother were excellent players, won the All-Ireland title. Championship dancers frequented the scene, including Deirdre Goulding and Liam Harney. Sean Curran, son of radio personality John Curran and his wife Kitty, became a lead dancer in the Mark Morris Modern Dance troupe in New York City and later started his own troupe.

Comhaltas helped restore the atmosphere that many immigrants missed about Ireland. The group met the first Sunday of every month at the Canadian American Club in Watertown. The club had a bar but also offered coffee, tea, and soda bread, turning the music session into a

Irish step dancers perform at the Irish Cultural Centre's annual festival.

family affair that sometimes included participants from four generations. One could hear white-haired flutist Gene Preston, who emigrated
from Sligo in the 1920s, playing alongside fiddler Brendan Tonra, who
came from Mayo in the 1950s. They played with accordionists Mike
Reynolds from Waltham and Chris Bulger from South Boston. The
session also attracted Canadian players Sally Kelly and Mary Irwin,
and Scottish fiddler Johnny Cunningham, which led to the beginnings
of a pan-Celtic scene that included Irish, Scottish, and Cape Breton
musicians.

The explosion of music coming out of Ireland and Scotland buoyed
Boston's music scene, and soon dozens of Irish radio programs flour-
ished in the Boston area. Longtime radio hosts John Curran, Bernie
McCarty, John Latchford, and Tommy Cummings were joined by a new
generation of disc jockeys like Brian O'Donovan, Gail Gilmore, and
Seamus Mulligan. Tom Clifford's popular cable TV show *Ireland on the
Move* was joined in 1995 by Celtic Vision, a full-time but short-lived Irish
television station.

In publishing, Quinlin Campbell Publishers of Boston published its
third edition of *Guide to the New England Irish* in 1994, listing 1,200 Irish
organizations and activities in the region. It more than tripled the size of

Irish Dancing Today

Thanks to dance revues like *Riverdance*, *Lord of the Dance*, and *Inishaneill*, Irish dancing is more popular than ever around Boston. A series of step dancing competitions (feis) are held in the area each year, with winners moving on to national and international stages. Forty-eight certified Irish dancing schools in Massachusetts teach step dancing, ceili dancing, or both.

Comhaltas Ceoltoiri Eireann holds dances throughout the year, and the **Irish Cultural Centre of New England** in Canton hosts a regular set and ceili dancing event weekly. The **Burren Pub** in Davis Square in Somerville holds set dancing lessons every Monday at 8:00 P.M.

the first edition published in 1985. In 1991, when Don Mooney's *Boston Irish News* went defunct, Ed and Mary Forry launched the *Boston Irish Reporter*, a bright monthly newspaper that catalogued the activities and personalities of the Irish community. The *Reporter* added editor Peter Stevens, a noted author with a unique appreciation of Boston Irish history. Connell and Siobhan Gallagher of Donegal, in association with Liam Ferrie of Galway, launched the *Irish Emigrant* green pages in South Boston, providing a weekly update on the bustling pub scene in greater Boston. For a time the two New York City papers, the *Irish Echo* and the *Irish Voice*, ran news bureaus in Boston that flourished but then faded after several years.

A number of excellent books about the Boston Irish emerged during this time. Political and social histories of the Boston Irish by Thomas H. O'Connor, Ruth Ann Harris, and Dennis P. Ryan charted the nineteenth-century Boston Irish experience. Jack Beatty's biography of James Michael Curley and William Bulger's political memoirs added considerable insight into Boston Irish politics. Novelists George V. Higgins, James Carroll, and Dennis Lehane brought to life a cast of larger-than-life characters holding court in the side streets of Boston.

Preserving the Culture

Despite the flourishing of Irish activity in greater Boston, one thing was missing: a central gathering spot that drew everyone together, the way Dudley Street had. The 1965 immigration laws had cut off the flow of new Irish coming into Boston, stripping away the vibrancy that newcomers brought to stock Irish neighborhoods like South Boston, Dorchester, Charlestown, and Brighton. New immigrant groups moved into these enclaves as Irish-American families headed for the suburbs. In the mid-1970s several Irish neighborhoods in Boston got ensnared in a school busing controversy that pitted working-class Blacks and whites against each other.

Just as previous generations left the South End and Roxbury for Jamaica Plain and West Roxbury, Irish-Americans continued to move west into towns like Dedham and Norwood. They also migrated south into Quincy, Scituate, and Hingham, making the South Shore the state's most heavily populated Irish region today.

The dispersion caused a tangible sadness about losing the community cohesiveness that had come to define the Boston Irish persona since the 1840s. Irish leaders began discussing the notion of building a cultural center as a way of recreating that sense of community being lost. Other cities—Chicago, Pittsburgh, and San Francisco—had created Irish centers with much smaller populations. Why couldn't Boston?

Bill McGowan, immigration leader and Gaelic Athletic Association official, outlined his ideas to "establish a Gaelic Center in Boston" during an interview with Vincent O'Sullivan of the *Boston Irish Press* in 1981. A few years later *Comhaltas Ceoltoiri Eireann* proposed a Traditional Irish Music Center "as a means of cultural identity and as an influence on the development of America's own music."

In 1989 a committee of Irish leaders announced plans to build an Irish Cultural Centre, led by Noel Connolly, Mike O'Connor, Eddie Barron, and others. Their goal was to create a place "where present and future generations can participate in activities that promote Irish cultural, education, sporting and social events." The group launched the annual Irish Festival at Stonehill College and a golf tournament to raise funds, and within five years the group had pulled together enough funds for a down payment on some land.

Where to locate such a center was a point of debate. Many of the organizers had moved out of Boston to surrounding towns, and they believed that a location south of Boston would be most convenient to the greatest number of Irish-Americans. Those who had stayed in Boston were pushing for a site within the city, with Mayor Ray Flynn offering to locate city property that could suffice. Even the *Boston Globe* weighed in on the debate with an editorial in 1993 stating:

> *The Irish center belongs in Boston, where emigres like trade unionist*
> *Daniel Tobin and folk hero John Boyle O'Reilly served the cause of*
> *social justice, a city that was home to the beloved Irish-American*
> *President John F. Kennedy. It is time to collect and preserve local Irish*
> *artifacts, books and museum-quality pieces now in private hands.*

But after examining more than one hundred sites, including the
Water & Sewer facility at Columbia Point and an old rope building at
Charlestown Navy Yard, in 1995 the group purchased a plot of land in
Canton, about 20 miles southwest of downtown Boston. With the site
issue settled, the project gained momentum.

Organizers of the Centre joined forces with the Gaelic Athletic
Association, which had outgrown Dilboy Field in Somerville, to create
the forty-six acre campus. Between 1995 and 1998 thousands of volunteers from both groups—laborers, carpenters, electricians, painters, and
trades people—cleared the land, cut the road, created the playing
fields, and built a 17,000-square-foot, two-story facility. The Centre officially opened in 1997, and today is a bustling, year-round gathering
place as originally envisioned.

Remembering the Famine

Despite the shifts in population, downtown Boston still mattered to the
Irish, if not for the future then at least for the past. In the early 1990s
plans got underway to commemorate the 150th anniversary of the Irish
Famine in Irish enclaves throughout the world. Because Boston was one
of the main ports where famine refugees fled in the 1840s, the local
Irish felt obliged to create a significant and permanent memorial. In
1991 Mayor Flynn and his press secretary Francis Costello selected a site
for the memorial at Faneuil Hall near Long Wharf, where the Famine
ships docked. But in 1993 Flynn was appointed ambassador to the
Vatican and moved to Rome, and Costello moved to Belfast. The
Memorial project languished until 1996, when Mayor Thomas Menino
asked developer Thomas Flatley to carry the project through.

Flatley agreed, and on May 1, 1997, he convened a meeting of leaders from the Irish community and business world to undertake the $1
million project. Flatley's point man was Mike Cummings, who had been
active in Irish circles since the 1950s. One afternoon they walked the

city of Boston and found the perfect spot for the Memorial at the corner of Washington and School Streets. It was along the city's Freedom Trail, which some two million people walked each year. It was nestled between two book-stores, across from the Old South Meeting House, and a few yards away from the International Institute of Boston, which helps new immigrants and refugees settle in Boston. And coincidentally, it was steps from the place in which the first Catholic Mass in Boston was publicly celebrated in 1788. The committee chose noted sculptor Robert Shure to undertake the project, and he delivered it on time and under budget just fourteen months later.

On June 28, 1998, the Boston Irish Famine Memorial was unveiled in front of 7,000 people, including Seamus Brennan, Ireland's Minister of State. The eight narrative plaques encircling the statues were read aloud by historian Thomas O'Connor, who was joined by an Irish immigrant, an Irish American, an Irish native, a Vietnamese girl, a Rwandan boy, a Medal of Honor winner, and a sur-vivor of the Jewish Holocaust. Some grumbling surfaced from local art critics about the Memorial and the selection process itself, but the pro-ject was deemed an immense success, as thousands of people journey to see it each year.

The 150th anniversary of the Famine commemoration was also embraced by neighboring communities. The Museum of Our National Heritage in Lexington, Massachusetts, created a Famine exhibit that ran from July through December 1996. In June 1997 a religious service was held on Deer Island to honor the 5,000 immigrants who had been quar-antined on the island. The City of Cambridge, led by John Flaherty and

A Cultural Hub for the Irish

The **Irish Cultural Centre** at 200 New Boston Road in Canton was established as a headquarters for the promotion and preservation of Irish culture for the New England region. The forty-six-acre campus includes a state-of-the-art new building with function rooms, a library and genealogical research room, a pub, classrooms, and a banquet room for large events. On its three playing fields a variety of Irish and American sports are played, including football, soccer, rugby, hurling, and camogie. The Centre has more than 4,000 members, who enjoy a year-round schedule of classes, performances, competition, and gather-ings in the areas of music, dance, theater, and athletics. Educational programs and social activities are also common throughout the year. For details about the Irish Cultural Centre, call (781) 821–8291 or visit the Web site www.irishculture.org.

John O'Connor, organized a Famine Memorial in Cambridge and commissioned Maurice Harmon of Derry, Northern Ireland, to create the
twin statues. The Cambridge memorial was unveiled in July 1997 before
5,000 people, with Mary Robinson, president of Ireland, presiding
along with Governor William Weld.

In a poignant way, the worldwide commemorations of the Great
Hunger helped to knit together, even for a brief time, Ireland's sprawling diaspora. It focused attention on the famines still taking place in
many African countries and put the spotlight on Irish relief groups like
CONCERN and GOAL. And in the broadest sense, it reminded the
world of the pain, loss, promise, and redemption inherent in the
human condition. In 1997 Tony Blair became the first British prime
minister in history to publicly acknowledge the British government's
role in the catastrophe. The unofficial apology occurred on June 1 at a
Famine commemoration in Mill Street, County Cork, Ireland. The ceremony was attended by American ambassador Jean Kennedy Smith and
British ambassador Veronica Sutherland. Mr. Blair's statement, read
aloud to the participants, said in part:

> *Those who governed in London at the time failed their people through
> standing by while a crop failure turned into a massive human
> tragedy. We must not forget such a dreadful event.*

The close of the Boston Irish century ended the way it started, with
a burst of creative energy. In 2000 the newly formed Boston Irish
Tourism Association (BITA) launched a year-round campaign to promote Irish cultural activities and businesses to the convention and visitors industry. BITA believed the city and state's Irish heritage would be
of interest to the millions of visitors who came here each year. The
group created a walking map called the Irish Heritage Trail, listing sixteen Irish memorials in downtown Boston and Back Bay, along with
dozens of others throughout the state. Starting at the Rose Kennedy
Garden on the waterfront, the Trail winds its way through the very life
of the city, overlapping with the Freedom Trail, the Black Heritage
Trail, and the Women's Heritage Trail. Charting cemeteries, churches,
battlefields, athletic fields, libraries, museums, the trail showed how the
Irish had become an indelible part of the city's history.

CHAPTER FIFTEEN

Who's Irish?

FICTION WRITER Gish Jen posed the poignant question, "Who's Irish?" in her 1999 short story about interethnic marriages. Jen's modern-day tale about a Chinese grandmother's snobbery toward her Irish-American in-laws strikes a chord with anyone who has married outside their own racial, religious, or ethnic tribe and discovers the tension that underlies assimilation.

In a humorous exchange, the Chinese daughter defends her Irish husband's clan, saying, "You know, the British call the Irish heathen, just like they call the Chinese . . . You think the Opium War was bad, how would you like to live right next door to the British."

The Chinese and Irish, it turns out, lived next door to each other in Boston and began intermarrying around 1875, when there was an abundance of single Irish women and single Chinese men. Sarah Deutch, in her book *Women and the City,* recounts an 1895 *Boston Globe* story in which a group of conventioneers wondered why a "rather good-looking" Irish girl was riding her bike around Chinatown, when suddenly a Chinese man opened a nearby door and called out "Lil, come quickly." The reporter explained that "the girl was probably the Chinaman's wife and that there were several more of her kind in the colony."

In 1906 a Boston almanac reported that the Irish were converting local Chinese, who crossed over the bridge from Chinatown to become Catholics in South Boston. Reverend Walter J. Browne of Saints Peter and Paul Church had "twenty-six baptized converts and fourteen neophytes," who "looked very well in European dress." The religious instructors were Muldoon, Coholan, Whalen, Conboy, Breen, and Cunningham.

What it means to be Irish in Boston has changed dramatically over the past three centuries. President Theodore Roosevelt was right in predicting that Irish immigrants would eventually become more American than Irish. In an 1897 letter to James J. Roche praising the newly formed American Irish Historical Society, Roosevelt wrote:

> We [Americans] are a new people, derived from race strains, and different from any one of them, and it is a good thing to have brought before us our diversity in race origin. . . . In time the different strains of blood will all be blended together, English, Irish, German and French. When that time comes the chief thing for all of us to keep in mind is that we must be good Americans, purely as such, no matter what be our creed, or our ancestry in Europe.

The strains of blood began blending early in America, and not just among Europeans. In the eighteenth century, when Irish and Scottish servants escaped into the wilderness with Indians and Africans, they began a process of racial intermingling that became the stock for America's melting pot. Race and religion emerged as the twin methods of establishing some definition of American society. The Irish, as "papists and foreigners," were perceived as twin threats to a fledgling Anglo-American nation and were stigmatized on both counts. Other groups—notably Blacks, Chinese, and Italians—faced similar rejection by nativists who were hoping that America might remain a homogenous white Anglo-Saxon Protestant nation. Those hopes were not realized.

The Civil War was the first true test since the American Revolution of what the nation would become. More than 10,000 Irish joined the state's regiments that fought to preserve the Union. Patrick Guiney from Tipperary, who lost an eye at the Battle of Wilderness while leading the Ninth Regiment, was a devout believer in Abraham Lincoln and was likely familiar with the president's viewpoint when it came to Blacks and Irish. In a letter to Joshua I. Speed in 1855, Lincoln wrote:

> I am not a Know-Nothing . . . how could I be? How can any one who abhors the oppression of Negroes be in favor of degrading any classes of white people? Our progress in degeneracy appears to me to be pretty rapid. As a nation, we began by declaring that 'all men are created equal.' We now practically read it all men are created equal, except Negroes and foreigners—and Catholics.

After the Civil War, leaders like John Boyle O'Reilly cultivated Irish

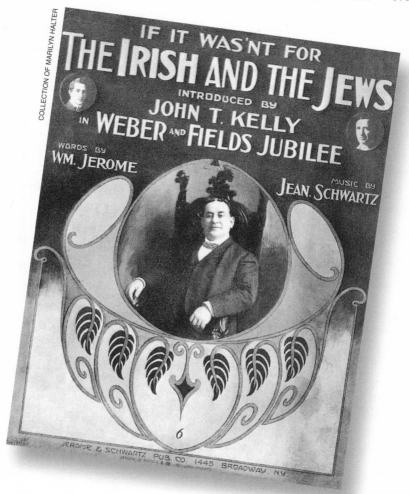

Ethnic sheet music in the early twentieth century
attests to the American melting pot concept.

solidarity with Blacks, Chinese, Jews, and Indians during his twenty years
of community leadership in Boston. A shared sense of oppression and
proximity among these groups led to interracial alliances. Deutsch
wrote, "In the 1870s and 1880s, black Bostonians married whites—
largely Irish women—at a higher rate than Irish Catholics married
Yankee Protestants."

In the early twentieth century, popular culture lauded alliances
among different groups in America, churning out songs like "My
Yiddish Colleen," the "Arrah Wanna (An Irish Indian Matrimonial

Venture)," or the "Irish-Dutch Argument." The Irish often became paranoid about their identity being appropriated. In 1900 the *Republic* newspaper ran an article entitled "Criminals Take Celtic Names," suggesting
a plot among criminals to give false Irish names when being arrested. A
few months later it ran an article entitled "Irish Melodies Stolen," accus-
ing English and Scots of taking credit for ancient Irish melodies.

Who is Irish today has more to do with sensibility than birthplace or
geography. As Ireland's former President Mary Robinson noted,
"Irishness is not simply territorial." In an odd way, Irishness is open to
anyone who desires it on Saint Patrick's Day, though that celebration is
often squandered by obnoxious clichés and stereotypes put forth by
marketers, bigots, and faux Irish. One of the most interesting parades
of recent years takes place in Lawrence, a mill city originally settled by
Irish immigrants but today a polyglot of Hispanics and Asians from all
over the world. "La Parade del Dia de San Patrico" is still run by the
local AOH, but the bands from local high schools are almost all
Hispanic, dressed in green uniforms, and playing a hybrid of jigs and
salsa as they march down the avenue behind Mayor Michael J. Sullivan,
who is himself half Irish and half Italian.

That openness to embrace a broader definition of Irishness was at
play in Cambridge's Saint Patrick's Day parades in 1995 and 1996, held
in solidarity with Irish gays who were prevented from marching in South
Boston. Cambridge organizer John Flaherty, a Galway native, said that
anyone who was proud to be Irish, no matter their affiliation, faith, or
preference, could march in the parade, and thousands did just that.

Who's Not Irish?

Not everyone wants to be Irish, even people living in Ireland. Many
Unionists in Northern Ireland profess allegiance to Great Britain and
prefer to be called British. It was not always so.

In the 1700s, Ulster Presbyterians arriving in Boston were proud to
call themselves Irish. Reverend John Moorhead's Presbyterian Church
was simply known as the Irish Church when established in 1729. The
Charitable Irish Society, formed in 1737 to help their fellow countrymen in times of distress, was initially comprised entirely of Protestants

Participants enjoy the Saint Patrick's Day parade in Lawrence, Massachusetts.

who helped anyone with an Irish name, regardless of their religion. "Kingdom of Ireland" was etched into tombstones at Copp's Hill and Central Burying Grounds in Boston.

By the early nineteenth century the descendants of these Ulstermen, Kevin Kenny writes, "eagerly embraced the term Scots-Irish as a way of distinguishing themselves from the incoming waves of Catholic Irish immigrants." And historian Michael J. O'Brien notes, "Scotch-Irish or Ulster Scots connotes in a snobbish way a racial superiority, while Irish implies an inferiority that originates primarily in a differing religious belief."

By the end of the nineteenth century, Professor John Fiske comments, "The antipathy between the Scotch-Irish and the true Irish is, perhaps, unsurpassed for bitterness and intensity."

In recent years, many Irish in Boston have sought to address the bitterness between the varieties of Irish identity. McCormack Institute scholar Padraig O'Malley brought nationalists and loyalists from Northern Ireland to Boston to talk to each other in the 1980s and at one point brought in South African Bishop Desmond Tutu to give a lecture on reconciliation. In 1998 Ulster Protestant minister Brian Dixon

joined Father Ted Linehan from Kerry in a homily on the 150th
anniversary of the Irish Famine on Deer Island. When the Dunfey family brought a group of loyalist paramilitaries to speak at Boston College
in 1997, the Ulstermen were surprised to discover that so many Irish
Americans were interested in what they had to say, even while not
agreeing with them. The two Congressional leaders on the issue of Irish
visas, Brian Donnelly and Bruce Morrison, are Irish Catholic and Irish
Protestant, respectively.

There are hopes that the "bitterness and intensity" that Fiske noted
will diminish in the new millennium. Local groups like the American
Ireland Fund and Irish-American Partnership support cross-community
initiatives in Northern Ireland. The Walsh Visa Program finds jobs and
housing in Boston for Irish Catholics and Protestants from Ireland and
Northern Ireland. Administered by the Irish Immigration Center, the
program exposes participants to pluralism, tolerance, and equality in
work and social settings, with hopes that they can transfer those skills
when they return home. If nothing else, a city like Boston widens the
horizons for people who've spent their lives in tiny villages where centuries of memories drench the countryside—where there is, to para-
phrase Yeats, great hatred and little room.

Redefining the Boston Irish

Boston's demographics have changed dramatically. Between 1900 and
2000, Boston's Irish population went from 40 percent to 14 percent.
Where did everyone go? Mostly the Irish moved beyond the Hub to
surrounding cities and towns, and today Massachusetts remains the
most Irish state in America, with 23 percent of the population claiming
Irish roots.

Amid the shifting demographics, however, are signposts of the Irish
promenade through Boston's history. The Rose Kennedy Garden in the
North End recalls an era in the nineteenth century when that neighborhood was heavily Irish. On Dorchester Avenue in Savin Hill, now a thriving Vietnamese community, there is a small plaque honoring Irish-born
Peter Nee, who lived there briefly in the 1960s before enlisting in the
United States Marines. The Connemara man died in Vietnam in 1969.

Flags adorn the streets of South Boston during the Saint Patrick's Day parade.

The Yankee cobblestones that the Irish paved over in the twentieth century are now being replaced by a new mosaic of ethnicity and race. Hibernian Hall on Dudley Street in Roxbury, once the centerpiece of the Irish cultural and social scene in greater Boston, is being converted into an arts center for Boston's African-American community. The working name of this new enterprise is Roxbury Center for Arts at Hibernian Hall; although the name of the center is not yet finalized, its developers want to find a way to acknowledge the building's Irish past.

Politics and religion were the anchors of the Boston Irish experience for much of the twentieth century. Both of these "militant and triumphant" institutions have been altered dramatically in recent years, and the politicians and priests no longer provide the comfort and assurance they once offered for Irish immigrants or Irish Americans.

What will sustain the Boston Irish in the future? Culture and education, long overshadowed by politics and religion, are increasingly the reference points of Irish-American identity and expression.

And a heightened cultural sensibility is helping to revamp Boston's Irish marketplace. In her book *Shopping for Identity: The Marketing of*

Ethnicity, Professor Marilyn Halter of Boston University notes how ethnic groups across America today now "look to the marketplace to revive and re-identify with ethnic values." The shift away from "Kiss Me I'm Irish" T-shirts and green beer toward more authentic products like Kara Irish pottery is contributing to an Irish revival. Exploring an authentic culture beyond the stereotypes and clichés is a hopeful sign. Stores like Aisling Gallery and Lorica Artworks feature Irish landscapes, not dancing leprechauns. *Comhaltas Ceoltoiri Eireann* instructs youngsters in traditional music and dance, which is in danger of being marginalized by the dominant pop ethos. Sugan Theatre brings a needed authenticity to Irish drama, while The Irish Ancestral Research Association (TIARA) and the New England Historic Genealogy Society encourage family history research projects.

Such a return to ethnic identity has antecedents in Boston history. Poet and editor John Boyle O'Reilly's generation spearheaded an Irish revival in the 1880s that lasted for more than two decades; it was fueled by a nationalistic pride and marked the beginnings of a hyphenated Irish-American identity. A similar revival occurred between 1945 and 1965, when a wave of new immigrants worked with Irish-American leaders to create a vibrant cultural scene in the Boston area that revitalized Gaelic sports, drama, set dancing, and the Irish language.

The present Irish revival in greater Boston, which began in the 1980s, is equally vibrant and widespread, not unlike those previous eras. The final section of this book, "A Visitor's Guide to Irish Boston," provides an overview of the variety of Irish activities and resources available today. It reflects the current chapter of the Irish experience in Boston that began nearly three centuries ago, when indentured servants and artisans gingerly set down roots in what would become America's most Irish city.

Part Two:
A Visitor's Guide to
IRISH BOSTON

All Things Irish In and Around Boston

Visitors to Irish Boston will find a great variety of attractions, historical monuments, exhibits, and programs related to Irish history and culture in the city. A selection of cultural and educational groups, businesses, historical sites, and other places worth exploring is provided here. More details on Irish organizations, museums, gift shops, pubs, and hotels as well as annual Irish events can be obtained by visiting the Web site www.irishmassachusetts.com, run by the Boston Irish Tourism Association. That Web site also has links to travel opportunities to Ireland or to other Irish-related sites in the States. For more details on Irish historical sites found on the Boston Irish Heritage Trail, visit the Web site www.irishheritagetrail.com.

For general tourist information on the Boston area, visit the Greater Boston Convention & Visitors Bureau Web site at www.bostonusa.com, which links to other regional tourist and travel agencies. For more information on travel to Ireland, visit Tourism Ireland's Web site at www.irelandvacations.com.

Bagpipe players at an Irish festival.

Tourist Information

Blackstone Valley Chamber of
Commerce
110 Church Street
Whitinsville, MA 01588
(508) 234–9090

Boston Irish Tourism Association
P. O. Box 341
Milton, MA 02186
(617) 696–9880

Cape Cod Chamber of Commerce
307 Main Street
Hyannis, MA 02601
(508) 862–0700

Crystal Travel
100 Spring Street
West Roxbury, MA 02132
(617) 327–4242

Crystal Travel
8 Chestnut Hill Avenue
Brighton, MA 02135
(617) 254–4900

Greater Boston Convention &
Visitors Bureau
Two Copley Place, Suite 105
Boston, MA 02115
(800) SEE–BOSTON

Massachusetts Convention Centers
Authority
900 Boylston Street
Boston, MA 02116
(617) 954–2000

Massachusetts Office of Travel
& Tourism
10 Park Plaza, Suite 4510
Boston, MA 02116
(800) 447–6277 (800–447–MASS)

Massachusetts Port Authority
One Harborside Drive, Suite 200S
East Boston, MA 02128
(617) 428–2800

Massachusetts Turnpike Authority
10 Park Plaza, Suite 4160
Boston, MA 02116
(877) MASS–PIKE

North of Boston Convention &
Visitors Bureau
17 Peabody Square
Peabody, MA 01960
(978) 977–7760

Plymouth Convention & Visitors
Bureau
32 Court Street, 2nd Floor
Plymouth, MA 02360
(508) 747–0100

Tourism Massachusetts
44 Broomfield Street, 8th Floor
Boston, MA 02108
(617)542–0015

JFK and daughter Caroline.

Museums and Library Collections

Archdiocese of Boston Archives
2121 Commonwealth Avenue
Boston, MA 02135
(617) 746–5797
Parish records and historical and genealogical resources on the Irish are available by appointment.

Boston Athenaeum
10½ Beacon Street
Boston, MA 02108
(617) 227–0270
Formed in 1808, the Athenaeum is a research library with an impressive collection of materials on Boston history.

Boston Museum Project
55 Court Street
Boston, MA 02108
(617) 367–1955
This address is the office of the planners working to create a museum dedicated to Boston's history. Call for information on the current status of the project.

Boston Public Library
700 Boylston Street, Copley Square
Boston, MA 02116
(617) 536–5400
The BPL has more than 13,000 Irish items, including collections of the 1798 Uprising, Abbey Theatre and Seamus Heaney, plus Irish newspapers, music, and photographs.

Bostonian Society Library
15 State Streeet
Boston, MA 02109
(617) 720–1713
The Bostonian Society Library owns 7,000 books; 35,000 photos; 400 maps; manuscript collections; ephemera; and scrapbooks about Boston history.

Captain Forbes House
215 Adams Street
Milton, MA 02186
(617) 696–1815
Contains memorabilia and documents on the USS Jamestown's humanitarian voyage to Cork in 1847.

City of Boston Archives
30 Millstone Road
Hyde Park, MA 02136
(617) 364–8679
The city's official papers, including birth and death records, are available here.

Commonwealth Museum
Columbia Point
Dorchester, MA 02125
(617) 727–9268
Contains treasures from the state's history, like Paul Revere's copperplate engraving of the Boston Massacre.

Harvard University
Widener Library
Cambridge, MA 02138
(617) 495–2411
Harvard has more than 10,000 books in the Celtic field.

Hull Public Library
9 Main Street
Hull, MA 02045
(781) 925–2295
Formerly the summer home of John Boyle O'Reilly, the library has a fine collection of Irish materials.

Maritime and Irish Mossing Museum
Driftway
Scituate, MA 02066
(781) 545–1083
*In the nineteenth century, immigrants cre-
ated a small industry gathering Irish
moss (carrageen) along the beaches in
Scituate; that process is captured in an
exhibit at this maritime history museum.*

JFK Birthplace
National Historic Place
83 Beals Street
Brookline, MA 02146
(617) 566–7937
*JFK was born and lived in this house
from 1917 to 1931.*

JFK Library and Museum
Columbia Point
Boston, MA 02125
(617) 514–1600
*The official repository for papers,
artifacts, and materials of the nation's
thirty-fifth president includes many Irish
items including Commodore John Berry's
sword.*

JFK Museum and Park
397 Main Street
Hyannis, MA 02601
(508) 790–3077
*An intimate recollection of JFK's love of
Cape Cod includes eighty photos and a
video narrated by Walter Cronkite.*

John J. Burns Library
Boston College
Chestnut Hill, MA 02467
(617) 552–3287
*The library has important papers of
Samuel Becket, W. B. Yeats, Eamon De
Valera, and Nuala Ni Dhomhnaill. The
Irish Music Center at the library is an
archival and listening center for Irish
music in America.*

Lawrence Public Library
135 Parker Street
Lawrence, MA 01843
(978) 794–5789
*The AOH contributed more than 6,000
items to the Irish Collection, including
rare broadsheets, pamphlets, newspapers,
and ephemera.*

MacPháidín Library
Stonehill College
N. Easton, MA 02357
(508) 565–1000
*Named for Donegal native and former
college president Bartley MacPhádín, the
library has an extensive collection of Irish
government documents.*

Massachusetts Historical Society
1154 Boylston Street
Boston, MA 02115
(617) 536–1608
*One of America's most important histori-
cal repositories, the Society was formed in
1791. It holds the Charitable Irish Society
records from 1737 through 1939.*

Massachusetts State Archives
220 Morrissey Boulevard
Boston, MA 02125
(617) 727–2816
*Contains legislative papers, vital records,
and genealogical information as well as
photos, maps, paintings, and audiovisu-
al materials on Massachusetts history.*

McMullen Museum of Art
Boston College
140 Commonwealth Avenue
Chestnut Hill, MA 02467
(617) 552–2237
*The museum works closely with BC's Irish
Studies Programs and brings in contempo-
rary art from Ireland.*

Museum of Fine Arts
465 Huntington Avenue
Boston, MA 02115
(617) 267–9300
Among the MFA's many Irish holdings are paintings by John S. Copley, early Irish silver, and a set of rare uilleann pipes belonging to the famous piper John Egan.

Museum of Our National Heritage
33 Marrett Road
Lexington, MA 02420
(781) 861–6559
Founded by the Scottish Rite Freemasons, the museum presents exhibits and concerts relevant to the Irish.

Newburyport Public Library
94 State Street
Newburyport, MA 01950-6619
(978) 465–4428
Formerly the home of Patrick Tracy, famous privateer during the American Revolution.

Quincy Historical Museum
8 Adams Street
Quincy, MA 02169-2002
(617) 773–1144
The Quincy Historical Society includes artifacts from the shipbuilding and granite industries which were heavily Irish in the nineteenth century.

Thomas P. O'Neill Library
Boston College
Chestnut Hill, MA 02167
(617) 552–8000
Named for U.S. Congressman Tip O'Neill, the library includes congressional records, photos, and video clips of O'Neill's career in politics.

LIBRARY OF MICHAEL P. QUINLIN

The John Boyle O'Reilly Memorial.

Irish Heritage Trail

Boston's *Irish Heritage Trail* provides an illustrated history of the Boston Irish experience through a series of statues, memorials, and landmarks that tell the Irish story. Here are the stops along the trail with their locations. Maps of the Irish Heritage Trail, which is a self-guided tour, are available at visitors kiosks at Boston Common Visitors Information Center, Prudential Center, or Massachusetts Turnpike visitor centers. Details can also be obtained on the Web site www.irishheritagetrail.com.

Downtown/Back Bay

Rose Kennedy's Rose Garden
Columbus Park, Atlantic Avenue

James Michael Curley Park
Congress and North Streets

Irish Famine Memorial
School and Washington Streets

Granary Burying Grounds
Tremont Street near Park Street

Colonel Robert Shaw Memorial
Beacon and Park Streets

Massachusetts State House
Beacon and Park Streets

Soldiers and Sailors Memorial
Flag Staff Hill, Boston Common

Commodore John Barry Plaque
Tremont Street, Boston Common

Boston Massacre Memorial
Tremont Street, Boston Common

Colonel Thomas Cass Statue
Boylston Street, Public Garden

David I. Walsh Statue
Charles River Esplanade at Hatch Shell

Maurice Tobin Statue
Charles River Esplanade at Hatch Shell

Patrick Collins Memorial
Commonwealth Avenue Mall near Dartmouth Street

Copley Square
Boylston and Dartmouth Streets

Boston Public Library
Boylston Street between Dartmouth and Exeter Streets

John Boyle O'Reilly Memorial
Boylston Street and the Fenway

Charlestown

USS *Constitution*
Charlestown Navy Yard

Charlestown Civil War Soldier and Bunker Hill Tablets
Winthrop Square, Winthrop Street

Bunker Hill Monument
Monument Avenue

The Irish Famine Memorial

The Irish Famine Memorial was unveiled in Boston on June 28, 1998, as part of the 150th anniversary of the Great Hunger. More than 7,000 people attended the ceremony on that warm Sunday afternoon, including many African guests who experienced modern-day famines in Rwanda and Sudan. The memorial's twin statues are encircled by eight narrative plaques recounting the history of the Irish Famine. The final plaque, Lest We Forget, brings the story to the present time: "The conditions that produced the Irish famine—crop failure, absentee landlordism, colonialism, and weak political leadership—still exist around the world today. . . . The lessons of the Irish famine need to be constantly learned and applied until history finally ceases to repeat itself."

East Boston

Colonel Edward L. Logan Statue
Logan International Airport

Dorchester

John F. Kennedy Library and
Museum
Columbia Point

John W. McCormack Memorial Park
Columbia Road

South Boston

Congressman J. Joseph Moakley Park
Old Colony Avenue

James B. Connolly Statue
Moakley Park, Old Colony Avenue

Dorchester Heights Memorial
G Street

Cambridge

Irish Famine Memorial
Cambridge Common, Massachusetts
Avenue

Annie Sullivan Plaque
Brattle and James Streets, Radcliffe
College

Brookline/Chestnut Hill/Newton

JFK Birthplace
83 Beals Street, Brookline

Boston College
140 Commonwealth Avenue,
Chestnut Hill

Johnny Kelley Statue
Commonwealth Avenue, Newton

Jamaica Plain

James Michael Curley House
350 Jamaica Way

Forrest Hills Cemetery
Route 203

Cemeteries

These cemeteries are among the largest and most historic burying grounds in the Boston area. The burial places of famous Irish Bostonians are noted.

Forest Hills Cemetery
95 Forest Hills Avenue
Jamaica Plain, MA 02130
(617) 524–0128
Sculptors Martin and James Millmore and writer Eugene O'Neill are buried here.

Holyhead Cemetery
587 Heath Street
Brookline, MA 02146
(617) 327–1010
John Boyle O'Reilly, Hugh O'Brien, Patrick Collins, and Rose Fitzgerald Kennedy are buried here.

Mount Auburn Cemetery
580 Mount Auburn Avenue
Cambridge, MA 02138
(617) 547–7105
Poet Fanny Parnell and Civil War hero Colonel Thomas Cass are buried here.

Mt. Calvary Cemetery
366 Cummings Highway
Roslindale, MA 02131
(617) 325–6830
Boxer John L. Sullivan and Mayor James Michael Curley are buried here.

Old Granary Burying Grounds
Tremont Street near Park Street
Boston, MA 02108
(617) 635–4505
Boston Massacre victim Patrick Carr, Governor James Sullivan, and Governor John Hancock are buried here.

Rest Haven Cemetery
Deer Island
Boston Harbor, MA
(781) 585–8181
More than 700 Irish immigrants are buried here. They were among those newcomers quarantined on the island from 1847 to 1849.

Saint Augustine's Cemetery
225 Dorchester Street
South Boston, MA 02127
The city's oldest Catholic cemetery, opened in 1818. Reverend Thomas O'Flaherty is buried here.

Saint Joseph's Cemetery
900 LaGrange Street
West Roxbury, MA 02132
(617) 327–1010
U.S. Congressman John W. McCormack, mayor and state senator John Francis "Honey Fitz" Fitzgerald, and labor leader Mary Kenny O'Sullivan are buried here.

FleetBoston Pavilion.

Theaters and Concert Venues

Boston Playwright's Theatre
949 Commonwealth Avenue
Boston, MA 02116
(617) 358–7529 (PLAY)
Dedicated to the writing and production of new works, the Theatre has featured Irish playwright Ronan Noone and others.

Boston Symphony Hall
301 Massachusetts Avenue
Boston, MA 02115
(888) 266–1200
The Chieftains play Symphony Hall every March, and Celtic Night at the Pops each summer features stars like Eileen Ivers and Natalie McMasters.

FleetBoston Pavilion
290 Northern Avenue
Boston, MA 02127
(617) 728–1600
This summer concert venue overlooking Boston Harbor features Irish performers such as Van Morrison, the Irish Tenors, the Cranberries, and Mary Black.

Huntington Theatre
264 Huntington Avenue
Boston, MA 02115
(617) 266–0800
Boston's leading theater company has produced plays in recent years by Frank McGuinness and Brian Friel.

North Shore Music Theatre
P. O. Box 62
Beverly, MA 01915
(978) 232–7200
The Irish Tenors, Barrage, and John McDermott perform here regularly.

Rogers Center for the Arts at
Merrimack College
315 Turnpike Street
North Andover, MA 01845
(978) 837–5355
The Center hosts plays, storytelling, and concerts by noted Irish artists year-round.

Súgán Theatre Company
Boston Center for the Arts
539 Tremont Street
Boston, MA 02116
(617) 497–5134
Boston's award-winning resident theater troupe at the BCA produces contemporary Irish and Scottish plays by Tom Murphy, Martin McDonagh, and others.

Wang Center for the
Performing Arts
270 Tremont Street
Boston, MA 02116
(617) 482–9393
International touring productions like Riverdance and Lord of the Dance are staged at Boston's most glorious concert venue.

The Last Hurrah at the Omni Parker House.

Accommodations

Boston Harbor Hotel
Rowes Wharf
Boston, MA 02110
(617) 439–7000

Boston Marriott
Copley Place
110 Huntington Avenue
Boston, MA 02116
(617) 236–5800

Boston Wyndham Hotel
89 Broad Street
Boston, MA 02110
(617) 556–0006

Doubletree Club Hotel Bayside
240 Mount Vernon Street
Boston, MA 02125
(617) 822–3600

Doubletree Hotel Downtown
821 Washington Street
Boston, MA 02111
(617) 956–7900

Embassy Suites Hotel
207 Porter Street
East Boston, MA 02128
(617) 567–5000

Fairmont Copley Plaza Hotel
138 Saint James Avenue
Boston, MA 02116
(617) 267–5300

Hilton at Dedham Place
25 Allied Drive
Dedham, MA 02026
(781) 329–7900

Holiday Inn
30 Washington Street
Somerville, MA 02143
(617) 628–1000

Boston Irish Hostelries

Several Boston hotels have colorful Irish connections. The **Omni Parker House** at the corner of Tremont and School Streets opened its doors in 1855 and was frequented by nineteenth-century writers Ralph Waldo Emerson and Charles Dickens. In the twentieth century, Irish chieftains like James M. Curley and John "Honey Fitz" Fitzgerald held their victory parties there. In 1946 Fitzgerald's grandson John F. Kennedy announced his candidacy for the Senate at the hotel, and rumor has it he proposed to Jacqueline Bouvier in the dining room! Aer Lingus once had an office there, and the hotel bar is affectionately named the *Last Hurrah*, after the novel of the same name by Edwin O'Connor.

The **Copley Plaza** on St. James Street is a longtime favorite of visiting dignitaries, from Eamon De Valera to John McCormack. The new **Jurys Hotel** in Boston's Back Bay is part of the well-known Jurys Doyle Hotel Group in Ireland. Jurys is located at the former headquarters of the Boston Police Department.

Hotel Commonwealth
500 Commonwealth Avenue
Boston, MA 02215
(617) 933–5000

Jurys Boston Hotel
350 Stuart Street, Back Bay
Boston, MA 02116
(617) 266–7200

Kendall Hotel
350 Main Street
Cambridge, MA 02142
(617) 577–1300

Langham Hotel Boston
250 Franklin Street
Boston, MA 02110
(617) 451–1900

The Mary Prentiss Inn
6 Prentiss Street
Cambridge, MA 02140
(617) 661–2929

Millennium Bostonian Hotel
26 North Street
Faneuil Hall Marketplace
Boston, MA 02109
(617) 523–3600

Omni Parker House Hotel
60 School Street
Boston, MA 02109
(617) 227–8600

Ramada & Comfort Inns Boston
800–900 Morrissey Boulevard
Dorchester, MA 02122
(617) 287–9100

The Black Rose in downtown Boston.

Dining

These pubs and restaurants are the favorites of Irish Bostonians; in many of them, an Irish ambience is created through the decor, the cuisine, and/or the entertainment.

Black Rose
160 State Street
Boston, MA 02109
(617) 742–2286

Blackthorn Pub
471 Broadway
South Boston, MA 02127
(617) 269–1159

Brendan Behan Pub
378 Centre Street
Jamaica Plain, MA 02130
(617) 522–5386

Burren Pub
247 Elm Street, Davis Square
Somerville MA 02144
(617) 776–6896

Cellar Pub
991 Massachusetts Avenue
Cambridge, MA 02138
(617) 876–2580

Clery's Bistro & Bar
113 Dartmouth Street
Boston, MA 02109
(617) 262–9874

Coogan's
171 Milk Street
Boston, MA 02109
(617) 451–7415

Crossroads Irish Pub
495 Beacon Street
Boston , MA 02021
(617) 262–7371

Dillon's
955 Boylston Street
Boston, MA 02115
(617) 421–1818

Doyle's Cafe
3484 Washington Street
Jamaica Plain, MA 02130
(617) 524–2345

Druid Pub
1357 Cambridge Street, Inman Square
Cambridge, MA 02139
(617) 497–0965

Flann O'Brien Pub
1619 Tremont Street
Boston, MA 02118
(617) 566–4148

Grafton Street Pub & Grille
1230 Massachusetts Avenue
Cambridge, MA 02138
(617) 497–0400

Grand Canal
7 Canal Street
Boston, MA 02114
(617) 523–1112

Green Briar
304 Washington Street
Brighton, MA 02135
(617) 789–4100

Hurricane O'Reilly's
150 Canal Street
Boston, MA 02114
(617) 722–0161

Independent
75 Union Square
Somerville , MA 02143
(617) 440–6022

J. J. Foley's
117 East Berkeley
Boston, MA 02117
(617) 728–0315

James' Gate
5-11 McBride Street
Jamaica Plain, MA 02130
(617) 983–2000

Jose McIntyre's
160 Milk Street
Boston, MA 02109
(617) 451–9460

Kells Restaurant & Pub
161 Brighton Avenue
Allston, MA 02134
(617) 782–9082

Kinvara Pub
34 Harvard Avenue
Allston, MA 02134
(617) 783–9400

Kitty O'Sheas
131 State Street
Boston, MA 02109
(617) 725–0100

Last Hurrah
60 School Street
Boston, MA 02108
(617) 227–8600

Littlest Bar
47 Province Street
Boston, MA 02108
(617) 523–9766

M. J. O'Connor's
27 Columbus Avenue
Boston, MA 02116
(617) 482–2255

Matt Murphy's
14 Harvard Street
Brookline, MA 02445
(617) 232–0188

McCann's
197 Portland Street
Boston, MA 02114
(617) 227–4059

O'Leary's
1010 Beacon Street
Brookline, MA 02146
(617) 734–0049

Plough & Star
912 Massachusetts Avenue
Cambridge, MA 02139
(617) 492–9653

Purple Shamrock
One Union Street
Boston, MA 02108
(617) 227–2060

Skellig
240 Moody Street
Waltham, MA 02453
(781) 647–0679

Sweeney's Retreat
18 Atlantic Avenue
Marblehead, MA 01945
(781) 631–6469

Tiernan's Pub and Restaurant
99 Broad Street
Boston, MA 02110
(617) 350–7077

Hot cross buns.

Gift Shops

These boutiques, studios, and shops in the Boston area offer Irish imports, crafts, and souvenirs. Call ahead for hours.

Aisling Gallery & Framing
229 Lincoln Street/Route 3A
Hingham, MA 02043-1732
(800) 752–9389

Bridget's—An Irish Tradition
Route One, Walpole Mall
East Walpole, MA 02032
(508) 660–8634

Bridget's–An Irish Tradition
10 Cordage Park Circle, Suite 110
Plymouth, MA 02360
(508) 747–2273

Bygones of Ireland
89–91 Canal Street
Salem, MA 01970
(978) 745–4999

Celtic Revival
P. O. Box 268
Medford, MA 02155
(781) 295–7828

Celtic Weavers
316 Faneuil Hall Marketplace
Boston, MA 02109
(617) 720–0750

Copley Place
100 Huntington Avenue
Boston, MA 02116-6506
(617) 262–6600, ext. 236

The Irish Cottage Gift Shops
21 Ledin Drive
Avon, MA 02322
(887) 39–IRISH

The Irish Cottage Gift Shops
Nashua Mall
4 Colliseum Avenue, Unit E6
Nashua, NH 03063-3215
(603) 598–5240

The Irish Cottage Gift Shops
South Shore Plaza
250 Granite Street
Braintree, MA 02184
(781) 848–8609

The Irish Cottage Gift Shops
Hanover Mall
1775 Washington Street
Hanover, MA 02339-1701
(781) 829–0098

The Irish Cottage Gift Shops
1898 Centre Street
West Roxbury, MA 02132
(617) 323–4644

The Irish Cottage Gift Shops
Burlington Mall
75 Middlesex Turnpike
Burlington, MA 01803-5310
(781) 272–1044

Irish Imports Limited Corporation
1737 Massachusetts Avenue
Cambridge, MA 02138
(617) 354–2511

Irish Imports Limited Corporation
39 Bowen's Wharf
Newport, RI 02840
(401) 847–3331

Kara Irish Pottery
64 Pleasant Street
Methuen, MA 01844
(800) 430–2008

Lorica ArtWorks
90 Main Street
Andover, MA 01810
(978) 470–1829

The Tinker's Cart
787 Main Street, Route 70
Clinton, MA 01510
(978) 365–4334

Wexford House Irish Imports
9 Crescent Street
West Boylston (Worcester), MA 01583
(800) 835–6677

COURTESY OF MASSACHUSETTS
OFFICE OF TRAVEL & TOURISM
KINDRA CLINEFF PHOTOGRAPHER

Onlookers enjoying a Saint Patrick's Day Parade.

Annual Events

This list includes events that are typically scheduled each year in the Boston area. Call for current information or visit www.irishmassachusetts.com.

March

Boston College Irish Film Series
Presents contemporary and historical films about Ireland and Irish America.
(617) 552–3966

Boston Massacre Reenactment
The Bostonian Society reenacts Boston's most famous episode around March 5 of each year in the downtown historic district.
(617) 720–1713

Charitable Irish Society Banquet
Held on March 17, the Society's banquet raises funds that are distributed year-round to immigrant programs.
(508) 655–8430

Famine Memorial Commemoration
An annual candlelight vigil, first held in 1999 at the Memorial in Boston, remembers famine victims around the world.
(781) 848–2000

Irish American Partnership Breakfast
A gathering of business leaders who support year-round programs in Ireland.
(800) 722–3893

Irish Food & Culture Celebration
Irish cuisine is the focus of greater Boston's newest St. Patrick's Day festivities as hotels, restaurants, and pubs present a variety of dining specials and host visits by Irish master chefs.
(617) 696–9880

Saint Patrick's Day Parade
Started in 1901, the annual parade is Boston's most popular Irish event, drawing up to half a million spectators. It begins in South Boston the Sunday before or after March 17.
(617) 268–7955

April/May

Eire Society Gold Medal Award Dinner in Boston
The prestigious Gold Medal award dinner is one of many Eire Society activities through the year.
For more information, contact info@eiresociety.org.

June

Irish Connections Festival
The most popular Irish fest in New England takes place each June in Canton, Massachusetts, hosted by the Irish Cultural Centre.
(781) 821–8291

John Boyle O'Reilly Commemoration
The Ancient Order of Hibernians holds a ceremony every June at Holyhood Cemetery in Brookline to honor Boston's greatest Irishman.
(617) 327–1010

June/July

Celtic Night with the Boston Pops
From Arthur Fiedler to Keith Lockhart, the Pops has a rich tradition of staging the finest Celtic performances. Celtic Night takes place annually in Boston in June or July as a lead-up to July Fourth celebrations.
(617) 266–1200

July

Irish Festival
This festival, held in Lowell, Massachusetts, is sponsored by the Billerica Irish American Social Club.
(978) 663–3900

Irish step dancers await their turn.

Keith Lockhart, conductor of the Boston Pops.

Blackstone Valley Celtic Festival
A one-day gathering in Whitinsville of the finest musicians, dancers, and craftsmen.
(508) 234–9090

August/September

Milford Irish Festival
An annual gathering in one of Massachusetts' most Irish towns to raise money for the historic St. Mary's Cemetary, built in 1840.
(508) 478–9087

Newport Irish Festival
Rhode Island's Labor Day weekend Irish extravaganza overlooks scenic Newport Harbor.
(401) 846–1600

October

American Conference of Irish Studies, New England Conference
Academics from throughout New England present their research at this annual gathering, held at a different college campus each year.
(508) 565–1000

Boston Irish Film Festival
Founded in 1999, the BIFF exposes Bostonian audiences to new Irish films, actors, and directors.
For more information, contact irishunex@earthlink.net.

Comhaltas Ceoltoiri Eireann Concert
Ireland's top musicians, singers, dancers, and storytellers perform each year in Waltham, Massachusetts, as part of a nationwide tour.
(781) 899–0911

Commemoration of *St. John* Famine
Ship Passengers
*The Ancient Order of Hibernians holds a
memorial service at Central Cemetery in
Cohasset for the ninety-three famine refugees
who perished when their ship, St. John,
sank in 1849 during a coastal storm.*
(781) 857–2495

Harvard's Celtic Colloquium
*Scholars and graduate students from
around the world gather in Cambridge to
present their latest findings on Celtic languages and literatures.*
(617) 495–1206

November

American Ireland Fund
*The Fund holds its Boston soiree to raise
money for peace and charity projects in
Ireland and Northern Ireland.*
(617) 574–0720

December

Celtic Sojourn Christmas Concert
*Radio personality Brian O'Donovan of
WGBH-FM hosts a wonderful musical
pageant celebrating Christmas in Ireland.*
(617) 300–5400

Gaelic Roots Christmas Concert
*Held at Boston College, this concert fea-
tures outstanding Celtic musicians,
singers, and dancers.*
(617) 552–0490

Irish Cultural Centre Christmas Ball
*The annual Christmas ball in Boston
supports cultural activities throughout the
year at the Centre in Canton.*
(781) 821–8291

The Connolly House at Boston College.

Academic Programs

These institutions offer under-graduate and/or graduate degree Irish Studies programs.

American Conference of
Irish Studies
Richard Finnegan
Stonehill College
Easton, MA 02357
(508) 565–1000
Founded in 1960, ACIS is an academic group with more than 1,500 members worldwide, most of whom are college pro-fessors. It publishes the Irish Literary Supplement *twice a year and holds a national conference each spring, followed by regional conferences in the fall.*

Boston College Irish Programs
Thomas E. Hachey
Connolly House
300 Hammond Street
Chestnut Hill, MA 02467
(617) 552–3937
BC's Irish programs include its Irish Studies department, the Irish Institute, the Burns Library Irish Collection, the Center for Irish Programs in Dublin, and Gaelic Roots activities year-round.

Bridgewater State College Irish
Studies Program
Patricia Fanning
Hart Hall, Room 310
Bridgewater, MA 02325
(508) 531–2648
Undergraduate minor in Irish-American Studies is offered in an eighteen-credit program with Massasoit Community College.

Harvard University Celtic Languages
and Literatures
Patrick Ford
Barker Center
12 Quincy Street
Cambridge, MA 02138
(617) 495–1206
Harvard gave its first Celtic course in 1896. Today the department offers graduate-level degrees in Celtic languages and literatures and hosts an annual Colloquium of scholarly papers by graduate students and researchers.

Stonehill College
Irish Studies Program
Richard Finnegan
320 Washington Street
Easton, MA 02357
(508) 565–1000
Stonehill offers a minor in Irish Studies, a study-abroad program at the National University of Ireland in Galway, and internships in Dublin.

UMass/Boston Irish Studies Program
Thomas O'Grady
100 Morrissey Boulevard
Boston, MA 02125-3393
(617) 287–6752
This interdisciplinary program offers his-tory and literature courses from ancient times to the present.

The Irish Cultural Centre in Canton.

IRISH CULTURAL CENTRE
OF NEW ENGLAND

Civic, Cultural, and Community Organizations

This list includes charitable organizations, social clubs, cultural and educational groups, and political organizations.

American Ireland Fund
211 Congress Street, 10th Floor
Boston, MA 02210
(617) 574–0720
Funds projects of peace and reconciliation, arts and culture, education and community development in Ireland and Northern Ireland.

Ancient Order of Hibernians
60 Longwood Road
Quincy, MA 02169
(617) 770–9006
Established in 1857 by Edward Riley, the Massachusetts AOH advances Irish Catholic heritage and lobbies for peace and justice in Northern Ireland.

Boston History Collaborative
650 Beacon Street, Suite 403
Boston, MA 02215
(617) 350–0358
The Collaborative promotes Boston's immigrant, maritime, literary, and innovation history.

Charitable Irish Society
319 Western Avenue
Sherborn, MA 01770
(508) 655–8430
Formed in 1737, the Society is the oldest Irish group in North America.

Comhaltas Ceoltoiri Eireann
239 Grove Street
Waltham, MA 02454
(781) 899–0911
The Irish Musicians Association's Boston chapter, formed in 1975, promotes Irish traditional music, song, and dance.

Cuman na Gaeilge I mBoston
P. O. Box 164
Dedham, MA 02027-0164
(617) 734–7472
Dedicated to the preservation and active use of the Irish language, the group holds classes throughout New England.

Eire Society of Boston
10 Ladd's Way
Scituate, MA 02066
info@eiresociety.org
The Eire Society perpetuates Irish culture and education in Boston area.

Emerald Society of the Boston Police
10 Birch Street
Roslindale, MA 02131
(617) 323–9018
The Society's Gaelic Column of Pipes and Drums performs at all notable Irish events in Boston.

Gaelic Athletic Association
Northeast Division
200 New Boston Drive
Canton, MA 02021
(781) 329–9288
The GAA promotes Irish games including Gaelic football, hurling, and camogie. The Boston chapter has 45 teams and nearly 2,000 players.

Gaelic Roots
300 Hammond Street
Chestnut Hill, MA 02467
(617) 552–0490
The Gaelic Roots program at Boston College offers instruction in traditional music and dance. Concerts and other special events are offered on occasions throughout the year.

Globe Citizens Circle
230 Commerce Way, Suite 300
Portsmouth, NH 03801
(603) 929–9851
The Circle promotes dialogue and reconciliation among various global factions, with a special focus on Northern Ireland.

Irish American Club of Cape Cod
248 Surf Drive
Mashpee, MA 02649
Cape Cod, one hour south of Boston, has a vibrant Irish-American community year-round.

Irish American Cultural Institute
165 Grove Street
Westwood, MA 02090
(781) 326–9319
Founded in 1962 by Eoin McKiernan, the IACI enhances the many voices of Irish culture and heritage, with twenty-two chapters throughout the United States.

Irish American Unity Conference
611 Pennsylvania Avenue, SE, # 4150
Washington, D.C. 20003
(800) 947–4282
This nationwide human rights group works for peace and justice in Northern Ireland.

Irish Cultural Centre of New England
200 New Boston Drive
Canton, MA 02021
(781) 821–8291
With a membership of more than 4,000, the Irish Cultural Centre is the region's largest and most active organization.

Irish Foundation of Lawrence
6 Mount Vernon Terrace
Lawrence, MA 01843
(978) 683–9007
Formed in 1999, the Irish Foundation promotes Irish history, culture, and heritage in the Merrimack Valley.

Irish Georgian Society
145 Pickney Street
Boston, MA 02108
(617) 367–0013
The Boston chapter is dedicated to restoring eighteenth-century architecture in Dublin.

Irish Networking Society
P. O. Box 1317
Boston, MA 02117
(781) 446–8074
A group of Irish professionals meet and network to enhance their careers, build their businesses, and make new friends.

Irish Social Club of Boston
119 Park Street
West Roxbury, MA 02132
(617) 327–7306
Formed in 1945, the Social Club has an active calendar of dances, concerts, and other activities for Irish families.

Patrick S. Gilmore Society
P. O. Box 341
Milton, MA 02186
(617) 696–9880
Promotes the music and life of the nineteenth-century musical impresario from Galway.

South Boston Irish-American Society
P. O. Box 388
South Boston, MA 02127
This society is dedicated to the history and culture of the South Boston Irish.

Radio and Television Programs

Celtic Sojourn/WGBH 89.7 FM
125 Western Avenue
Boston, MA 02134
Saturday; Noon–3:00 P.M.
(617) 300–5400

Celtic Twilight/WUMB 91.9 FM
UMass/Boston
Dorchester, MA 02125
Saturday; 4:00–9:00 P.M.
(617) 287–6919

Comhaltas Ceoltoiri Eirann Show/
WNTN 1550AM
239 Grove Street
Waltham, MA 02454
Saturday; Noon–1:30 P.M.
(781) 899–0911

Feast of Irish Music/950 WROL AM
308 Victory Road
Quincy, MA 02171
Sunday; 1:00–5:00 P.M.
(617) 770–3030

Four Green Fields/WCUW 91.3 FM
910 Main Street
Worcester, MA 01610
Saturday; 9:30–11:00 A.M.
(508) 753–2284

Ireland on the Move/Cable TV Show
P.O. Box 583
Hyde Park, MA 02136
Friday; 8:00 P.M. Boston Cable
(617) 264–3041

Irish Hit Parade/950 WROL AM
308 Victory Road
Quincy, MA 02171
Saturday; 10:00 A.M.–7:00 P.M.
(617) 328–0880

Sound of Erin/WNTN 1550 AM
P.O. Box 12
Belmont, MA 02478
Saturday; 1:30–4:30 P.M.
(617) 484–2275

The Irish Hour/WUNR 1660 AM
9 Dean Road
Milton, MA 02186
Thursday; 8:00–10:00 P.M.
(617) 698–2585

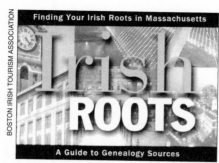

Genealogy guide Irish Roots.

Publications

Boston Irish Reporter
150 Mount Vernon Street
Dorchester, MA 02125
(617) 436–1222
Monthly newspaper covering Boston-area activities.

Irish America Magazine
875 Sixth Avenue, Suite 2100
New York City, NY 10001
(212) 725–2993
Bimonthly magazine with a national scope. Hosts Top 100 Irish-American awards each year.

Irish Connections
305 Madison Avenue, Suite 1223
New York, NY 10165
(212) 490–8061
Quarterly magazine with a national scope.

Irish Echo
309 Fifth Avenue
New York, NY 10016
(212) 686–1266
Established in 1928, the weekly newspaper covers Irish-American and Irish news.

Irish Emigrant
P. O. Box 1549
Boston, MA 02127
(617) 268–8322
The weekly "green pages" is distributed for free in Boston and New York pubs.

Irish Literary Supplement
P. O. Box 265
Wading River, NY 11792
(631) 929–0224
The biannual newspaper is the official publication for the American Conference of Irish Studies.

Irish Voice
875 Sixth Avenue, Suite 2100
New York, NY 10001
(212) 684–3366
A weekly newspaper based in New York City, and sister publication of Irish America *magazine.*

Agencies and Social Services

This list includes companies, organizations, and government agencies that can assist travelers, immigrants, and investors.

Aer Lingus
538 Broadhollow Road
Melville, NY 11747
(800) 474–7424 (1–800–IRISH AIR)
Ireland's national airline began its Boston route in October 1958 and today flies directly to Shannon and Dublin. The airline's local address in the United States is listed above with the U.S. toll-free phone number. For addresses and phone numbers in Ireland, visit the Web site www.aer lingus.com.

British Consulate General
One Memorial Drive
Suite 1500
Cambridge, MA 02142
(617) 245–4500
The consulate supplies information and contacts on Northern Ireland, Wales, Scotland, and England while representing Britain's interests in the United States.

Enterprise Ireland
101 Federal Street, Suite 1900
Boston, MA 02110
(617) 342–7124
Working on behalf of the Irish Government, Enterprise Ireland helps Irish companies set up businesses in America.

Industrial Development Authority of Ireland
20 Park Plaza, Suite 520
Boston, MA 02116
(617) 482–8225
IDA Ireland seeks American companies to invest in and open businesses in Ireland.

International Institute of Boston
One Milk Street
Boston, MA 02109
(617) 695–9990
Since 1924 the Institute has helped immigrants and refugees get settled in America.

Invest Northern Ireland
545 Boylston Street, 2nd Floor
Boston, MA 02116
(617) 266–8839
INI operates the Northern Ireland Technology and Development Center in Boston to help Northern Ireland companies do business in the United States.

Ireland's Consulate General
535 Boylston Street
Boston, MA 02115
(617) 267–9330
The Consulate provides services to Irish and American citizens, such as issuing passport renewals and granting Irish citizenship and represents the Irish Government in New England.

Irish American Partnership
33 Broad Street
Boston, MA 02109
(617) 723–2707
IAP supports science and technology education, job creation, and entrepreneurial projects in Ireland and Northern Ireland.

Irish Chamber of Commerce USA
New England Chapter
80 Mansur Street
Lowell, MA 01852
*This business group with chapters
throughout the United States promotes
Ireland as a gateway to the European
Union.*

Irish Immigration Center
59 Temple Place
Boston, MA 02111
(617) 542–7654
*The Center helps new immigrants get
acclimated in Boston, offering citizenship
workshops, legal advice, counseling,
and connections to the job and housing
markets.*

Irish Pastoral Center
953 Hancock Street
Quincy, MA 02170
(617) 479–7074
*A resource and referral agency affiliated
with the Archdiocese of Boston, dedicated
to helping new Irish immigrants.*

Tourism Ireland
345 Park Avenue
New York, NY 10154
(800) 223–6470
*Tourism Ireland is the official agency for
marketing Ireland and Northern Ireland
in the United States, working with travel
agents, tour operators and the general
public.*

Bibliography/Notes

Chapter One

Boston Newsletter, May 8, 1704.

New England Courant, August 21, 1721.

New England Weekly Journal, November 6, 1727; November 22, 1737; January 23, 1738; February 28, 1738; March 17, 1738; May 23, 1738; June 20, 1738; November 28, 1738.

Records of Suffolk Court, 1671–1780. Boston: Colonial Society of America, Volume XXIX/XXX.

Selectman's Minutes, City Document No. 77 (August 9 and September 15, 1736) and *No. 87* (December 3 and February 11, 1740).

Adams, James Truslow. *Provincial Society 1690–1763,* Vol. 3 of *A History of American Life;* edited by Arthur M. Schlesinger and Dixon Ryan Fox, New York: The MacMillan Company, 1927.

Barker, Charles A. *American Convictions: Cycles of Public Thought 1600–1850.* Philadelphia: J. B. Lippincott Company, 1970.

Burke, Charles T. *A History of the Charitable Irish Society.* Boston: Charitable Irish Society, 1973.

Cullen, James B. *The Story of the Irish in Boston.* Boston: James B. Cullen and Company, 1889.

Doherty, J. E. and D. J. Hickey. *A Chronology of Irish History Since 1500.* Savage: Barnes and Noble Books, 1990.

Dunn, Richard S. *Sugar and Slaves: The Rise of the Planter Class in the English West Indies: 1624–1713.* New York: W.W. Norton, 1972.

Erikson, Kai T. *Wayward Puritans: A Study in the Sociology of Deviance.* New York: MacMillan Publishing Company, 1966.

Evan Thomas Interview. *Naval History Magazine* 17, no. 3 (June 2003) Annapolis: U.S. Naval Institute.

Fender, Stephen. *American Literature in Context: 1620–1830.* New York: Methuen, 1983.

Ford, Henry Jones. *The Scotch-Irish in America.* Princeton: Princeton University Press, 1915.

Howe, M. A. DeWolfe. *Boston Common: Scenes from Four Centuries.* Boston: The Atlantic Monthly Press, 1910.

Jennings, Francis. *The Invasion of America: Indians, Colonialism, and the Cant of Conquest.* New York: W.W. Norton & Company, 1975.

Johnson, Harriett E. *The Early History of the Arlington Street Church.* Boston: Arlington Street Church, 1937.

Kenny, Kevin. *The American Irish, A History.* London: Longman, 2000.

Leyburn, James G. *The Scotch Irish: A Social History.* Chapel Hill: University of North Carolina Press, 1962.

Linebaugh, Peter. *The London Hanged: Crime and Civil Society in the Eighteenth Century.* New York: Cambridge University Press, 1992.

Lucey, Charles. *Harp and Sword: 1776.* Washington, D.C.: Charles Lucey, 1976.

McDonnell, Frances. *Emigrants from Ireland to America 1735–1743.* Baltimore: Genealogical Publishing Company, 1992.

Moorhead, Rev. John. *Marriages Performed at Church of Irish Presbyterian Strangers.* Harvard University Divinity School, 1730–1770.

Moorhead, Rev. John. *Baptisms Performed at Church of the Irish Presbyterian Strangers.* Harvard University Divinity School, 1730–1770.

Morgan, Edmund S. *The Puritan Family: Religion and Domestic Relations in Seventeenth-Century New England.* New York: Harper & Row, 1966.

Murdock, Kenneth B. *Literature and Theology in Colonial New England.* New York: Harper and Row, 1949.

O'Connor, Thomas H. *The Irish in New England.* Boston: New England Historic Genealogical Society, 1985.

Quinlin, Michael P. *Finding Your Irish Roots in Massachusetts.* Boston: Boston Irish Tourism Association, 2004.

Riley, Arthur J. *Catholicism in New England to 1788.* Washington, D.C.: Catholic University of America, 1936.

Sellin, J. Thorsten. *Slavery and the Penal System.* New York: Elsevier Scientific Publishing, 1976.

Simmons, R. C. *The American Colonies: From Settlement to Independence.* New York: W.W. Norton, 1976.

Smith, Abbott Emerson. *Colonists in Bondage: White Servitude and Convict Labor in America 1607–1776.* Chapel Hill: University of North Carolina Press, 1947.

Sweetser, M. F. *King's Handbook of Boston Harbor.* Boston: Applewood Books, 1882.

Whitmore, William H. *Notes Concerning Peter Pelham: The Earliest Artist Resident in New England.* Cambridge: John Wilson and Sons, 1867.

Chapter Two

Boston Globe, March 5, 2001.

Draper's Gazette, September 21, 1775.

Selectman's Minutes, City Document, No. 42 (October 5, 1769 and January 5, 1775).

Ballad Entitled, Patrick's Hearty Invitation to His Countrymen to the Tune of "Paddy Whack." Dublin: Academy Press, 1976.

Ireland and Irishmen in the American War of Independence. Dublin: Academic Press, 1976.

Painters and Engravers of New England. Boston: Massachusetts Historical Society, 1866.

Boston Prints and Printmakers 1670–1777. Boston: The Colonial Society of Massachusetts, 1971.

Adams, John. *John Adams: Diary and Autobiography 1775–1804.* Cambridge: Harvard University Press, 1961.

Adams, Thomas Boylston. *A New Nation.* Chester: Globe Pequot Press, 1981.

Bucke, Gerald L. "The Irish Contribution to the American Nation," *Eire Society Bulletin* (December 1976).

Cahill, Robert Ellis. *The Irish of Old New England.* Peabody: Chandler-Smith Publishing House, Inc., 1985.

Copley, John Singleton. Letter to Henry Pelham, August 1775, *Letters & Papers of John Singleton Copley and Henry Pelham, 1739–1776.* Boston: Massachusetts Historical Society, 1914.

Danforth, Mildred E. "The Indomitable Sullivans," *Eire Society Bulletin* (January 1977).

Doyle, David Noel. *Ireland, Irishmen and Revolutionary America: 1760–1820.* Dublin: Mercier Press, 1981.

Ford, Henry Jones. *The Scotch-Irish in America*. Princeton: Princeton University Press, 1915.

Pelham, Henry. Letters of Henry Pelham to John Singleton Copley, May 1775, *Letters & Papers of John Singleton Copley and Henry Pelham, 1739–1776*. Boston: Massachusetts Historical Society , 1914.

Jones, E. Alfred. *The Loyalists of Massachusetts: Their Memorials, Petitions and Claims*. London: The Saint Catherine Press, 1930.

Maas, David Edward. "The Return of Massachusetts Loyalists." Ph.D. diss., University of Wisconsin, 1972.

Marquis de Chastellux. *Ireland and Irishmen in the American War of Independence*. Dublin: Academic Press, 1976.

O'Brien, Michael J. *The Irish at Bunker Hill*. New York: Devin-Adair Company, 1968.

O'Brien, Michael J. *A Hidden Phase of American History: Ireland's Part in America's Struggle for Liberty*. Baltimore: Genealogical Publishing Co. Inc., 1973.

O'Brien, Michael J. "America's Debt to Ireland," *The Gaelic American*, June 21, 1919.

O'Brien, Michael J. "The Kellys, Burkes and Sheas of the Massachusetts Line," *American Irish Historical Society*, Vol. XXI, 1922.

Prown, Jules David. *John Singleton Copley*. Cambridge: Harvard University Press, 1966.

Ryan, George E. "Patrick Carr," *Eire Society Bulletin*, November 1, 1970.

Ryan, George E. "The Eire Society Bulletin," *Eire Society Bulletin*, March 1978.

Stark, James H. *The Loyalists of Massachusetts and the Other Side of the American Revolution*. Boston: James H. Stark, 1910.

Thomas, Evan. *John Paul Jones: Sailor, Hero, Father of the American Navy*. New York: Simon and Schuster, 2003.

Zobel, Hiller B. *The Boston Massacre*. New York: W.W. Norton, 1970.

Chapter Three

The Intelligencer, March 23, 1832.

The Jesuit, March 16 and 23 and November 23, 1833.

The Pilot, February 19, 1853.

Bartlett, John. *Familiar Quotations*, Fifteenth and 125th editions, Boston: Little Brown and Company, 1980.

Benedict Fenwick. Letter to Massachusetts General Court, March 1832, *Archdiocese of Boston Archives*, 1832.

Boston Catholic Directory. Boston: Archdiocese of Boston, 1995.

Coyle, Henry, Theodore Mayhew, and Frank Hickey. *Our Church, Her Children and Institutions*. Boston: Archdiocese of Boston, 1908.

Cullen, James B. *The Story of the Irish in Boston*. Boston: James B. Cullen, 1889.

Daly, Marie. Interview by Michael P. Quinlin. Boston, June 26, 2003, and December 8, 2003.

Dauwer, Leo P. *I Remember Southie*. Boston: Christopher Publishing House, 1975.

Ellis, John Tracy, and Robert Trisco. *A Guide to American Catholic History*, 2d ed. Santa Barbara: ABC-Clio, 1982.

Gurney, William J., *A Short History of St. Augustine's Cemetery*, South Boston; 1953.

Mooney, Thomas. *A History of Ireland from Its First Settlement to Its Present Time*. Volume I. Boston: Patrick Donahoe, 1853.

Murray, Thomas. *Papers of Thomas Murray.* Boston: John J. Burns Archives, Boston College, 1814–48.

O'Connor, Thomas H. *South Boston: My Home Town.* Boston: Quinlan Press, 1988.

O'Connor, Thomas H. *Boston Catholics: A History of the Church and Its People.* Boston: Northeastern University Press, 1998.

O'Toole, James M. "Sources for Irish-American History in the Archives of the Archdiocese of Boston," *Eire Society Bulletin,* November 1982.

Quincy, John Jr. *Quincy's Market: A Boston Landmark.* Boston: Northeastern University Press, 2003.

Walsh, Francis. "*The Boston Pilot:* A Newspaper for the Irish Immigrant, 1829–1908." Boston University thesis, 1968.

Chapter Four

The Intelligencer, March 23, 1832; November 23, 1833; January 18, 1834.

Adams, John Quincy. *Ireland's Conquest.* Columbus: Isaac N. Whiting, 1849.

Court transcript, *Bunker Hill Aurora,* November 30, 1833; December 12, 21, and 28, 1833; January 18, 1834.

Ellis, John Tracy. *The Pilot: 1829–1979.* Boston: Archdiocese of Boston, 1979.

Grimes, Robert, R. *How Shall We Sing in a Foreign Land?* South Bend: University of Notre Dame Press, 1996.

Jones, Howard Mumford. *The Many Voices of Boston: A Historical Anthology: 1630–1975.* Boston: Little Brown and Company, 1975.

Lord, Robert H., John E. Sexton, and Edward T. Harrington. *History of the Archdiocese of Boston.* Vol. 2. New York: Sheed & Ward, 1944.

Schultz, Nancy Lusignan. *Fire and Roses: The Burning of Ursuline Convent, 1834.* Boston: Northeastern University Press, 2000.

Tager, Jack. *Boston Riots: Three Centuries of Social Violence.* Boston: Northeastern University Press, 2000.

Whittier, John Greenleaf. "The Emerald Isle," *Newburyport Free Press,* 1826.

Wolkovich-Valkavicius, William. *Immigrants and Yankees in Nashoba Valley, Massachusetts.* W. Groton: St. James Church, 1981.

Chapter Five

American Signal, May 20, 1847; July 24, 1847.

Boston Daily Bee, January 1, 1847; February 18, 1847; May 10, 1847.

Boston Herald, April 24, 1851; April 28, 1851; May 5, 1853.

Boston Medical and Surgical Journal, March 3, 1847.

Boston Pilot, March 16, 1850; February 12, 1859; March 15, 1862; August 29, 1863.

Boston Whig, May 25, 1847.

Abbott, Edith. *Historical Aspects of the Immigration Problem: Selected Documents.* Chicago: University of Chicago Press, 1926.

Boston Society for the Prevention of Pauperism, Annual Report, 1865.

Clark, Henry Grafton, M.D. *Typhus Fever: Its History, Nature and Treatment.* Boston: Ticknor, Reed, and Fields, 1850.

Drake, Dan, M.D. "The Irish Immigrants' Fever." *Boston Medical and Surgical Journal,* August 27, 1847.

Forbes, R. B. *An Interesting Memoir of the Jamestown Voyage to Ireland.* Boston: James B. Cullen and Company, 1890.

Hale, Edward Everett. *Letters on Irish Emigration.* Boston, 1852.

Hanlin, Oscar. *Boston's Immigrants: 1790–1880.* Cambridge: Harvard University Press, 1941.

Harris, Ruth Ann. *The Search for Missing Friends.* Boston: New England Historic Genealogical Society, 1995.

Lee, Henry. *Massachusetts Help to Ireland During Famine.* Milton: Captain Robert Bennet Forbes House, 1967.

Loughran, William J. "Calamity off Cohasset," *Eire Society Bulletin,* November 1987.

Lover, Samuel. *War Ship of Peace, an Irish Melody.* New York: Firth and Hall, 1847.

Maguire, John Francis, M.P. *The Irish in America.* London: Longmans, Green & Co., 1868.

McColgan, John. "Boston 1847: What Really Happened?" *Boston Irish Reporter,* August 1997.

Quinlin, Michael P. "The Boston Medical Society's Response to Typhus Fever During the Irish Famine." Paper delivered at American Committee for Irish Studies conference, Suffolk University, October 1997.

Sullivan, Louis. *The Autobiography of an Idea.* New York: Dover Publications, 1956.

Upham J. B., M.D. *Records of Maculated Typhus, or Ship Fever.* New York: John F. Trow, Printer, 1852.

Woodham-Smith, Cecil. "Ireland's Hunger, England's Fault?" *Atlantic Monthly,* January 1963.

Woodham-Smith, Cecil. *The Great Hunger.* New York: Harper & Row, Publishers, 1963.

Chapter Six

Boston Herald, April 1851; May 1853.

Boston Evening Transcript, August 3, 1868.

Boston Traveler, August 19, 1853.

Boston Pilot, March 12, 1859.

Clark, Dennis. *Hibernia America: The Irish and Regional Cultures.* Westport: Greenwood Press, 1986.

Coffey, Michael, and Terry Golway. *The Irish in America.* New York: Hyperion, 1997.

Coyle, Henry, Theodore Mayhew, and Mathew Hickey. *Our Church, Her Children and Institutions.* Boston: Archdiocese of Boston, 1908.

Curran, Michael. *Life of Patrick Collins.* Norwood: Norwood Press, 1906.

Jensen, Richard. "No Irish Need Apply: A Myth of Victimization," *Journal of Social History,* Vol. 36, Nov. 2, 2002.

Kobel, Dale. *Paddy and the Republic: Ethnicity and Nationality in Antebellum America.* Middletown: Wesleyan University Press, 1986.

Lane, Roger. *Policing the City: Boston, 1822–1885.* New York: Athenaeum, 1971.

O'Connor, Thomas H. *The Call to Arms,* Vol. 1 in *Massachusetts in the Civil War.* Massachusetts Civil War Centennial Commission, 1960.

O'Connor, Thomas H. *Civil War Boston: Home Front and Battlefield.* Boston: Northeastern University Press, 1997.

Page, N. Clifford. *Irish Songs: A Collection of Airs New and Old.* Boston: Oliver Ditson Publishing, 1907.

Quill, Edward. *Deer Island Death/Burial Registry 1847–1850.* Boston: City of Boston Archives, 1990.

Ryan, Thomas. *Recollections of an Old Musician.* New York: E.P. Dutton, 1899.

Von Franks, Albert J. *The Trials of Anthony Burns: Freedom and Slavery in Emerson's Boston.* Cambridge: Harvard University Press, 1998.

Wilson, Susan. *Boston Sites and Insights.* Boston: Beacon Press, 1994.

Chapter Seven

Boston Herald, April 14, 1871.

Irish American Weekly, July 5, 1868.

Cobbe, F. P. "No Irish Need Apply," *Every Saturday Magazine,* July 25, 1868.

Coyle, Henry, Theodore Mayhew, and Matthew Hickey. *Our Church, Her Children and Institutions.* Boston: Archdiocese of Boston, 1908.

Gilmore, P. S. *History of the National Peace Jubilee and Great Musical Festival.* Boston: P. S. Gilmore, 1871.

Gilmore, Patrick S. *When Johnny Comes Marching Home Again.* Boston: Lee and Shephard, 1863.

Kammen, Michael. *Meadows of Memory: Images of Time and Tradition in American Art and Culture.* Austin: University of Texas Press, 1992.

McNamara, Daniel. Christian Samito, editor. *The History of the Ninth Regiment Massachusetts Volunteer Infantry.* New York: Fordham University Press, 2000.

National Peace Jubilee Festival Official Program, June 15, 1869.

Obituary, "Death of Martin Milmore," *The Pilot,* July 30, 1883.

Roche, James Jeffrey. *John Boyle O'Reilly: Life, Poems and Speeches.* New York: Cassell Publishing Company, 1891.

Rohdenburh, Ernest III. *A Bid for Immortality: The Sculpture and Life of Martin Milmore.* Chatham Historical Society, n.d.

Saint-Gaudens, Homer. *The Reminiscences of Augustus Saint-Gaudens.* New York: Garland Publishers, 1913.

Samito, Christian, ed. *Commanding Boston's Irish Ninth: The Letters of Colonel Patrick R. Guiney.* New York: Fordham University Press, 1997.

Shannon, Mary. *Passport to Public Art in Boston.* Boston: City of Boston Printers, 1980.

Chapter Eight

Donahoe's Monthly Magazine, Volume XII, Nos. 1–6, July–December 1884; Volume XXIII, Nos. 1–6, January–June 1890; Volume XXVII, No 1–6, January–December 1892.

Irish-American Weekly, June 15, 1878.

Irish Echo, January 1886; September 1890.

Irish World, August 5, 1881.

Boston Pilot, May 6, 1871.

Quincy Patriot Ledger, September 19–20, 1992.

Republic, March 25, 1882; March 18, 1896.

The American Irish Historical Society Proceedings. Bowie: Heritage Books, 1991.

Exercises at the Dedication and Presentation of the O'Reilly Monument, June 20, 1897. Boston: Boston City Council, 1897.

Casey, John S. *Journal of a Voyage from Portland to Fremantle on Board the*

Convict Ship Hougoumont. Bryn Mawr: Dorrance & Company, 1988.

Cullen, James B. *The Story of the Irish in Boston.* Boston: James B. Cullen, 1889.

Cummings, Michael. "100 Years Later, Copley Square Still Echoes Gilmore's Giant Jubilee," *The Pilot,* April 19, 1969.

Fanny Parnell, *The Pilot,* August 5, 1882.

Galvin, John T. *"Patrick J. Maguire: Boston's Last Democratic Boss, " The New England Quarterly,* Vol. IV, No. 3, September 1985.

Golway, Terry. *For the Cause of Liberty: A Thousand Years of Ireland's Heroes.* New York: Simon & Schuster, 2000.

Joyce, William Leonard. *Editors and Ethnicity: A History of the Irish-American Press 1848–1883.* New York: Arno Press, 1876.

Logan, Edward L. *The Clover Club of Boston, Golden Jubilee Year Book.* Boston: The Clover Club, 1933.

O'Connell, Shaun. *Imagining Boston: A Literary Landscape.* Boston: Beacon Press, 1990.

O'Reilly, John B. *The Pilot,* September 30, 1871.

Quinn, Peter. "How the Irish Stayed Irish," *America,* March 16, 1996.

Solomon, Barbara Miller. *Ancestors and Immigrants: A Changing New England Tradition.* Boston: Northeastern University Press, 1989.

Stein, Charles W. *American Vaudeville: As Seen by Its Contemporaries.* New York: De Capo, 1985.

Stevens, Peter. *The Voyage of the Catalpa: A Perilous Journey and Six Irish Rebels' Escape to Freedom.* New York: Carroll & Graf Publishers, 2002.

Chapter Nine

Boston Globe, April 8, 1896.

Republic, March 25, 1882; May 1882.

The Boston Marathon: 100 Years of Blood, Sweat and Cheers. Chicago: Triumph Books, 1996.

Anderson, Jack. *John L. Sullivan: The First Irish American Boxing Champion.* [On-line] Available at http://www.hoganstand.com/general/identity/geese/stories/sullivan.htm. Copyright 2004.

Bush, George. Letter to Baseball Hall of Fame, February 14, 2001, Houston.

Concannon, Joe. "The Elder's 50th Jaunt," *Boston Globe,* April 1980.

Connolly, James B. *Limelight Magazine.* Boston: Wood Company, 1933–34.

Cooper, Pamela. *Twenty-Six Miles in America.* Syracuse: Syracuse University Press, 1998.

Cullen, James B. *The Story of the Irish in Boston.* Boston: James B. Cullen, 1889.

Daley, Arthur. "Sports of the Times: A Vote from Afar," *New York Times,* January 19, 1949.

Donovan, Charles M. and Ellenora Donovan O'Brien. *Nomination to the Committee on Baseball Veterans National Hall of Fame, Patrick J. Donovan.* Pottstown, 2000.

Donovan, Charles M. *Irish America Magazine,* April-May, 2003.

Dunn, Joseph and P. J. Lennox. *The Glories of Ireland.* Washington, D.C.: Phoenix Ltd., 1914.

Gersham, Michael, ed. *125 Years of Professional Baseball.* Chicago: Triumph Books, 1994.

Joe Concannon, *The Boston Globe,* 1980.

Kaplan, Ron. "The Sporting Life: From King Kelly to Mark Maguire," *Irish America Magazine,* February–March 2003.

Kissal, Gary. "New Life for an Old Salt? The Renaissance of James Brendan Connolly," *Eire Society Bulletin,* November 1991.

Obituary, "Patsy Donovan," *New York Times,* December 26, 1953.

Obituary, "Thomas E. Burke," *Boston Sunday Post,* February 15, 1929.

Olmsted, Frederick Law. *Civilizing American Cities: Writings on City Landscapes.* New York: De Capo Press, 1997.

Power, Jerome W. *The Boston Strong Boy, 1937–38.* American Life Histories: Manuscripts from the Federal Writers Project 1936–1940. Library of Congress [online] Available at http://memory.loc .gov/ammem/wpaintro/ wpahome.html. October 19, 1998.

Riess, Steven A. *City Games: The Evolution of Urban Society and the Rise of Sports.* Urbana: University of Illinois Press, 1989.

Roche, James Jeffrey. *John Boyle O'Reilly: Life, Poems and Speeches.* New York: Cassell Publishing Company, 1891.

Schaefer, John. *The Irish American Athletic Club: Redefining Americanism at the 1908 Olympic Games.* New York: Archives of Irish America, 2001.

Wilcox, Ralph C. *The English as Poor Losers, and Other Thoughts on the Modernization of Sports.* Unpublished manuscript, 1908. Available on-line at http://www.rms-republic.com /connolly.html. May 1, 1997.

Chapter Ten

Republic, June 2, 1900; May 5, 12, and 19, 1905; March 22, 1919.

Boston Globe, February 16, 18, and 21, 1900; December 20, 1901; December 4, 1905; April 25–29, 1916.

Boston Herald, March 18, 1896.

Boston Sunday Post, September 22, 1912.

Gaelic American, December 30, 1905.

Irish World, June 22, 1919; July 5, 1919; March 26, 1927; May 7, 1927; December 31, 1927; July 2, 1932.

Ayers, Brenda A. "'Honey Fitz' In Search of a 'Bigger, Better and Busier Boston,'" *Eire Society Bulletin,* March 1981.

Classon, Herbert N. "The Irish in America," *Munsey's Magazine,* April 1906.

Cummings, Michael. "The Logans of Logan Airport," *Eire Society Bulletin,* November 1983.

Cummings, Michael. "The Life and Times of Brigadier-General Lawrence James Logan," Unpublished article, 1981.

Gaelic Alliance of Boston Program Book, Dublin: National Library, 1912.

Harty, Patricia. "Irish Americans of the Century," *Irish America Magazine,* November 1999.

MacManus, M. J. *Eamon De Valera: A Biography.* Dublin: Talbot Press Ltd., 1945.

McCabe, John. *George M. Cohan: The Man Who Owned Broadway.* New York: De Capo Press, 1973.

Norton, Elliot. *Broadway Down East: An Informal Account of the Plays, Players and Playhouses of Boston from Puritan Times to the Present.* Boston: Boston Public Library, 1978.

O'Connell, Lenahan, and James W. Ryan. *The O'Connell Family of Massachusetts.* Boston: Elizabeth James Press, 1994.

Ryan, Dennis. *Beyond the Ballot Box: A Social History of the Boston Irish, 1845–1917.* Amherst: University of Massachusetts Press, 1983.

Wayman, Dorothy. *David Walsh: Citizen-Patriot*. Milwaukee: Bruce Publishing Company, 1952.

Chapter Eleven

Boston City Paper, April 5–18, 1997.
Boston Sunday Globe, October 5, 1958.
Irish World, September 26, 1931; May 27, 1933; March 29, 1941; June 2, 1947; February 28, 1948.
Newsweek, January 8, 1951.
Republic, January 15, 1910, March 26, 1910.
Roxbury Gazette, May 30, 1913; June 7, 1913.
Allen, John. "John McCormack: Master Singer," *Ireland Today,* June 1984.
Beatty, Jack. *The Rascal King: The Life and Times of James Michael Curley (1874–1958)*. Reading: Addison-Wesley Publishing Company, 1992.
Carroll, James Robert. *One of Ourselves: John F. Kennedy in Ireland*. Bennington: Images from the Past, 2003.
Cummings, Michael. *Gaelic Athletic Association History*. Unpublished, 1983.
Garvey, Thomas. "Dancing on Dudley Street," *Guide to the New England Irish,* 2nd ed., 1987.
Hughes, Herbert. *Irish Country Songs*. London, 1909.
Johnson, H. Earle. *Symphony Hall, Boston*. Boston: Little, Brown and Company, 1950.
Maier, Thomas. *The Kennedys: America's Emerald Kings*. New York: Basic Books, 2003.
McCormack, John. *John McCormack Song Album*. New York, Boosey & Hawkes, 1932.
McCormack, John. Boston Symphony Hall Archives.
McCormack, John. John J. Burns Library Archives, Boston College.
McCormack, Lily. *I Hear You Calling Me*. Milwaukee: Bruce Publishing Company, 1949.
O'Connor, Thomas H. *The Boston Irish*. Boston: Northeastern University Press, 1995.
O'Neill, Francis. *Irish Minstrels and Musicians*. Cork: Mercier Press, 1913.
Obituary, "Jazz priest N. O'Connor dead at 81," *New York Times,* July 7, 2003.
Ryan, George E. "Irish Notes on American Music," *Eire Society Bulletin,* March 1988.
Sullivan, Mark. *Our Times: Pre-War America,* Vol. 3. New York: Charles Scribner & Sons, 1971.
Swan, John C. *Music in Boston: Readings from the First Three Centuries*. Boston: Boston Public Library, 1977.
Victor Records Catalog, 1919.
White, Robert. "John McCormack's Recordings," *Cara Magazine,* May/June 1984.
Williams, William H. A. *'Twas Only an Irishman's Dream: The Image of Ireland and the Irish in Popular Song Lyrics: 1800–1920*. Chicago: University of Illinois Press, 1996.

Chapter Twelve

Boston Business Journal, October 17–23, 2003.
Boston Evening American, November 27, 1959.
Boston Globe, October 1, 1958; January 27, 1968.
Boston Traveler, October 9, 1956.
Irish Echo, April 3, 1982; October 31, November 27, and December 5, 1987; February 13, 1988.

Irish World, June 22, 1946; August 29, 1950.

Roxbury Citizen, March 8, 1951.

Roscommon Herald, July 25, 1969.

Feis Program Book. Boston: Central Counties Committee, 1950.

Harvard–National Library of Ireland Irish Manuscripts Microfilm Project, *Eire Society Bulletin,* Speech of President Jimmy Carter, October 20, 1979.

"First Boston Visit of the Pete Brown Band coming to the New State Ballroom Direct from Ireland," Circular, May 24–26, 1962.

"Irish American Committee for the John F. Kennedy Memorial Library Fund in Boston," Correspondence, April 15, 1964.

Forty-sixth Annual Directory. Central Council of Irish County Clubs, March 17, 1951.

Fifty-fifth Annual Reunion Program. County Donegal Association, November 21, 1963.

Daley, Marie E. "Nationalism, Sentiment and Economics: Relations Between Ireland and Irish America in the Postwar Years," *Eire-Ireland,* Spring/Summer 2002.

Fahey, Joseph J. *Boston's Forty-Five Mayors.* Boston: City of Boston Printers, 1975.

Feis Mor Greater Boston Feis Program. July 30, 1950.

Ford, James J. "Some Records of the Irish Language in the Greater Boston Area," *Eire Society Bulletin,* November 4, 1973.

Annual Reunion and Ball Program. Gaelic Athletic Association, December 3, 1953.

Hennessey, Maurice N. *I'll Come Back in the Springtime.* New York: Ives Washburn, Inc., 1966.

Eleventh Annual "Night in Ireland" Program Book. Irish Talent Club, November 1, 1959.

Kennedy, John F. "On Poetry and National Power," *Massachusetts Review,* Winter 1964.

Kennedy, John F. *A Nation of Immigrants.* New York: Harper and Row, 1964.

Lyons, Louis M. "The Legend of John F. Kennedy," *Massachusetts Review,* Winter 1964.

MacBride, Sean. "Greetings to Boston Feis," *Eire Society Bulletin,* 1951.

Mitchell, Arthur. *JFK and His Irish Heritage.* Dublin: Moytura Press, 1994.

O'Connor, Edwin, *The Last Hurrah.* Boston: Atlantic Monthly Press, 1956.

Chapter Thirteen

Boston Globe, September 25, 1980; May 5, 2001.

Irish Echo, April 22, 1989.

Irish People, December 2, 1989.

Irish Times, February 19, 1985; March 25, May 6, and June 17, 1989.

Irish Voice, January 18, 1987.

Quincy Patriot Ledger, March 15–16, 2003.

Massachusetts House of Representatives. Resolution Demanding the Recall and Withdrawal of the British Consulate. June 15, 1981.

Symposium on Northern Ireland Program. Boston: University of Massachusetts, March 18–19, 1983.

Selectman's Minutes, City Document No. 77 (December 28, 1737).

U.S. Congress, Resolution to make additional immigrant visas available for immigrants from certain foreign countries. 99th Cong., 1st sess., H. R. 2606, *Congressional Record* (May 23, 1985).

U.S. Congress, A bill to amend the Immigration and Nationality Act to provide for additional immigrant visa numbers . . . , 99th Cong., 2nd sess., S 2219 by Mr. Kerry. *Congressional Record,* Vol. 132, No. 36 (March 21, 1986).

U.S. Congress, A bill to amend the Immigration and Nationality Act to effect changes in the numerical limitation and preference system. 99th Cong., 2nd sess., S 2768 by Mr. Kennedy. *Congressional Record,* Vol. 132, No. 114 (August 15, 1986).

Guide for the New Irish. Ancient Order of Hibernians, March 1988.

Devlin-McAliskey, Bernadette. "Eight Hundred Years for Freedom," *Forward Motion Magazine,* March/April 1998.

Flatley, Thomas J. *Testimony of Thomas J. Flatley.* U.S. House of Representatives Subcommittee on Immigration, Refugees and International Law (September 7, 1988).

Kennedy, Edward M. *Statement of Senator Edward M. Kennedy Opposing the Use of Plastic Bullets in Northern Ireland and Calling for a Ban on the Ulster Defence Association,* Press Release, June 15, 1982.

McGowan, William. *Massachusetts Immigration Committee Objectives,* 1985.

O'Hanlon, Ray. *The New Irish Americans.* Niwot: Roberts Rinehart Publishers, 1998.

Obituary. "Leo Cooney, 74; fought for equal rights in N. Ireland," *Boston Globe,* June 23, 2003.

William McGowan. Interview by Michael P. Quinlin. "The Irish in Boston Are on the Move," *Boston Irish Press,* No. 1, January 1981.

Chapter Fourteen

Boston Globe, March 15, 1990; March 17, 1994; March 11, 1995; March 19, 2001; March 24, 2002.

Irish Echo, December 30, 1989; September 16–22, 1992; March 8–15, 1995; April 12–18, 1995; November 27–December 3, 1996; March 5–11, 1997; June 17–23, 1998; March 13–19, 1996; November 22–30, 1998; May 28–June 3, 2003.

South Boston Tribune, April 11, 1991.

Bulger, William M. *While the Music Lasts: My Life in Politics.* Boston: Houghton Mifflin, 1996.

Carroll, James. *The City Below.* Boston: Houghton Mifflin, 1994.

Davis, William A. *Boston Globe,* March 17, 2001.

Ford, James J. "From the North End to the Fenway: An Irish Walk Through Central Boston," *Eire Society Bulletin,* December 1991.

Quinlin, Michael. "Irish Music as an Emigrant Language," Paper delivered at ACIS conference, Boston University, October 2001, and at Gaelic Roots, June 2003.

Quinlin, Michael P. *Guide to the Boston Irish.* Boston: Quinlin Campbell Publishers, 1985.

Quinlin, Michael P., and Colette Minogue Quinlin. *Guide to the New England Irish,* 3rd ed. Boston: Quinlin Campbell Publishers, 1994.

Quinlin, Michael P. "Boston Public Library: The People's Palace," *Irish America Magazine,* January/February 1998.

Chapter Fifteen

Boston College Chronicle, March 4, 1993.

Boston Globe, March 17 and 19, 1996; July 10, 1999.

Boston Herald, January 8, 2001.

Christian Science Monitor, December 19, 1994.

Republic, February 24, 1900.

Boston Pilot, March 22, 1834; Aug 29, 1863.

Home & Away, April 28, 2003.

International Irish Dancing Magazine, July 2002.

U.S. Congress, *Irish Peace Process Cultural and Training Program Act of 1998.* 105th Cong., 2nd sess., H.R. 4293, 1998.

U.S. Congress, *To amend and extend the Irish Peace Process Cultural and Training Program Act of 1999.* 108th Cong., 1st sess., H.R. 2655, 2003.

Bowen, Kevin. *In Search of Grace O'Malley.* Dorchester: West Cedar Street Press, 1997.

Coyle, Henry, Theodore Mayhew and Frank Hickey. *Our Church, Her Children and Institutions.* Boston: Archdiocese of Boston, 1908.

Deutsch, Sarah. *Women and the City: Gender, Space and Power in Boston 1870–1940.* Oxford: Oxford University Press, 2000.

Dezell, Maureen. *Irish America Coming into Clover.* New York: Doubleday, 2000.

Gen, Jish. *Who's Irish.* New York: Vintage Books, 2000.

Halter, Marilyn. *Shopping for Identity: The Marketing of Ethnicity.* New York: Schocken Books, 2000.

Kenny, Kevin. *The American Irish, A History.* Boston: Longman Publishers, 2000.

Lincoln, Abraham. *The Collected Works of Abraham Lincoln,* Vol. 2. Roy Basler, ed. New Brunswick: 1953.

MacDonald, Michael Patrick. *All Souls: A Family Story from Southie.* New York: Ballantine Books, 1999.

Robinson, Mary. "Address to the Irish Parliament," February 2, 1995.

Roosevelt, Theodore. *American Irish Historical Society,* January 13, 1897.

Wilson, Susan. *The Omni Parker House: A Brief History of America's Longest Continuously Operating Hotel.* Boston: Omni Parker House, 2001.

Index

About the Author

MICHAEL P. QUINLIN is the founder of the Boston Irish Tourism Association and creator of the Boston Irish Heritage Trail. He is the author of *Guide to the New England Irish,* and his many articles and op-ed pieces have appeared in the *Boston Globe,* the *Boston Herald, Irish Echo,* and *Irish America Magazine.* He is currently editing *Classic Irish Stories* (The Lyons Press, forthcoming). He lives in Milton, Massachusetts, with his wife, Colette, and sons Leo and Devin.